THE IRISH-AMERICAN IN POPULAR CULTURE
1945–2000

THE IRISH-AMERICAN IN POPULAR CULTURE 1945–2000

STEPHANIE RAINS

IRISH ACADEMIC PRESS

DUBLIN • PORTLAND, OR

First published in 2007 by
IRISH ACADEMIC PRESS
44 Northumberland Road, Dublin 4, Ireland

and in the United States of America by
IRISH ACADEMIC PRESS
c/o ISBS, Suite 300, 920 NE 58th Avenue
Portland, Oregon 97213-3786

www.iap.ie

© 2007 Stephanie Rains

British Library Cataloguing in Publication Data
An entry can be found on request

ISBN 978 0 7165 2830 2 (cloth)
ISBN 978 0 7165 2831 9 (paper)

Library of Congress Cataloging-in-Publication Data
An entry can be found on request

All rights reserved. Without limiting the rights under copyright
reserved alone, no part of this publication may be reproduced, stored
in or introduced into a retrieval system, or transmitted, in any form or
by any means (electronic, mechanical, photocopying, recording or
otherwise), without the prior written permission of both the
copyright owner and the publisher of this book

Typeset in 11pt on 13pt Sabon
by FiSH Books, Enfield, Middx
Printed by Creative Print and Design, Gwent, Wales

For Nick

Contents

Acknowledgements

This book began its life as my PhD thesis at Dublin City University, and my first acknowledgements must therefore go to those funding organisations whose generosity made that work possible. The Dublin City University School of Communications, as well as the IRCHSS, both provided early sources of funding which were much appreciated. The majority of my graduate funding, however, came from The Dublin City University Educational Trust Research Scholarship, for which I am extremely grateful.

Several different libraries and archives have been essential to this research over a number of years, and the assistance and support of their staff has been invaluable. I would particularly like to thank the staff of Dublin City University Library, Trinity College Dublin Library, the National Library of Ireland, the Pearse Street Library, the Irish Film Archive, the Bobst Library of New York University and New York Public Library.

During my time at DCU School of Communications, a number of people frequently provided the less tangible but equally necessary forms of support which were essential to my day-to-day life. Thanks are due to all of them, particularly, but not exclusively, Maeve Connolly, Michael Cronin, Luke Gibbons, Debbie Ging, John Horgan, Peadar Kirby, Stephanie McBride, Des McGuinness, Barbara O'Connor and Brian Trench. Most of all, of course, I would like to thank Farrel Corcoran for his patient and endlessly supportive supervision, as well as for his personal kindness and support. He was a calming and cheering influence throughout my research, and never failed in his generosity of time and thought. Martin McLoone's advice on the finished thesis has also proved very valuable.

I would also like to thank my colleagues from the Department of Humanities at Dundalk Institute of Technology, who provided friendship and advice during my first experiences of teaching, and have continued to supply both ever since. Special thanks are due to Fiona Fearon, Mark Fearon and Caroline O'Sullivan, as well as the

Department's students, who had the dubious pleasure of teaching me how to teach.

I'm also very grateful for the encouragement and support I've received during my time in the School of Business and Humanities at Dun Laoghaire Institute of Art, Design and Technology. I'd like to thank all of my colleagues, but most especially Josephine Browne, Justin Carville, Maeve Connolly, Grainne Elmore, Paula Gilligan, Therese Moylan, Sylvia Wrynn and everyone from 'the typing pool', not least for proving just how essential a sense of humour is to academic life. I also owe great thanks to my students on the BA in English Media and Cultural Studies, who have not only been a pleasure to teach, but whose lively class discussions have also helped me work through some of the ideas in this book.

I am also very grateful for the encouragement and assistance of the Irish Academic Press, especially Lisa Hyde, for her friendly and valuable editorial advice. I would also like to express my gratitude to Irish Academic Press' copy-editors, Sian Mills and Manuela Tecusan, whose painstaking work on the manuscript resulted in so many improvements. Any remaining errors are, of course, my own.

An article based upon parts of Chapter 2 has been published as 'Roots and Routes: Irish-American Interest in Genealogy, 1945-2000', in Diane Negra (ed.), *The Irish In Us: Irishness, Performativity, and Popular Culture*, (Durham, North Carolina: Duke University Press, 2006). Articles based upon parts of Chapter 3 have appeared as 'Celtic Kitsch: Irish-America and Irish Material Culture', in *Circa*, Issue 107, Spring 2004, and 'Home from Home: Diasporic Images of Ireland in Film and Tourism', in Barbara O'Connor and Michael Cronin (eds.), *Tourism in Ireland: A Critical Study*, (Clevedon: Channel View Publications, 2003).

The jacket image of this book is the illustrated cover of the theme song to *The Quiet Man*, 'Isle of Innisfree', words and music by Richard Farrelly, © 1950, Peter Maurice Music Co Ltd, London WC2H 0QY.

Many individuals have provided the affection and encouragement which, over the years, have enabled me to persevere with this and other projects. I would like to thank Stuart Murray for his enduring friendship, along with Valerie and the boys, especially Lucas, of course. I owe a special debt to Katy Mullin, both for her contribution to my sanity under the 'other country' rule, and for her particularly expert insights into cosmopolitanism. Maeve Connolly has been wonderful company on and off an extraordinary number of campuses, and similar thanks go to Grainne Elmore and Paula Gilligan at IADT, whose friendship is much appreciated. Further advice, support and essential email distractions have been generously provided by Andy Auge, Diane Negra and Ray Ryan. Thanks are also particularly due to my parents, Ann and Tony, who while I was doing my PhD never once asked when I was going to get a proper job.

    I am of course especially grateful to Nick Daly, to whom this book is dedicated. I greatly appreciate his spirited encouragement and support, and also Pola's equally spirited determination that playing with your cat is just as important as working on footnotes. She was quite right, of course.

Stephanie Rains
Dublin, 2007

List of Illustrations

Abbreviations and Acronyms

CEEC   Committee of European Economic Cooperation

DCU   Dublin City University

FARA   Foreign Agents Registration Act (US)

IADT   Institute of Art, Design and Technology

INLA   Irish National Liberation Army

IRA   Irish Republican Army

IRCHSS Irish Research Council for the Humanities and Social Science

IRSP   Irish Republican Socialist Party

NICRA   Northern Ireland Civil Rights Association

Noraid Irish Northern Aid Committee

RTE   Radio Telefis Eireann

UIDA   United Ireland Development Authority*

UPI   United Press International

*The UIDA was proposed as part of one suggested solution to the Troubles, discussed in Chapter 1. However, it has never actually existed, or seemed likely to.

Introduction

IN ONE OF their 'priceless' series of television advertisements of recent years, Mastercard highlighted the apparently unquantifiable nature of Irishness. Seen through the eyes of a Dublin man moving through the city, the advert watches identifiably American tourists buying leprechaun hats and green trousers, the voice-over noting the cost of each item. Eventually, as the Dublin man settles into a pub with a pint of Guinness, the voice-over intones, 'knowing what it means to be Irish – priceless'. This advertisement picks up on a major theme of popular discussion in Irish culture from the 1990s onwards – the nature of Irish identity, its connections to or separation from the processes of commodification, and the role (if any) to be played in that identity-construction by the Irish-American diaspora.

This book developed out of similar concerns with Irish identity-construction, and especially the nature of contemporary Irish-American identities and their connections to contemporary Ireland. One of the notable features of Irish and Irish-American popular culture from the mid-twentieth century onwards is a recurring figure: that of the Irish-American in Ireland. Furthermore, there seem to be recurring themes and forms of representation which are particular to texts in which this figure appears. These include a strong emphasis upon the issues of identity, ethnicity and memory, as well as notably filmic narrative formats in tourist texts which do not deploy such devices when dealing with other visitors to Ireland. These particularities are noticeably increased when the depicted Irish-American, as is very often the case, is of second-, third-, or even later-generation birth in the United States, and therefore has no personal knowledge of Ireland prior to their visit.

In attempting to interrogate this recurring figure of the Irish-American in Ireland, I became convinced of its importance in the definitions and performances of Irishness in global popular culture. This seemed an area particularly worthy of attention, given the extraordinary degree of interest in Irish culture and identity around the world, but especially in the United States, during the 1990s. As a result, this project shifted its emphasis to an examination of the Irish-American diaspora's construction and performance of their ethnic identity, a process still, it will be argued, principally conducted through the media of film and tourism, but also through other aspects of popular cultural practice, such as family history, political and social activism, and consumerism.

Due to the geographical and historical scale of the Irish diaspora in the United States, this book necessarily approaches the subject within fairly strict boundaries of discussion. The setting of all of these boundaries involved a process of selection which is outlined below.

POST-SECOND WORLD WAR IRISH AMERICA

First, this book deals with the period between the end of the Second World War and the end of the twentieth century. There are a number of reasons for this, the principal one being that it has been an important but so far under-researched half-century in terms of Irish diaspora formation and representation. From the 1980s onwards, there has been a growing interest in critiquing the histories of Irish America during the late nineteenth and early twentieth centuries. This has taken the form of examining both the social and cultural histories of the diaspora, as well as their important contributions to wider American society and culture of the time.[1] This period was of course a crucial one in American history, as it coincided with the nation's absorption of vast numbers of other European immigrant groups, and the ways in which this absorption process was negotiated and represented, for the Irish as for other groups, is highly revealing of the ways in which modern America was formed.

The period following the end of the Second World War, however, has been relatively neglected within examinations of the Irish-American diaspora. There is no doubt that, following the social, political and cultural upheavals caused by the war, the position within American society of white European ethnic groups such as the Irish changed enormously. Their access to social and economic mobility was for the most part increasingly assured, and the very serious questions which had been raised during and after the First World War about their identity within and allegiance to the United States appeared an irrelevance by the 1950s. So ethnic groups such as Irish America were seen as progressively more American and less Irish over the decades following 1945, as it was largely assumed they had an ever-decreasing need or desire to engage with an Ireland which was no longer part of their national or cultural identity. Instead, in the post-war years, and especially from the 1960s onwards, it was other ethnic groups, particularly African Americans, Native Americans and, later, non-European immigrants, whose ethnicity and negotiation of American identity became the focus of the social interest and even, in the more extreme cases, the moral panics which had earlier applied to groups such as Irish America.

Despite this historical shift, it is very specifically within the post-Second World War period that the figure of the Irish-American 'returning' (often for the first time) to Ireland begins to recur with growing frequency in films, novels and memoirs, as well as tourism texts. As early as 1952, this was being reflected in the plot of *The Quiet Man*, and over the coming decades this theme would proliferate, in the burgeoning genealogy industry in which Irish-Americans have played a significant role, the waves of interest among Irish America in political causes back in Ireland, and other popular cultural practices, including the development of a new genre also popular among Irish-Americans, the 'family memoir'. This genre typically traces a family's social and emotional trajectory from the migrant generation up until the current, diasporic, author's generation. The enormous commercial success of Irish cultural products within the United States during the 1990s, from U2's music through to *Riverdance*, and including Irish theme pubs and Seamus Heaney's poetry along the way, has only served to confirm the levels of interest among Irish America in their cultural inheritance. The precise meaning of this interest, and the extent to which it is reflective of any real impact upon identity formation within the diaspora, is of course highly contested, and will be discussed in detail throughout the following chapters. This contestation in itself, however, highlights the importance of continuing research into Irish-American ethnicity during the post-Second World War period.

IRISH AMERICA AND IRELAND

A second defining feature of this project is that it focuses on the Irish-American diaspora's relationship to Ireland itself, and examines the ways in which contact of various kinds with the 'homeland'

and its culture has continued to structure and inform their diasporic identity-construction. This process is importantly distinct from an examination of the now well-established Irish-American cultural forms and practices developed and circulated *within* the United States, which do not look 'back' to Ireland itself. Due to the size and degree of establishment which the Irish-American diaspora already had by the end of the Second World War, these cultural forms and practices were already numerous during the second half of the twentieth century. Developed to express the American experience of Irish immigrants and their descendants, these cultural practices often have few if any equivalents within Ireland, and may indeed be among the most influential grounds of Irish critiques of Irish America's 'inauthentic' Irishness. This crucial distinction between such 'American' Irish-American cultural practices and those which continue to engage with Ireland itself therefore profoundly informs the choice of texts, practices and events which this book uses to examine the relationship of later-generation Irish America to their ethnic homeland.

Based upon the decision to examine Irish America's relationship to and interaction with Ireland itself, the texts and practices chosen for this book therefore all involve this element of contact or engagement with Ireland by the diaspora. Film texts, for example, were selected if they were concerned with some aspect of later-generation Irish America's experience of Ireland, rather than with Irish-American life or culture entirely within the United States. Films such as *The Quiet Man, Shake Hands With The Devil, Patriot Games, The Luck of the Irish* or *This Is My Father*,[2] all of which are key texts within this study, each contain such an encounter between Irish America and Ireland as a key element of their narratives and representations. By comparison, other significant Irish-American films, such as *The Brothers McMullen*,[3] are not discussed here, due to their concentration upon an Irish-American experience exclusively within the United States.

Tourist texts concerning the Irish-American market in Ireland, by their nature, involve an interaction between the diaspora and its ethnic homeland. A variety of such texts are examined, ranging from promotional films such as *The Irish In Me* and *O'Hara's Holiday*,[4] to the diasporic consumption of material culture such as Waterford Crystal and Irish linen. Also considered, while not technically tourist texts, are popular publications such as *National Geographic* magazine, as well as *Time* and *Life* magazines. These publications have a long-established role in presenting the rest of the world to the American public, and *National Geographic* in particular has published special features on Ireland over the course of this book's entire period of study, very often features which highlight the connection between Ireland and Irish America.

Cultural practices or events also form an important part of this study. The significant levels of interest and participation in the genealogy industry among Irish America is a cultural practice given particular consideration, as are the 1990s phenomena of Irish theme pubs within the United States (and elsewhere), and the show *Riverdance*. The Rose of Tralee competition, given its particularly strong links to the Irish-American diaspora, is also examined as a long-running and popular source of continuing links between later-generation Irish America and Ireland itself.

Political, activist and charitable movements or organisations within Irish America are also included in this study where they have been specifically engaged with events or causes relating to Ireland, north or south. These include diverse ideological positions, ranging from Noraid to American government involvement in the Northern Ireland peace process, as well as charitable or philanthropic organisations such as the American–Ireland Fund.

However, there are a number of texts or cultural practices, many of them regarded as central features of Irish-American identity, which are not included in this study. Most noticeably, perhaps, St Patrick's Day celebrations, commemorations and parades are not discussed. This is because, as several critical and historical studies of the subject have demonstrated, Irish America's participation in St Patrick's Day celebrations, such as parades and carnivals, has traditionally been a primarily American activity, reflective above all else of Irish America's relationship to the United States.[5] Equally, the long tradition of Irish bars (as opposed to Irish theme pubs) in American towns and cities with large Irish-American populations is not explored in this study, as a clear differentiation is made between 'Irish bars', a fundamentally American-based Irish-American cultural practice, and the newer 'Irish theme pubs', which seek to export a version of Irish public houses to other parts of the world, including those with diasporic communities. For the same reasons, there is no detailed discussion of the important contribution made to American public and political life by the Irish-American community, except where that contribution has been mobilised to engage with political issues concerning Ireland.

THE 'LATER-GENERATION' DIASPORA

A further aspect of this project's selectivity is that of the generational groups chosen for consideration. Due to the patterns of Irish migration to the United States, as well as the length of time for which this has been occurring, the majority of Americans who, by the end of the Second World War or later, would identify themselves as ethnically Irish were themselves born in the United States. It is this group, members of the diaspora of the second, third, or even later generations, who are the subject of this book. For an examination of cultural and ethnic performativity such as this, it seems self-evident that members of the Irish-American diaspora who were themselves born in Ireland and emigrated to the United States will have an importantly different relationship to their ethnicity and cultural identity to that of the members of the diaspora who were born and brought up in the United States. The cultural representation of the 'returning' Irish-American in Ireland, for example, whose persistent recurrence originally initiated this project, is most frequently delineated as American-born, and often on their first 'return' to their ethnic homeland. Given that the American-born diaspora has been more numerous in the post-Second World War period, and must engage in a more complex and nuanced process of identity formation, it seemed useful to concentrate upon their highly particularised performance of ethnicity. In doing so, I hope that many of the complicating elements of cultural transmission, inherited memory, and transnational identity will be illuminated through the prism of their experiences and cultural products.

The nature of diasporic identities such as those of later-generation Irish-Americans is founded specifically in the detail and ellipses of the hyphen itself, and against the unhyphenated terms such as 'Irish' and 'American'. One of the principal aims of this book therefore is to examine the ways in which late twentieth-century later-generation Irish-Americans both define and perform their Irishness; this inevitably occurs in a social and cultural context consisting of other, equally delineated identities, both hyphenated and unhyphenated.

IRISH ETHNICITY AND RELIGION

Such close attention to definitions of national, cultural or ethnic identity is, of course, particularly pertinent to discussions of any aspect of Irishness, where slippages and oppositions, as well as deeply embedded political meaning within language and imagery, are especially central to any discussion of identities. The use of the very term 'Irish', when discussing identities within Northern Ireland, for example, carries with it a weight of implication and opposition, as well as the shadow of a very real violence which throws into relief more abstracted discussions about the 'violence of language'. While this actual violence has not been translated into the Irish-American diaspora's experience during the post-Second World War period of this study, the difficulties of defining Irishness itself have been very clearly absorbed into the discussions and performances of Irish-American identities. The size, variety, and centuries-long time-frame of Irish emigration to the United States have inevitably ensured that the contemporary diaspora is highly varied in its ethnic, religious and regional Irish inheritance. Irish America, in its broadest definition, consists of descendants of immigrants who might have described themselves as Catholic, Protestant, Gaelic, Ulster-Scots and Anglo-Irish; and who arrived in the United States at different historical moments and for different socio-economic, political and religious reasons. As was mentioned above, a considerable amount of the research into Irish-American history and sociology conducted over the last few decades of the twentieth century has concentrated upon these differences, and has attempted to delineate the numbers and motivations of each group of emigrants from Ireland. There have also been, throughout the twentieth century, historians of the Irish in America, who have approached the topic through the prism of Catholic and, more rarely, Protestant, religious history within the United States.

This emphasis upon Irish America's varied religious, political and ethnic background is of course a worthwhile enterprise, especially when considering the processes by which the wider diaspora was established, during the eighteenth, nineteenth and early twentieth centuries. Nevertheless, it is not the approach taken in this study. The following chapters quite deliberately do not discuss religious affiliation of any kind, whether Protestant or Catholic, among Irish-Americans. This decision is closely related to the explanation, above, of the historical and textual boundaries of this particular project. Given that the opening questions of this book centre upon the popular cultural connections with Ireland expressed and performed within Irish America, the book itself has concentrated its analysis upon the cultural concerns and identities expressed within those texts.

To include religious practices and the myriad 'texts' that those practices produce, as 'popular culture', seems neither appropriate nor useful. Equally, as the historians of both Catholic and Protestant affiliations among those of Irish descent in the United States have suggested in much of their work, by the starting point of this study, all of these denominations had established themselves as integral parts of *American* society and religious practice, without significant reliance upon their Irishness as such, in either their forms or conventions.

IRISH AMERICA AND IRISH STUDIES

Recent examinations of contemporary Irish-American identity have tended to focus on the ways in which this theme has related to a wider reworking of ethnic identities within American society. In particular, there has been an emphasis upon Irish ethnicity as an 'innocent' version of whiteness, which has allowed Irish-Americans to maintain the inherent privileges of whiteness within American society while simultaneously making claims of ethnic victimhood and exclusion, based upon the historical experience of both Ireland's colonisation and the discrimination experienced by earlier generations of Irish Catholics in the United States.[6]

I find these arguments profoundly convincing, and would suggest that they form the most coherent and socially important contributions to contemporary studies of Irish-American culture. This project, however, approaches Irish-American identity from a slightly different perspective – and one which, I hope, can usefully be read alongside these other studies as an extra dimension to the understandings they produce. By definition, the studies mentioned above primarily examine Irish-American identity formation and its ideologies from within an American perspective – they are examinations of the ways in which Irish-American identity is a function of wider American identities.

This book, however, is an examination of the continuing encounters between Irish America and Ireland itself. Of course it is the case that these two approaches are indivisible from each other at many levels – it is through reference to Irish history and culture that Irish America distinguishes itself from other American ethnicities, after all. However, there is a meaningful distinction between Irish-American popular cultural forms and those of Ireland itself. And it is useful, I hope, to examine the very particular ways in which

Ireland – as opposed to Irish America – has continued to function within the processes of ethnic identity construction during the later twentieth century.

One particular use which it is hoped may be made of this focus upon moments of contact, both literal and imaginative, between Irish America and Ireland, is to attempt an examination of the tensions which exist between these two cultures. This tension is not unique to the contemporary era, and now as previously appears to revolve around questions of the 'ownership' of Irishness, as well as very deeply embedded questions about what constitutes 'authenticity' within expressions of that Irishness. I would argue therefore that a full examination of Irish-American identity within the United States needs to take into account the ways in which it is structured by ongoing Irish-American encounters with Ireland itself. The elements of tension which such an examination reveal will, I would suggest, add an important additional layer to understandings of the uses to which Irish-American identity is put within the United States. Equally, Irish identity and culture within Ireland cannot be fully understood – especially in the contemporary era – without reference to the connections with, and divisions from, Irish-American identity and culture.

The following chapters are arranged thematically rather than chronologically. The first chapter considers the political economy of Irish America's relationship to Ireland, focusing upon financial and political influence between the two nations. Chapter 2 moves on to discuss the nature of later-generation diasporic identity, through an examination of the Irish-American search for Irish 'roots', along with the ways in which this cultural practice reflects wider changes in the concepts of history and memory. The third chapter focuses on Irish-American cultural consumption, with a particular emphasis upon material culture, and discusses the ways in which these cultural objects transmit and influence concepts of diasporic identity. Chapter 4 is a discussion of the ways in which popular representations (especially film) of the relationship between Irish America and Ireland have had a strong emphasis upon gendered national and diasporic identity, and examines the ways in which this has operated during the late twentieth century. The fifth and final chapter examines the theoretical understanding of diasporic identities and maps the influences and elisions within considerations of Irish America and other global diasporas.

NOTES

1   The range of scholarship produced since the 1980s on earlier Irish-American history and culture is obviously too great to list in detail here. However, even a cursory examination would include works such as Tim Pat Coogan, *Wherever Green Is Worn: The Story of the Irish Diaspora* (New York: Palgrave Press, 2000), Kevin Kenny, *The American Irish: A History* (London: Longman, 2000), Andy Bielenberg (ed.), *The Irish Diaspora* (London: Longman, 2000), Arthur Gribben (ed.), *The Great Famine and the Irish Diaspora in America* (Amherst: University of Massachusetts Press, 1998), and Charles Fanning (ed.), *New Perspectives on the Irish Diaspora* (Carbondale: Southern Illinois University Press, 2000). More specifically statistical studies have included Kerby A. Miller, *Emigrants and Exiles: Ireland and the Irish Exodus to North America* (Oxford: Oxford University Press, 1985), and Donald Harman Akenson, *The Irish Diaspora: A Primer* (Belfast: Institute of Irish Studies, 1996), while the development of detailed studies of specific aspects of Irish-American history has included Noel Ignatiev, *How the Irish Became White* (London: Routledge, 1995), Kevin Kenny, *Making Sense of the Molly Maguires* (Oxford: Oxford University Press, 1998), Steven P. Erie, *Rainbow's End: Irish-Americans and the Dilemmas of Urban Machine Politics, 1840–1985* (Berkeley: University of California Press, 1988), Timothy J. Meagher, *Inventing Irish America: Generation, Class and Ethnic Identity in a New England City, 1880–1928* (Notre Dame: University of Notre Dame Press, 2001), and William Leonard Joyce, *Editors and Ethnicity: A History of the Irish-American Press, 1848–1883* (New York: Arno Press, 1976). Irish-American women's history has also been specifically addressed, in studies such as Hasia Diner, *Erin's Daughters in America: Irish Immigrant Women in the Nineteenth Century* (Baltimore, MD: Johns Hopkins University Press, 1983), and Ide O'Carroll, *Models for Movers: Irish Women's Emigration to America* (Dublin: Attic Press, 1990). While some of these studies do include some discussion of Irish America in the latter half of the twentieth century, their emphasis has tended to be upon the rediscovery of the earlier history of the diaspora.

2   *The Luck of the Irish*, dir. Henry Koster (20ᵗʰ Century Fox, 1948), *The Quiet Man*, dir. John Ford (Republic Studios, 1952), *Shake Hands With the Devil*, dir. Michael Anderson (United Artists, 1958), *Patriot Games*, dir. Phillip Noyce (Paramount Pictures, 1992), *This Is My Father*, dir. Paul Quinn (Filmline International/Hummingbird Communications, 1998).

3   *The Brothers McMullen*, dir. Edward Burns (20th Century Fox, 1995).

4   *O'Hara's Holiday*, dir. Peter Bryan (Tribune Films Incorporated, 1960), *The Irish In Me*, dir. Herman Boxer (Universal International Colour/Dudley Pictures Corporation, 1959).

5   Mike Cronin and Daryl Adair, *The Wearing of the Green: A History of St Patrick's Day* (London: Routledge, 2002).

6   See Diane Negra, 'Irishness, Innocence, and American Identity Politics Before and After September 11', *The Irish In Us: Irishness, Performativity, and Popular Culture* (Durham, NC: Duke University Press, 2006) and Bronwen Walter, *Outsiders Inside: Whiteness, Place and Irish Women* (London: Routledge, 2001).

1

The Political Economy of the Diaspora: Irish-American Politics and Capital in Ireland

INTRODUCTION

IN 1956, the then Senator John F. Kennedy gave a St Patrick's Day address to the Irish Fellowship Club of Chicago, in which, after making reference to the Soviet Union's current threat to 'man's desire to be free', he went on to highlight the complexity of this situation for America as a whole and ethnic groups such as Irish America in particular. Describing the international alliances by which the perceived Soviet threat was to be resisted, Kennedy also acknowledged the divisions of political thought within those alliances, in particular highlighting the continued colonial involvement of many of America's Western partners. As a result of the developing Cold War, Kennedy explained:

> we have found our destiny to be closely linked with that of the British and the French...nations which still hold under their subjugation large areas of the world upon which they feel their ultimate security depends. And thus we have been caught up in a dilemma which up to now has been insoluble. We want our allies to be strong, and yet quite obviously a part of their strength comes from their overseas possessions. And thus our dilemma has become a paradox. We fight to keep the world free from Communist imperialism – but in doing so we hamper our efforts, and bring suspicion upon our motives, by being closely linked with Western imperialism.[1]

Although Kennedy then went on to speak specifically of French involvement in North Africa as well as the Islamic world's growing anti-colonialism, rather than the issue of Irish partition, his message, delivered to an Irish-American audience on St Patrick's Day, also contained a scarcely veiled acknowledgement of Irish nationalism as it intersected with the 'special relationship' between Britain and the United States. In effect, the Irish-American dilemma Kennedy was clearly signalling in 1956 – that of the competing interests of anti-colonial diasporas and anti-communist superpowers – would be the continuing dilemma to face American involvement in Irish affairs for the rest of the century. From the relatively free position of being a young senator, Kennedy was able to articulate the issue in a way which neither he – nor any other post-war president – would feel able to do so explicitly again.

Irish-American support for the Irish nation, both political and economic, had a long and often tempestuous history by 1956. This chapter will explore the developments and setbacks of that support between the end of the Second World War and the end of the twentieth century. In so doing, it will attempt to track the complex intersections and oppositions between Irish America's economic and civic involvement with Ireland, crucially placing these within the international context in which diasporic connections must always be made. This examination of the political economy of Irish America's relationship to Ireland is a necessary precursor, I would argue, to an understanding of the cultural relationships which are the subject of later chapters in this book.

Beginning with the end of the Second World War and the Marshall Plan era this initiated, this discussion follows Irish America's political-economic evolution through the development of the Cold War, the beginning of the Troubles at the end of the 1960s, the highly charged symbolism of the early 1980s hunger strikes, and on towards the Peace Process and Good Friday Agreement of the late 1990s.

Throughout this discussion, political and economic connections between Ireland and its United States diaspora are analysed in tandem with each other rather than separately. This approach has been taken because the evidence suggests that not only have political and financial developments often been explicitly connected with each other, but even apparently discrete financial interventions have often had an ideological motivation and vice versa.

Contemporary diasporic engagements with the politics of ethnic homelands are beginning to attract increasing scholarly attention, on the grounds that, as Jolle Demmers has noted, 'by living their lives across borders diaspora find themselves confronted with and engaged in the nation-building processes of two or more nation-states. Their identities and practices are likely to be configured by hegemonic categories, such as race and ethnicity, that are deeply embedded in the nation-building processes of these nation-states'.[2]

Such a statement has clear validity in the case of the Irish-American diaspora during the nineteenth and early twentieth centuries, particularly for its many members during that era who were first-generation immigrants from Ireland. In more recent times, however, as Adrian Guelke has pointed out with specific respect to the issue of Northern Ireland, because of the different scales of international power and wealth involved, it is inevitably easier 'to trace the effect of American actions and pronouncements on Northern Ireland than it is to gauge the impact of events in Northern Ireland on the opinion of Americans in general or even of those assumed to have a special interest in the situation, the Irish-Americans'.[3] This is particularly the case in the instance of the varying ideological positions taken by sections of Irish America towards Ireland. One of the most frequently made assertions about the Irish diaspora in the United States during the latter half of the twentieth century is that it has tended to display a striking lack of interest in the political and economic welfare and development of the 'old country'. This apparent lack of interest is compared negatively both to their own previous record of involvement in Irish affairs (during the eras of Parnell and de Valera, for example), and to the interventions in 'home' issues of other ethnic diasporas in the United States, most notably that of Jewish-American support for the state of Israel. To achieve the same financial power and political influence as the Jewish-American lobby in America was a clear ambition of Irish-American groups. The funds and political support raised by such groups as the United Jewish Communities and the Koret Foundation have become the benchmark of diasporic influence within the United States. Commenting on this phenomenon in 1997, Alvin Rabuska estimated that $7.7 billion out of Israel's economy of $80–85 billion per year consisted of 'unilateral gifts and transfers', the greatest donors of which were the government and private foundations of the United States.[4]

This chapter seeks to clarify the reasons for Irish America's distinctive engagement with Irish political economies since 1945. In particular, it attempts to highlight the ways in which apparent lack of interest may in fact have been a demonstration of the Irish-American 'dilemma' rather than of apathy, a situation largely due to the exceptionally complex global politics in which the governmental relationship between Ireland and the United States has been enmeshed during this period. The Irish-American diaspora has, in effect, embodied this web of competing interests and loyalties for much of the last fifty years, and as such the majority of its overt ideological activities have been muted by comparison to some other diasporas. This chapter attempts both to describe and to disentangle some of these complexities in order to shed light on the politics and economics of the contemporary Irish-American diaspora.

WORLD WAR TO COLD WAR

The aftermath of the Second World War, for Ireland as for the rest of Western Europe, was strongly affected by the introduction of Marshall Aid for reconstruction. Overseen by the Committee of European Economic Cooperation (CEEC), which first met in Paris in July 1947, Marshall Aid from the United States to all eligible European nations was undertaken in order 'to make Europe so prosperous that communism would have no attractions'.[5] As such, this United States intervention was an explicit recognition that almost from the very moment the Second World War ended the Cold War had begun.

The proportion of each European nation's GNP coming from United States aid for the duration of the Marshall Plan was significant (in 1948–49, foreign aid constituted 7.8 per cent of Irish GNP, a figure largely consistent with other countries' experience), and the overall cost of the project to America was huge. In 1948, Congress approved a payment of $5 billion, and it gave a further $12 billion over the next four years.[6] The scale and duration of the reconstruction project undertaken was therefore an early indication of the dominance which Cold War strategy would come to have over global politics for the following decades.

Ireland was eligible for Marshall Plan funding under the same terms as all other eligible Western European nations. However, loans and grants were only issued after investigation of individual states' economic circumstances and the submission of long-term forecasts regarding the potential benefits of funding. Despite some initial doubts about the project on the part of the Irish government, therefore, Sean Lemass travelled to Paris in 1947 to attend the initial CEEC meeting, and Sean MacBride presented Ireland's case at later meetings. The Irish government produced its benefits projection report as a White Paper headed *The European Recovery Programme: Ireland's Long Term Programme (1949–53)*. This programme sought to reassure the CEEC that the recommendations of its investigation into the Irish economy would be undertaken following the receipt of Marshall Aid. The Committee, while accepting the importance of agriculture to the Irish economy, had recommended that Ireland 'needs to mechanize its agriculture, obtain more fertilizers and animal feed stuffs, increase its imports of fuel and overhaul its transportation system'. In the event, few of the White Paper's projections for the use of reconstruction funds were realised, although they were directed towards land reclamation and rural electrification.[7] What is striking, however, about the eventual Irish share of reconstruction funds is how small it was, not only in the light of Ireland's economic problems, but also by comparison to the funding other European nations received and to the amounts the Irish government originally expected to be granted.

Ireland was eventually offered only a $10 million loan, by comparison to Britain's $100 million loan plus a $300 million non-repayable grant.[8] Even taking into account the difference in size of the two economies, this was an obvious anomaly in purely economic terms, as the Irish government vigorously objected. The political aspect of the financial allocations was thus made clear, as was the fact that they represented both retrospective and current Western preoccupations.

Ireland's position in the political affections of the United States had been severely damaged by its neutrality during the Second World War, compounded even further by de Valera's message of condolence following Hitler's death. Despite his protestations that neutrality was an honourable course of national action for Ireland and that the condolence message was merely an act of diplomatic courtesy in line with that policy, both the government and popular opinion in the United States (including the Irish-American community) tended to regard these actions as a betrayal during a time of international emergency.[9] Any aspect of Marshall Aid allocation which contained an element of 'reward' (however unspoken) for war efforts was therefore going to be unavailable to Ireland. The repercussions of Ireland's wartime neutrality would become even more pronounced during the protracted struggles over partition, as will be discussed below.

The other political aspect of reconstruction-fund allocation, that of maintaining Western Europe as a bulwark against communism, was signalled more clearly in CEEC documents. A briefing note to the Committee from Jack Hickerson of the State Department commented, following Irish objections to their allocation, 'there are no over-riding international political considerations which would warrant preferential treatment towards the Irish'.[10] The 'political considerations' which would have given rise to preferential treatment would clearly have been a perceived threat of significant communist activity or popularity in Ireland – in the marked absence of these, United States foreign aid would be directed to more 'unstable' regions.[11]

Post-war attempts to interest United States governments in the issue of Irish partition were also severely hampered by both memories of Irish wartime neutrality and the growing Cold War partnership between the United States and Britain. During the Second World War, the United States had been given use of British military bases in North Ireland, a facility which had been denied in the Free State due to its neutral status. Within the context of Cold War strategy, this continued to be an important factor in American foreign policy, and one of considerably more pressing concern than the debate about Irish unification. Another memo written by Hickerson in the State Department commented: 'We have, according to the past record, every reason to count on the use of bases in the area in the event of need . . . I am sure you will agree that this is a powerful argument for this government's favouring the continued control of Northern Ireland by the United Kingdom.'[12] The growing importance of the 'special relationship' between the United States and Britain throughout the 1940s and 1950s, forged by their wartime cooperation and stabilised by their common positions regarding Cold War strategy, therefore marginalised Irish attempts to capitalise on their own 'special relationship' with America.

That relationship was obviously at its strongest in the case of the Irish-American community, who might have been expected to support the unification cause. There were indeed one or two instances of pro-Irish campaigning in American national politics throughout this time, although they rarely received sufficient backing to result in legislation or policy changes. In 1950, for example, the House of Representatives supported an amendment to the Foreign Aid Appropriation Bill, intending to withhold all future aid to Britain until Irish partition was removed; this amendment was later defeated.[13] In both the House of Representatives and later in the Senate, John F. Kennedy spoke in favour of reunification on the grounds that it 'would do much to end an ancient injustice and is in accordance with the traditional American support of self-determination'.[14] Nevertheless, the general tone of Washington's policy towards Ireland throughout the 1950s was better reflected by the neutral wording of President Truman's official message of congratulation on the occasion of the Republic of Ireland Act in 1949, which merely conveyed 'sincere good wishes for the continued welfare and prosperity of your country', and was sent only after the United States Embassy in London had confirmed that the British government would be sending a similar message. As Sean Cronin comments: 'The State Department's attitude in this whole affair goes far to confirm the view held by many Irish-Americans that in its relations with Ireland the United States preferred to work through the British government.'[15] Cronin's statement therefore raises the question of both Irish-American opinion and levels of influence at the level of national politics during this time. The history and strength of Irish-American involvement in American politics from the nineteenth century onwards has been extensively documented; most of this political influence, however, was at local and municipal level within the Irish-dominated areas such as New York, Boston and Chicago, and was in itself seen to be in decline by the 1960s.[16]

The new global political and ideological climate following the Second World War, however, would have required Irish-American supporters of pro-Irish policies to wield considerable power at a national level, in the Congress and Senate. And, while the 1950s and 1960s saw the emergence into national politics of the Kennedy brothers, Daniel Moynihan and Tip O'Neill, their influence at this time was still extremely limited. Indeed, it has been frequently suggested that, just as the 'suburbanisation' of the Irish-American population during this time diluted and ultimately ended the Irish domination of ward politics, so the rise to national power of individual members of the community occurred, by necessity, at the expense of their strongly identifiable Irish concerns and identities. With particular reference to John F. Kennedy and Daniel Moynihan, George E. Reedy claims such politicians were 'not Irish-Americans but Americans of Irish descent. Even Woodrow Wilson would have been satisfied with their credentials'.[17] Any aspiring Irish-American politician of this era would have been conscious of the lessons to be drawn from Al Smith's 1928 presidential campaign, in which popular suspicions both of 'Tammany Hall' machine-style politics and of Smith's Catholicism had destroyed an otherwise credible candidate.

THE KENNEDY ERA

The career of John F. Kennedy, particularly his election in 1960 as the first Irish Catholic president, is a significant example of the complexity of the Irish-American diaspora's political engagement with Irish issues. Kennedy undoubtedly aimed to appeal to the Irish-American community in his election campaign (in a way which signalled some confidence that the era of Al Smith's defeat was now over), as evidenced by a *Time* magazine feature story on the family during the run-up to the election, which proclaimed that 'The Kennedy clan is as handsome and spirited as a meadow full of Irish thoroughbreds, as tough as a blackthorn shillelagh, as ruthless as Cuchulain, the mythical hero who cast up the hills of Ireland with his sword.'[18] The 1960 election itself showed predictable support for Kennedy from Irish-Americans, with one study showing that he won 75 per cent of Irish Catholic votes.[19] George E. Reedy, however, argues that 'whether Catholics voted for Kennedy because he was Catholic – or whether all Irish voted for Kennedy because he was Irish – is a question open to doubt'.[20]

An issue which was soon not open to doubt, however, was the question of whether the United States' first Irish Catholic president would participate in or facilitate greater support for Irish foreign policies or economic intervention. As president, he was now forced to confront the dilemma he had alluded to in 1956: whether to support anti-colonial movements on the international stage, or to support America's imperial anti-communist allies. It soon became clear that Kennedy placed the struggle against international communism above liberation struggles, in Ireland and elsewhere.

It is extremely difficult to judge the level of interest in, and commitment to, political issues in Ireland among the larger Irish-American community. As has frequently been pointed out, between the end of the Second World War and the outbreak of the Troubles in 1969, there was a striking lack of formal organisation among the diaspora. Membership of well-established groups such as the Ancient Order of Hibernians was stagnant at best, and the previously thriving Irish-American newspaper industry was also relatively dormant at this time.[21] There are a number of possible reasons for this era of muted politics among the diaspora.

A likely factor in their lack of involvement may have been the scarcity, in the United States' media, of powerful news stories which might have mobilised diaspora public opinion. As will be discussed below, the role of the mass media in opinion-forming and disseminating information is crucial to transnational diaspora political involvement, a fact which would become clear once the Troubles resumed at the end of the 1960s. Prior to that, only the IRA's border campaign of 1956–62 would have provided stories to mobilise diaspora support, and even those would have been unlikely to provide sufficient political imagery to generate significant interest among later-generation Irish-Americans.

As well as this reason for a general lack of active engagement with Irish politics among the diaspora, there was also the central question of the overwhelmingly anti-communist emphasis of American politics at this time. As was outlined above, this led to the strengthening of the 'special relationship' between the United States and Britain; and while few Irish-Americans are likely to have been actively pro-British, their anti-communism (spurred further perhaps by their Catholicism) is likely to have prevented large-scale political organisation against America's main strategic ally in the Cold War.

And finally, the move towards suburbanisation, degree-level education and white-collar employment which characterised this generation of Irish America also involved a (conscious or unconscious) turning away from specifically ethnic concerns, including Irish politics and current affairs – as with other aspects of ethnic identity, it would be the next generation who returned to such matters with enthusiasm, during the 1970s. As Kevin Kenny has claimed of this period, it could be argued that 'it was in 1960 rather than 1860 that the American Irish finally became "white", if by that term one means full racial and cultural respectability, a final acceptance by white American Protestants of Irish-American Catholics as their equals in all things important'.[22] However, this acceptance, it is argued, frequently came at the cost of considerable assimilation to the dominant Anglo-American value system, including that system's application to international politics. Indeed, President Kennedy himself has frequently been described in assimilationist terms. His ambassador to Ireland, Thomas J. Kiernan, not only asserted that, 'apart from his Americanism which was a hundred percent, [Kennedy] was more British than Irish', but also explained this allegiance by arguing that 'those with Irish names in America are still wanting to be accepted as part of the establishment, or at any rate not be regarded as outsiders'.[23]

Despite this assessment, however, Kennedy's 1963 visit to Ireland was not only the first of a presiding American president, but was also the first state visit by any American president to their ethnic homeland. That visit, both at the time and in historical retrospect, highlighted a number of the recurring themes of the diasporic relationship to Ireland. Kennedy's own statements, as well as the representations of his visit in the Irish press, are revealing of the relationship between Ireland and its diaspora at the time. The *Irish Press*, on the day of his arrival in Ireland, produced a specially re-designed front page, in which photographs of Kennedy and de Valera faced each other across a scroll-framed statement which announced: 'You have come to the home of your forefathers and history fulfils itself in your journey and your arrival and in the welcome from the heart that the Irish people offer you.'[24] The coat-of-arms effect which this design produced was therefore reflective of the determination to emphasise the powerful 'family' connections between Ireland and its diaspora.

Kennedy too was eager to reiterate this aspect of the relationship, as was shown in his very first speech upon arrival at Dublin Airport, when, discussing the Irish diaspora, he claimed: 'These sons and daughters are scattered throughout the world and they give this small island a family of millions upon millions...They have also kept a special place in their memory – in many cases their ancestral memory – for this grey and misty Ireland. So in a sense all of them who visit Ireland come home.'[25] Here, then, was the world's most famous representative of the Irish diaspora laying claim on behalf of that community to their 'homeland' across the generations that lay between them and their emigrating ancestors. The terms in which this particular diasporic hero was received, and the ways in which he responded to that reception, are interesting. Later commentators have argued that the language and imagery which Kennedy used on his Irish visit were romanticised and nostalgic in their emphasis upon the national struggle for independence and the tenacious resistance of imperial domination.[26] Certainly, he reiterated these themes in his many speeches.

However, Kennedy also drew specific attention to Ireland's growing participation in global politics, and to the rapid economic and social development of the country. This theme was particularly noticeable in his historic speech to the Dáil, in which he eulogised Ireland's progress since Independence, and emphasised the nation's importance on the modern world stage. In particular, although Kennedy used his Dáil speech to make reference to Ireland's successful struggle for independence and freedom as well as her 'independent course in foreign policy', he explicitly tied this history to the current United States' political concerns about the spread of communist influence across eastern Europe. Only a week earlier, he had made his famous speech at the Berlin Wall, and was utilising Irish history to further his attacks on Soviet policy. In a complex reworking of his 1956 St Patrick's Day theme, Kennedy now conflated the Irish struggle for independence (from the United States' main ally) with that of nations such as Hungary, whose uprising had recently been brutally suppressed by the Soviet military. Some commentators have argued that Kennedy was tacitly supportive of Irish neutrality, but his approval of its 'independent' foreign policy was only on the condition that 'it is not neutral between liberty and tyranny and never will be'.[27] In other words, Ireland's 'neutral' capitalist liberal democracy meant that, as The *New York Times* commented in its coverage, Kennedy's visit 'had no great diplomatic importance', as Irish cooperation with the Anglo-American alliance against the USSR was assured.[28]

THE TROUBLES

The beginnings of the civil rights movement in Northern Ireland in the late 1960s proved a crucial turning point for Irish-American political engagement with Ireland. The diaspora proved immediately responsive to press coverage of the civil rights marches across the province. One immediate result of this responsiveness was that the Northern Ireland Civil Rights Association leader Bernadette Devlin was invited on a speaking tour of the United States in August 1969. This trip, designed to raise both money and awareness of the NICRA campaign, was to become more notable for its underlining of ideological differences between Irish and Irish-American campaigners. Devlin insistently drew parallels between the civil rights movements in Ireland and the United States, meeting with African-American campaigners during her visit, and urging Irish-American supporters to explore the common ideological grounds of the two groups. This proved a highly unpopular approach among the more established Irish-American organisations who were hosting her tour, as shown by the reports of hostile audience receptions and the fact that she only succeeded in raising $200,000 out of the $1 million initially hoped for.[29]

It was Devlin's 1969 tour (as well as a subsequent one in 1971) which initiated the characterisation of Irish-American political involvement as conservative, exclusive and even racist. Devlin certainly did expose the divergence of ideological approaches between Irish and Irish-American campaigning groups during the decades after Independence, when their contacts had diminished. Where Irish groups had developed in tandem with the social radicalism of 1960s politics, as well as being influenced by the parallels between their own situation and that of other marginalised communities, Irish America, after several decades of disengagement, had remained ideologically rooted in the struggles of Independence and the Civil War, rather than making connections between themselves and other American groups such as the African-American civil rights campaigners. Devlin's visit highlighted the level of difference between the homeland and diasporic communities. She was frequently heckled as she spoke in support of African-American civil rights campaigners, publicly presented donation cheques were taken back in private, and African-American supporters were physically prevented from entering Irish-organised public meetings.[30] The chant of 'Niggers Out Of Boston, Brits Out Of Belfast', widely alleged to have been used by Irish-American protesters during the anti-bussing campaigns of the early 1970s, is also frequently presented as conclusive evidence of Irish-American refusal to engage with the radical politics of Irish campaigners such as Devlin.[31] One central reason for this divergence is likely to have been the unequal circulation of information between the two locations. The lack of political interaction between Ireland and the United States since the end of the Second World War had been matched by the lack of current affairs information about Ireland reaching the diaspora. By contrast, the emerging civil rights movement in Northern Ireland had been heavily influenced by the worldwide media coverage of the African-American civil rights campaign in the United States.[32]

Despite these events, the Irish-American communities which Devlin visited in 1969 were already more complex than they are often portrayed. The South Boston communities in particular are usually subject to specific condemnation because of their opposition to the bussing programmes of the early 1970s; and yet, as Seamus Metress has argued of these conflicts, 'the virulence of these local clashes, with race often playing a somewhat marginal role, has tended to obscure the important contributions of many Irish-Americans to the cause of social justice for African-Americans'.[33] Equally, Brian Dooley points to an early 1970s survey by the

National Opinion Research Center which not only found that Irish-Americans were the Gentile group most in favour of integration, but also noted that 89 per cent replied they would vote for a Jewish president.[34] Nevertheless, it is undoubtedly true that the sudden surge of interest in the Irish political situation among Irish-Americans at the outbreak of the Troubles came initially from a reconnection with the older tradition of Irish-American political movements, dating back to Parnell and de Valera, rather than from a recognition of ideological solidarity with other colonised or marginalised groups.

Following this resurgence of interest in the Irish political situation, Irish-American political and economic support organisations began to be established or rejuvenated on a significant scale during the early 1970s. While the history of these movements, and their interaction with both the United States and Irish governments, would come to be marked by schisms and crucial ideological differences, it is nevertheless clear that this era proved a turning point in the history of diasporic political and economic involvement.

Of these groups, one of the first and most controversial to be established was the Irish Northern Aid Committee (more popularly known as Noraid). This was begun in 1970 by Michael Flannery, a former IRA man who had left Ireland after the Civil War. As such, he was typical of the politicised Irish-Americans of the time; many were first generation immigrants who had had previous experience of direct action in Ireland itself.

The ways in which Noraid – and several other nationalist organisations such as the Irish National Caucus and the Irish-American Unity Conference – approached political campaigns and fund-raising initiatives were in themselves revealing of the diaspora's style of political engagement. In a pattern established by Bernadette Devlin's 1969 speaking tour, the most financially successful periods in all the campaigning groups' histories have been those involving high-profile visits to the United States by Irish figures already well known through mass media reporting. This shows the clear importance of both the media images of Ireland conveyed to Irish America and, by implication, the political–economic media structures which produce these images. These structures will be discussed below in some detail.

Where NICRA's attempts to involve Irish-American public opinion had become entangled in the different political context of the diaspora, organisations such as Noraid were rejected by the differing political approach of the Irish government. Successive Dublin administrations condemned the organisation's perceived support for IRA violence, and issued frequent appeals to Irish-Americans not to contribute to their fund-raising efforts. Despite noticeable fluctuations in their income over the decades, however, Noraid continued to be a major force in diaspora interventions into Irish affairs. This occurred despite the United States government's own attempts – at the behest of both British and Irish governments – to diminish their appeal and power. As an organisation raising money for use overseas, Noraid was obliged to register its interests under the terms of the 1938 American Foreign Agents Registration Act (generally known as FARA). In 1971 they did so, naming the Irish Northern Aid Committee as their principal foreign agent. This was in keeping with the organisation's consistent profession that their fund-raising in the United States was for the purpose of supporting the families and dependants of prisoners and others involved in the Troubles, rather than direct funding of IRA actions themselves. As has been pointed out by many commentators, this was a rather irrelevant distinction, as, even if it were strictly correct (a much disputed point), Noraid's support for dependants would allow the IRA to divert more of their other funds into direct action.

The United States' Justice Department challenged Noraid's registration under FARA on the grounds that not only did they believe the organisation's true foreign agent was actually the IRA, but they also believed the six-monthly financial disclosures legally required as a part of FARA registration were significantly incomplete. This resulted in a long-running court case, eventually settled in 1984, when Noraid agreed to name the IRA as their foreign agent, on condition of being allowed to state that they were doing so only under protest. Perhaps the most significant long-term result of this legal contest has been to further obscure the actual level of income Noraid was able to raise during the height of the Troubles, as they refused to submit full financial disclosure statements during the long trial and appeals process.[35]

Nevertheless, as the most forceful and well-publicised Irish-American political campaign of the 1970s and 1980s, an analysis of Noraid's disclosed fund-raising provides an interesting picture of the aspects of Irish politics which were supported or rejected by its American diaspora. Conflicting information occurs in different sources for almost all of the years discussed. However, the figures below represent the most commonly agreed upon totals for each financial period. As an example of the levels of confusion surrounding Noraid's income, Holland quotes a Noraid source as claiming that only $200,000 was raised throughout all of 1981, despite rumours that the true amount was considerably higher. However, in an article published in the *Christian Science Monitor* on 21 January 1985, Michael Flannery is quoted as saying that 'During the Hunger Strikes, for instance, we took in more money in two months than we did for a whole year before. It was almost $300,000 taken in.' Table 1.1 therefore illustrates only the best available figures for Noraid's income during the crucial period of the Troubles, between the organisation's FARA registration and the hunger strikes.

Table 1.1   Declared Income of Noraid, 1971–81[36]

Date	Declared income (US$)
1971 (second half only)	128,099
1972	463,000
1973 (first half only)	123,000
1974	211,000
1975	174,000
1976	119,500
1977	108,000
1980	130,000
1981	200,000

It must be accepted that these figures are almost certainly not full disclosures; Michael Flannery himself has been widely quoted as having declared that the organisation preferred cash donations because, 'with cash, the government didn't know how much we sent'.[37] Nevertheless, the fluctuations in income – rather than the income itself – are worthy of analysis in order to attempt a determination of the factors contributing to Noraid's relative popularity with the diaspora, who were their core constituency.

The sharp rise in income between the first financial declaration in December 1971 and that of the second disclosure in May 1972 indicates the profound effect the Bloody Sunday shootings of 30 January 1972 had upon Irish-American popular opinion. Where the civil rights movement had raised levels of awareness, it had been hindered not only by its sometimes unpopular connections to the African-American civil rights movement, but also by its relatively abstract arguments. Irish America – particularly members of later generations without personal contacts in Ireland – was largely

dependent upon mass media coverage of Ireland by foreign correspondents for its political knowledge of the country. As such,
detailed discussions of the finer points of civil rights campaign
demands were relatively rare. By contrast, the images of unarmed
protesters being shot in the street by the British army provided both
a powerful news story for the world's press and a clear and unam-
biguous cause for a nationalist diaspora.

Newly reinvigorated Irish-American campaigning groups, which
became both more numerous and more vocal in the aftermath of
Bloody Sunday, were no longer muted by the Kennedy-era dilemma
of anti-colonialism versus anti-communism. Instead, they placed the
British actions in Northern Ireland squarely within the rubric of
colonial oppression – even when they chose not to equate them with
other international examples, as Irish activists themselves were
doing. A more popular approach among Irish-American campaigners was the siting of Catholic resistance in Northern Ireland within
the ideological framework of America's own anti-colonial history. In
June 1972, for example, the American Committee for Ulster Justice
issued a statement declaring that 'The United States, which itself was
the first colony of Britain to successfully initiate its independence,
must look sympathetically on the fight of the people who of all
nations on earth are most identified with the historical movement of
national liberation and political independence.'[38] Such an explicit
connection between American and Irish histories of anti-colonialism
was to be increasingly common as the political engagement with
Ireland increased among its American diaspora.

This was in stark contrast, however, with the coverage of the
Troubles produced by the mainstream United States press, such as
the *New York Times*, the *Washington Post* and the *Chicago Tribune*.
Given the disparity of circulation and political influence between
even the reinvigorated Irish-American press of the 1970s and their
mainstream counterparts, the differences in their approach to this
issue are significant, and again point towards the ways in which
diasporic political activities are subject to complex international
webs of influence and loyalties.

The specific events of 30 January 1972 received fairly critical
press coverage and political responses. President Nixon expressed
'concern' at the 'tragic events', and the *New York Times* described
the Irish-American reaction as being 'understandably outraged at the
bloodshed in Ulster and would like someone to promise to do something about it'.[39] This was unusually sympathetic coverage, however

mildly worded the implied criticisms of British actions were. The general tone of mainstream American media coverage, following the fresh outbreak of the Troubles, was considerably more sympathetic to British concerns. In his analysis of Irish-American interventions in Ireland, Jack Holland has noted the distinctive frame of reference used to describe and assess Irish politics within the American press, commenting that 'The "inexplicable" Irish soon became a fixture of the coverage. Benignly, the inexplicable nature of the Irish could be expressed in terms of mystery. Or it could be seen malignantly, as an explanation for the religious hatred which the press regards as a cause of the violence.'[40]

This emphasis upon religious hatred continued to characterise the majority of reports concerning Ireland. The Troubles were routinely referred to in terms of sectarian warfare between fanatical religious groups, neither of which were prepared to participate in the modern processes of liberal democratic and constitutional government. This characterisation of Northern Ireland politics therefore positioned the British government and army as 'honest brokers' unwittingly caught between the warring factions. This was emphasised by the way in which American press coverage tended to refer to British soldiers stationed in Northern Ireland as 'Tommies', terminology which, as Holland has argued, 'conjured up a memory of the chirpy little Second World War trooper in a soup-plate helmet'.[41] As such, the contrasting images of Irish sectarian fanaticism and British heroic fairness continued through press coverage the Cold War 'special relationship' support which American governments had shown in their foreign policy since 1945. Describing the end of the Stormont government in 1974, for example, *Time* magazine combined all of these images in its statement that Britain 'was *forced* to reimpose direct rule from Westminster and the British Tommies once again were on the alert to prevent Irishman from killing Irishman' [emphasis added].[42]

Such coverage of Irish politics by the mainstream American media was possibly influenced by the structural basis under which most of it operated. The majority of American journalists covering Irish stories were doing so from their papers' London bureaux – and in many cases were even submitting their copy to London sub-editors before it was sent to America.[43] The results of this institutional as well as political structuring of Irish news was described by the *Daily News*' Jim Mulvaney, who, as a rare exception to this system, was based in Ireland. Of the other newspapers' approach, Mulvaney stated: 'If you came through London you would get the Foreign Office briefing and arrive in Northern Ireland scared stiff. The people who were not based in Ireland were writing pro-British stories.'[44] The decision taken by most of the American press to cover Ireland from London would in part have been a pragmatic decision based on the need to centre foreign correspondents in major bureaux from which they could cover a wide area. Nevertheless, the coverage of a serious political dispute only from the capital city of one major participant was clearly problematic, and must reflect deeper political sympathies as well as practicalities.

The emphasising of such structural biases within media coverage of Ireland became one of the most consistent policies of the Irish-American press. This relatively unusual process of media analysis within the media itself obviously reflected the Irish-American press' understanding that their own circulation and political influence – even among the diasporic community – would always be severely limited by comparison to that of the leading newspapers and television networks. Their campaign to highlight the political–economic influences of media institutions upon the reporting of Ireland within the United States was to continue throughout the 1970s and 1980s. The Philadelphia-based *Irish Edition*, for example, published an analysis of the role of the international wire-services in the reporting of Irish news, under the headline, 'All the News That's Brit We Print', in a clear parody of the *New York Times*' well-known slogan, 'All the News That's Fit To Print'. Focusing on the output of United Press International (UPI), the article complains of 'not only inaccuracies but also several instances of apparent bias' in stories produced by this news agency, whose bulletins were picked up and republished across the world. As well as pointing to the UPI's consistent characterisation of the conflict as being largely one of sectarian disputes, the *Irish Edition* pointed out that, whereas Bernadette Devlin McAliskey had been described as a 'Catholic firebrand', giving 'rabble-rousing' speeches, Ian Paisley was termed a 'Protestant leader'. The UPI, like most of the other international news agencies, was also based in London, through which office all Irish stories were routed prior to international release. The *Irish Edition* also maintained that 'many of UPI's wire photos from Northern Ireland are marked "strict embargo (can't use) for UK (United Kingdom) and all Ireland" ... this extensive embargo appeared mainly on pictures that could be considered favorable to the republican cause'.[45]

The growing commitment to political campaigning on Irish issues shown by some Irish-American newspapers and groups such as Noraid and Mario Biaggi's Ad Hoc Congressional Committee for Irish Affairs did not occur in simple opposition to Anglo-American alliances with Britain, however. The Irish government was almost equally opposed to the interventions of Irish America, particularly those of Noraid, whom it saw as directly supporting the IRA. Indeed, the Irish government, through its embassy in Washington, attempted to 'police' Irish-American activities with great care in order to prevent financial or political support for IRA campaigns having significant effects. Groups such as the Irish National Caucus and even long-standing organisations such as the Ancient Order of Hibernians were censured by the Irish Embassy for perceived IRA sympathies. This situation was described by Tim Pat Coogan as being symptomatic of 'the perennial difficulty, existing for over a century, as to who controls Irish-American policy, the Irish in Ireland or the Irish in America'.[46]

Despite the Irish government's failure to entirely discredit organisations such as Noraid, the calls from Dublin for a strictly constitutional response to Irish politics from the diaspora did result in the increasing development of alternative approaches to the issue, particularly from within American national politics. In 1977, the Friends of Ireland Declaration supporting peaceful solutions to the Northern Ireland conflict was signed by Tip O'Neill, Tom Foley, William Buckley and Hugh Carey – the high-profile Irish-American senators who would come to be known as the 'Four Horsemen' of Irish issues in the United States. In the same year, President Carter issued a statement endorsing political solutions to the Troubles, and asking Americans not to contribute to organisations with 'direct or indirect' connections to violence.[47] The previous year, in August 1976, Carter had promised United States investment in Northern Ireland in the event of a peaceful settlement.

Noraid and similar organisations in the United States attempted to portray the Friends of Ireland position as a betrayal of principle which should be rejected by Irish-Americans, but, as Table 1.1 shows, their income did drop significantly during this time from its previous high point of 1972. The combined effect of mainstream media representations of the Northern Ireland conflict as an internecine struggle, and the new directions taken by relatively powerful national politicians undoubtedly contributed to this decline in Noraid's influence. Here again the effects of media images upon diasporic engagements with Ireland are visible – high levels of 'direct' involvement such as Noraid activities, indicating a level of commitment to 'Irish' identity at least temporarily superseding 'American' identity, are created during the circulation of intensely dramatic media images such as those surrounding Bloody Sunday. This would happen again during the politically charged events surrounding the hunger strikes in the early 1980s, as will be discussed below. In between these periods of intense imagery from Ireland, however, when political debate became more abstract as well as more complex, and with Irish-American allegiances divided between different policies, the levels of direct involvement dropped.

Lawrence McCaffrey has argued, following the ideas of William V. Shannon, a former American ambassador to Dublin, that middle-class Irish-Americans found it difficult to identify with Catholics in Northern Ireland, due primarily to the economic and class differences between them.[48] Essentially, this is an extension of McCaffrey's often repeated argument that suburbanisation and economic advancement among Irish-Americans in the decades following the Second World War have 'diluted' their ethnic allegiances. His statement about divisions between the 'lace-curtain' Irish in American suburbs and the Catholic residents of inner-city Belfast implies the same underlying point – that by the 1970s, the majority of Irish-Americans defined their identity more through economic and social class than through ethnicity. He explains the support that organisations such as Noraid have received through the argument that, by 1969 and later, most Irish-Americans understood so little of the political situation in Ireland that they 'could not distinguish between the IRA and NICRA, so that much of the money that they contributed for Northern Ireland equality went into the wrong pockets'.[49] This argument is undermined, however, by the notable fluctuations in financial support shown for Noraid across the periods for which their accounts are available. Similarly, George E. Reedy's unsupported contention that Irish-American support for the IRA, 'if it does exist it probably involves people who have a terrorist psychology and would find some other outlet if there were no conflict in Ulster', fails to explain the ways in which Noraid's income rose and fell throughout the 1970s and 1980s.[50]

The nature of diasporic transmission of political allegiance through the channels of mass media seems a far more convincing explanation for the developing and changing Irish-American involvements with Ireland during this period. McCaffrey himself appears to acknowledge this factor when he argues that 'Reacting to terrorism in the Mideast and other places that have resulted in the murder or capture of Americans, most of the Irish in the United States are furious when the IRA ambushes British soldiers or assassinates British politicians. They are angrier when IRA bombs kill women and children.'[51] This statement contains many probable truths; nevertheless, McCaffrey's conflation of the Irish situation with other conflicts around the world, as well as his telling emphasis upon the effects of women and children's involvement in the Troubles, suggest the power of news imagery over a diaspora separated by both geography and generations from direct knowledge of their ethnic homeland. The evidence of Noraid's financial statements also suggests that ethnic allegiances had not worn away by this period, but were stimulated by very specific events and imagery. That Noraid (and, presumably, the IRA themselves) were aware of this factor in their campaigns is indicated by interviews given to the *Christian Science Monitor* by Michael Flannery in the mid-1980s, making a retrospective assessment of the nature of their appeal to Irish America. In this interview, Flannery is quoted as asserting that:

> 'We're never without something to excite the people here. When the Hunger Strike was over, it started up again with the St. Patrick's Day Parade.' He ticks off a list of controversial events beginning with the 1981 fatal Hunger Strike of Bobby Sands and nine other Republican prisoners in Northern Ireland. His list ends with the death of a Belfast man who had been shot by Northern Ireland security forces with a plastic bullet... 'All this excites the people. Right away they rally' Flannery says.[52]

SMALL-SCALE PHILANTHROPY

The development of the ideological split during the mid-1970s between the 'Four Horsemen's' approach to Irish issues and that of Noraid and similar groups such as the Irish-American Unity Conference also marked the beginning of a new form of financial involvement in Ireland for Irish America. This came in the shape of the growing number of fund-raising organisations dedicated to philanthropic or social development initiatives in Ireland.

The longest-established of these was the American-Irish Foundation, jointly founded by de Valera and President John F. Kennedy in 1963 as a commemoration of Kennedy's visit to Ireland.

Its remit was to raise money for cultural and educational projects in Ireland, in order to 'foster connections between Americans of Irish descent and the country of their ancestry'.[53] However, despite its origins in a high point of diasporic contact, and the involvement of the two current presidents, the Foundation had never achieved the income levels necessary to carry out significant agendas. By the mid-1970s, however, philanthropic ventures of this kind between Irish America and Ireland were becoming more numerous and more popular with donors.

In 1976, the Ireland Fund was established by Irish businessman Tony O'Reilly and Dan Rooney, the owner of the Pittsburgh Steelers American football team. The Fund declared it had 'a trinity of goals – Peace, Culture and Charity'.[54] This was followed in 1978 by the (less successful) O'Neill Trust, founded by Tip O'Neill, 'to canalise money from private American investors into employment-generating projects in Ireland'.[55] The establishment of the Ireland Fund (which was to be amalgamated with the rather neglected American-Irish Foundation on St Patrick's Day 1987, at a White House ceremony) marked a significant development in the economic involvement of the United States diaspora with Ireland. Previous sources of investment, loans, grants and charitable aid from America had been channelled – very limitedly – through national government. This had been the case for Marshall Aid and the American Irish Foundation. The establishment of the Ireland Fund in 1976 marked the beginnings of popular, non-governmental philanthropic relationships with Ireland from the Irish-American community.

As well as high-profile, high-income organisations such as the Ireland Fund, smaller and mainly community-based groups aiming to encourage peaceful development and social integration in Northern Ireland also began to appear during the mid-1970s. A popular form of such organisations were those dedicated to providing American holidays for children growing up within the worst affected areas of the Troubles. Among the first of these was the Rotary Club of Hibbing, Minnesota, who raised $47,000 to bring sixty Protestant and sixty Catholic teenagers from Belfast to stay with families in the Hibbing area during the summer of 1974. In his assessment of these ventures, Andrew Wilson has also cited 'the *Ulster Project*, based in the Midwest, the *Cape Cod Irish Children's Program*, and the *Irish Children's Summer Program* in Greensboro, North Carolina', all of which had begun operation by 1975.[56] As Wilson commented, 'the schemes have had an important effect on

Irish-Americans. The various groups provide an outlet for individuals who want to do something for Northern Ireland...Like the Ireland Fund, the children's schemes provide Irish-Americans with a means to project their concerns for Ulster into peaceful programs.'[57]

Such organisations and summer programmes have continued; the Northern Ireland Children's Enterprise, based in North White Plains, New York State, began providing holidays for children from Belfast in 1982. In 1998, their work was profiled in a *New York Times* article which characterised their efforts as an attempt to further sectarian reconciliation in Ireland through their practice of hosting Protestant and Catholic children with the same families during their stay in America. 'Children and teenagers in Northern Ireland live in a way that it's hard for some Americans to imagine', Jack Nelon, vice-president of *Children's Enterprises*, said. 'When they come here, everything is an event – going to the supermarket or the town pool, riding a bicycle down the street without worrying about being taunted or shot at.'[58] Clearly, the tone of such comments indicates the high motivation – and perhaps heightened interpretation of Belfast life – shown by such small-scale organisations willing to raise comparatively large sums of money for such projects.

Wilson's argument that both the Ireland Fund and the children's projects, despite their differing constituencies, were a sign of Irish America's increasing desire during the 1970s to find a 'peaceful' form of involvement with Irish issues is also supported by the fall in contributions at this time to more political organisations such as Noraid. This can be seen as an indication of the success of attempts to minimise the political and financial power of Noraid, particularly through the mobilisation of prominent national politicians such as Edward Kennedy and Tip O'Neill. Of their interventions from this point on in Irish-American politics, Sean Cronin has commented that, 'apart from their political influence, which was considerable, the Friends [of Ireland] helped the Irish government to isolate Noraid's supporters'.[59]

What is in fact particularly striking about all of the fund-raising groups established at this time is their deliberate lack of engagement with political topics. Instead, the emphasis was placed upon social and economic development programmes, attempts at 'reconciliation' between children and teenagers being only the most obvious of these. Equally, the framing of Irish social and economic problems entirely within the context of a need for such reconciliation between members of the Protestant and Catholic communities demonstrates the influence of the mainstream media's representation of the Troubles as a sectarian rather than a colonial conflict.

THE HUNGER STRIKES

The mid-1970s lull in Irish-American political interest and involvement with Ireland, by comparison to its sudden increase following Bloody Sunday in 1972, came to an end with the beginning of the hunger strikes in 1981. The protests of Bobby Sands and the other hunger strikers in the Long Kesh prison during 1981 attracted increasing amounts of international media coverage, particularly once Sands had been elected an MP during the final months of his life. His death, on 5 May 1981, provoked an unprecedented level of press and public interest in events in Ireland, an interest which continued throughout the rest of the year as other protesters died. The mainstream press in the United States continued, for the most part, to be highly critical of Irish republicanism throughout the hunger strikes; as the campaign continued, however, they also began to publish forthright criticism of the British government's position and handling of the situation.

The unprecedented rise in public feeling about Ireland within the United States generally and the Irish-American community in particular during the 1980–81 period prompted several shifts in activity and policy among those groups already involved in political lobbying. The national politicians such as Edward Kennedy, Tip O'Neill and Daniel Moynihan, presumably reassured by the Irish government's own desire to see British policy towards the protesters change, attempted to involve President Reagan in moves to apply pressure on Thatcher's government in London. This failed, due almost certainly to Reagan's continued privileging of the United States' 'special relationship' with Britain in international affairs.

The most obvious surge of public support from Irish America as a result of the hunger strikes was that reflected in Noraid's published fund-raising success. As Table 1.1 shows, their income during late 1980 to late 1981 was almost doubled from that of the previous twelve months. As was previously mentioned, both Noraid's legal battle with the US State Department and their certain under-declaring of income during this time makes assessment of their full fund-raising success at this time almost impossible. This situation was further complicated following the hunger strikers' deaths, when relatives of a number of the protesters toured the United States at the invitation of Noraid. This tour was intended to raise levels of awareness and support for the republican cause among Irish-Americans, as well as to raise funds. Those involved in the tour included Sean Sands, Malachy McCreesh and Liz O'Hara, all siblings of hunger strikers who had died that year.

Their speaking tour across Irish centres in the United States was undoubtedly popular and well attended. How much money their tour raised, however, is less clear. Widely believed rumours suggest that their speaking engagements alone raised more than $250,000, on top of other donations to Noraid during this period. Noraid, however, insists in its disclosed accounts that it received less than $200,000 in total during 1981; although some other readings of their complex accounts produce higher figures than this, they certainly do not match the suggested earnings of the hunger strike relatives' tour.[60]

The Irish-American press was particularly rejuvenated during the hunger striker's protest. In Philadelphia the *Irish Edition*, a new and highly republican newspaper, was launched in March 1981 with a front-page story condemning the British government under the headline 'Bobby Sands Is Going To Die'. By May of that year, the paper was printing a black border around its front page in honour of Sands.[61]

The Irish-American press coverage of the hunger strikers' deaths, and the Irish Republican movement's provision of news material relating to them, demonstrated a clear understanding of powerful news images. In particular, the concentration, in the aftermath of several of the deaths, upon the female mourners at the hunger strikers' funerals allowed for the further presentation of the men themselves as martyrs and family men. This coverage continued in the Irish-American press for some time after the hunger strikers' deaths, and was especially noticeable in the case of Bobby Sands' sisters and Joe McDonnell's wife and daughter. The IRA's understanding of the power of such images was underlined by their provision of press facilities such as camera scaffolds at the graveside for Sands' funeral. The British government was also well aware of the influence carried abroad by coverage of Sands' and the others' funerals. David Gilliland, the chief British spokesman on Northern Ireland at the time, was quoted as admitting that 'the crews from all over the world were well accommodated. Splendid scaffolding for the cameras was erected at the grave site. The IRA know the pictorial stuff has to be good, or it won't get on the air.'[62]

As was discussed above, it seems clear that the diaspora's political engagement with events in Ireland was significantly affected by particularly strong media images, usually those which emphasised individualised human suffering and oppression, rather than more abstract issues of human rights or political-historical disputes. This must already have been clear to fund-raisers on both sides of the Atlantic following the level of publicity given to Bernadette Devlin's 1969 and 1971 tours; despite the political difficulties her specific ideological message had caused during her visits to Irish-American communities, her position as a young female activist had provided a mass media profile few other campaigners could have achieved. As such, images of grieving young women – particularly photogenic ones – were obviously powerful tools for motivating Irish-American support following the hunger strikes.

Indeed, the effectiveness of these female media images may have been an influencing factor in Sinn Féin and Noraid's decision to include Liz O'Hara on the fund-raising tour of hunger strikers' relatives which visited the United States in 1981 after the strike was over. Her brother, Patsy O'Hara, had been a member of the INLA rather than the IRA, and her inclusion on the American tour was the subject of some controversy even before the visit began. This controversy only increased when the IRSP (the INLA's political wing), through Belfast city councillor Sean Flynn and O'Hara herself, attempted to demand one-third of the money raised in the United States. Noraid disputed this demand, and the ensuing conflict has only added to the difficulty in assessing exactly how much funding the tour as a whole raised. The possibility of this dispute arising, particularly if the tour was as financially successful as all parties concerned would have hoped, must have been clear before the group left Ireland. Equally, the chance of O'Hara attempting to advance the radical socialist agenda of the INLA during the tour itself must have occurred to Noraid as risking a repeat of Bernadette Devlin McAliskey's politically damaging visit.[63] Notwithstanding the stated sense of cross-party solidarity felt by all the hunger strikers' relatives, it therefore seems likely that Liz O'Hara's eventual inclusion in the tour despite such political differences may well have been influenced by the publicity advantages offered by the presence of a young woman grieving for her brother.

The Irish-American newspapers were particularly vigorous in their critical analysis of mainstream press reports and editorials during the hunger strikes; with an unprecedented coverage of Irish events by the national media in the United States, the framing and assumptions of their stories obviously carried even greater political weight than usual. Despite the national media's increasing criticism of British government policy as the protest continued, republican Irish-American newspapers were still highly critical of their perceived anti-Irish bias. On 23 May 1981, for example, the *Irish People* published a scathing attack on a *New York Times* review of the recently published *The Terror Network: The Secret War of International Terrorism*, by Clare Sterling. 'Oisin', a regular *Irish People* columnist, concluded his article with the question, 'Isn't it about time that the appropriate authorities requested the publishers of the *New York Times* to register as agents of a foreign government?'[64] This was, of course, a reference to the ongoing dispute at the time between the State Department and Noraid over its registration as representatives of a foreign agent.

This is merely one example of the many attempts by Irish-American republican media to highlight the selective reporting as well as the political–economic structural influences on coverage of Irish issues since the outbreak of the Troubles in 1969. By the 1980s, however, the network of diasporic political communication between Ireland and Irish America had become considerably more complicated than this. Not only was the mainstream American press reporting through a network of international news bureaux and agencies which transmitted Irish news through London, but the republican Irish-American press, which received information directly from Dublin and Belfast, was also producing coverage of Northern Ireland for the diaspora which was specifically different from that produced for Irish audiences in Ireland.

It has been argued that the Irish-American press, in reporting Irish nationalist policies, was filtering out apparently 'radical' viewpoints from their stories. In particular, it has been suggested, the Irish-American press during the 1980s was showing an increasing tendency to re-edit Irish stories in order to omit the more overtly socialist aspects of Sinn Féin ideology.[65] This process was particularly seen to apply to the *Irish People*, one of the most long-standing and most strongly nationalist of the Irish-American papers, with close links to Sinn Féin in Ireland and Noraid in the United States. The paper is, in effect, an American edition of *An Phoblacht*, the Sinn Féin newspaper, with a majority of each copy being a reprint of the articles published by *An Phoblacht* in Ireland a week earlier. Bearing in mind the *Irish People*'s blanket reprinting of large sections of *An*

Phoblacht, therefore, the undoubted evidence of difference in content between the two papers is significant.

Essentially, the editorial policy of the *Irish People* during the 1980s with regard to its selection and editing of articles from *An Phoblacht* frequently appears to have been one of removing references to Sinn Féin or the IRA's more socialist agendas, as well as of omitting of *An Phoblacht*'s frequently drawn parallels between the Irish situation and that of most other conflicts across the world. As Adrian Guelke has commented, 'in particular, the social conservatism and anti-Communism of the *Irish People* set it apart from the trends of radicalisation, secularisation and politicisation that have shaped Sinn Féin ideology since the late 1970s'.[66] This difference between the two papers was frequently achieved through the use of editing and re-headlining. For example, when covering the Sinn Féin Ard-Fheis of 1985, *The Irish People* printed excerpts from Gerry Adams' speech, where *An Phoblacht* had reproduced it in full. The omitted paragraphs, taken from throughout the speech, all refer either to perceived international parallels to the conflict in Northern Ireland, or to Sinn Féin's socialist policies for the island of Ireland. Of international conflicts, for example, Adams argued that:

> The natural and logical place for Ireland is alongside the Palestinians, the Chileans, El Salvadoreans and Nicaraguans. A government which truly represented the Irish people would be in opposition to Reagan's backing of repressive regimes in Central America, in opposition to Israel's policy of genocide against the Palestinian people, and in opposition to the British partition and occupation of this country.[67]

On domestic issues within Ireland as a whole, Adams, after attacking the, 'monetarist' policies of the Irish government as well as those of the British, goes on to assert that 'Sinn Féin supports demands for divorce and other legislation because we recognise it as a need and basic right for people'.[68] Neither of these paragraphs – nor several others dealing with socialist national or international party policy – were reproduced in the *Irish People*'s 'excerpts' version printed nine days later.[69]

Indeed, the *Irish People*'s editorial policy is particularly noticeable for its lack of international coverage, in contrast to *An Phoblacht*. *An Phoblacht* ran a regular 'World View' section covering republican and liberation stories from around the world. In September 1985, for example, this section published an account of President

Reagan's alleged activities as an FBI anti-communist informer during the 1940s.[70] The *Irish People* does not print *An Phoblacht*'s 'World View' section; its equivalent space is taken by a 'Community Events' calendar covering listings of functions and fund-raisers to be held in the greater New York area. In the edition of the *Irish People* which might have carried the claims about Reagan's FBI activities, the equivalent space contained a notice of an Ancient Order of Hibernians, 'prime rib dinner and dance...at Throggs Neck Country Club' in the Bronx.[71] Analyses of the *Irish People*'s editorial policies have therefore tended to conclude that these omissions and selections confirm the continuation of the Irish-American establishment's anti-socialist and anti-multicultural position, as forcibly demonstrated during Bernadette Devlin's visits.

In fact, the coverage of the Northern Ireland conflict and of its parallels with other contemporary political conflicts around the world in the Irish-American press was highly complex during the 1980s. While the *Irish People* had removed references to Nicaragua and Palestine from its copy of Gerry Adams' speech, it retained his opening statement in support of the ANC in South Africa, including the line, 'To the ANC, we extend our unconditional solidarity. To our black brothers and sisters in struggle we send this simple message of support: "Fight on!" '.[72] This willingness by the *Irish People*, an influential voice in Irish-American political commentary, to engage with another liberation struggle as being analogous to that in Ireland, while it strategically ignored others, had similar echoes at other times during the 1980s. During the extensive coverage of and comment on the hunger strikes, the *Irish People* had published a series of articles making very direct links between African-American and Irish history in the United States, dealing with topics such as racism in American inner cities and the history of correspondence between Marcus Garvey and Eamon de Valera during the campaign for Irish independence.[73] One of this series, an article by the African-American novelist Lionel Mitchell headlined 'A Black Writer's View on the Irish Freedom Struggle', contained Mitchell's statement that:

> there is a cloud over all matters Irish in America and I certainly believe it affects us all – including Irish-Americans. One effect is the dichotomy between the traditional conservative rhetoric we hear from them contrasted now during the crisis in Ireland with a new language of allusions to the African slave trade, to the Black freedom

struggle ... The Black Civil Rights movement has become a model, a blueprint ... [74]

Significantly, these articles were not published in *An Phoblacht* – they were produced solely for the diasporic audience. Taken in conjunction with the selective editing and reproduction of *An Phoblacht* articles, this would suggest a number of key conclusions about Irish-American ideological approaches to both Irish politics and the diaspora's role within them.

First, the consistent absence of *An Phoblacht*'s international stories from editions of the *Irish People*, along with the substitution of strictly local information in their place, points to a vital difference both in the mode of address and in the contextual framing of dias- poric current affairs news. While *An Phoblacht*, published in Ireland, may consider itself a national newspaper (albeit one of minority circulation) with all the opportunity and obligation to provide international news coverage which that position implies, the *Irish People*, published in New York, operates in a very different environment. Even leaving aside the fact that the United States does not have a structure of national newspapers in the way that European nations do, the *Irish People*'s readership is based largely on ethnic and regional identification rather than standard news provision. As such, its editorial policies would be affected by the knowledge that most of its readers would be acquiring the majority of their 'general' current affairs information elsewhere. The special- ist nature of the *Irish People*'s market position rests precisely on providing information of particular interest to the Irish-American diaspora. Inevitably, this kind of 'special interest' information falls predominantly into two categories; that of in-depth (and ideologi- cally distinctive) coverage of news from Ireland, and that of local Irish-American community news. These are the two categories of information which the *Irish People*'s readership cannot expect to receive from the mainstream media they also consume. International news, on the other hand, is regularly supplied by that mainstream media, and with greater resources than the *Irish People* could hope to achieve.

Second, the publication in the early 1980s by the Irish-American press of articles such as the one by Lionel Mitchell suggests that the press had significantly shifted its ideological position from that of the 1960s and 1970s. At that time, during speaking and fund-raising tours such as that by Bernadette Devlin, correlations between the

African-American and Irish Civil Rights movements had drawn sharp criticism and a telling lack of financial donations. While this attitude undoubtedly still existed among some of the politically active diaspora by the early 1980s, the publication of articles pointing to direct historical and political links between African-Americans and Irish-Americans by such a long-standing proponent of Irish-American nationalism as the *Irish People* is indicative of a significant widening of scope in political thinking within the diaspora.

Further indications that the Irish-American media's framing of Irish politics was not simply a conservative approach came from the coverage of President Reagan's official visit to Ireland in June 1984. The significant protests against and boycotts of his appearances around the country were covered in detail by *An Phoblacht*, and reprinted with little or no editing in the *Irish People*. These reports made extensive reference to Irish opposition to United States' foreign policy in Central America and the Middle East, even quoting criticism from Nancy Reagan's cousin, a visiting professor at Galway University, of Reagan's 'militaristic stance'.[75]

By the mid-1990s, this development was further demonstrated by the style of response from the Irish-American Unity Conference to David Trimble's official visit to the United States as part of the peace negotiations. The IAUC took out a quarter-page notice in the *New York Times*, headlined 'A Welcome to David Trimble, The "David Duke" of Ireland'. The text of the notice describes Trimble's participation in Orange marches through Catholic areas of Belfast, and argues that 'This behaviour is not unlike a KKK march through an African–American neighbourhood, or a neo-nazi march through a Jewish neighbourhood'.[76]

'PARALLEL ECONOMIES' AND THE PEACE PROCESS

The pattern of intense interest followed by a decline in campaigning activity, which characterised Irish-American responses to Bloody Sunday in 1972, also occurred again after the initial period of interest in the hunger strikes in 1981. Once more, the lack of comparable mass media images to maintain the surge of political feeling inspired both by the hunger strikers themselves and by their bereaved relatives visiting the United States led to a decline in diasporic commitment. While President Reagan's visit to Ireland in 1984 had provided some opportunity for Irish America to voice its political commitment, the complexities of feeling about Reagan's domestic and international policies both in Ireland and in the United States had prevented his visit from being a catalyst for any significant or ongoing developments. Similarly, the IRA's response to the hunger strikers' deaths had been an escalation of attacks and bombings on mainland Britain, most spectacularly including the near-assassination of Margaret Thatcher during the Conservative Party Conference in Brighton in October 1984.

The images produced by activities such as these would have been partly intended to maintain a high level of awareness among Irish-American supporters following the end of the hunger strikes. In 1985, the *Christian Science Monitor*, using an interview given in Dublin by senior IRA figure Joe Cahill, commented of the Brighton bombing: 'Such high-visibility bombings keep the IRA's struggle against Britain in the American public eye through widespread press coverage... This is the public-relations dimension of guerrilla warfare. "Every operation is planned for a specific purpose in mind, it is not just bombing for bombing's sake," said Cahill.' In the same interview, Cahill did however acknowledge that civilian deaths were potentially damaging to the IRA's support among Irish-Americans, but rather nonchalantly explained that they could be dismissed as accidents. 'Cahill likens civilian deaths in IRA operations to a foul being committed by a boxer in the ring. He says fans rooting for the boxer don't like it that a foul has been committed, but they continue to support and cheer for their boxer anyway.'[77] Nevertheless, by the mid-1980s, the Reagan government's concentration of policy and publicity on the campaign against 'international terrorism' meant that such IRA activities were likely to provoke disapproval among American audiences for exactly the same reasons that the images of the hunger strike provoked sympathy – they appeared to confirm the IRA as terrorists in just the same way that media images of the hunger strikes had appeared to confirm the British government's oppression of Catholic nationalists.

It was within this political context – as well as a social context of enormously increased Irish-American community wealth and influence – that the mid-1980s saw a rapid increase in the development of charitable and philanthropic enterprises on behalf of Ireland. As was discussed above, some of these organisations had their genesis in the lull in overtly political activity occasioned by the lack of Irish-American support for 'traditional' nationalist direct action during the mid-1970s. However, most of these organisations were locally based, such as the children's holiday schemes, and therefore inevitably small-scale. Those which had the potential for large-scale fund-raising, such as Tony O'Reilly's Ireland Fund, had nevertheless not begun to approach the scale of financial power which the Irish-American diaspora's size could have supported, and certainly did not rival the fund-raising scope of similar diasporic organisations such as those operated by Jewish America for the support of Israel. In just one of many negative comparisons between the two diasporas, for example, it was reported in 1985 that Irish nationalist campaigners in the United States were 'seeking to gain support in the US Congress by raising the awareness of Irish-Americans on the Northern Ireland issue and organizing an Irish-American voting bloc. They seek to emulate the success that Israeli-Zionist groups have had in the US in both mobilising American-Jewish support and translating that support into political influence on Capitol Hill'.[78] Indeed, according to one report, by 1984 the Irish Republic was spending $5.5 million on lobbying in Washington, making it the fifth-largest such lobbying group to the United States government, although certainly without quite the level of success achieved on behalf of Israel.[79]

However, in 1986, the British and Irish governments jointly established the International Fund for Ireland in order to raise investment and capital for social development in Northern Ireland and the border counties of the Republic. The establishment of the Fund was closely related to the signing of the Anglo-Irish Agreement between the British and Irish governments, and the financial contributions it receives from the United States are the fulfilment of President Carter's 1976 pledge to provide funding in the event of peaceful negotiations between the two governments. The International Fund for Ireland's diasporic connections are clear from the list of major international donor governments, which includes the United States, Canada, Australia and New Zealand, as well as the European Union. Of these governmental donations, that from the United States is by far the largest; between 1997 and 2000, US$19.6 million per year was received by the Fund. The Fund objectives are stated as being 'to promote economic and social advance; and to encourage contact, dialogue and reconciliation between Unionists and Nationalists throughout Ireland'.[80] The Fund distributes grants to community-based organisations whose work aims to foster social and economic development in the hope of leading to reconciliation between different communities in the North and South of Ireland.

The scale of the Fund's operations is large, with a total of around IR£950 million invested up to September 1997. The Fund aims to improve employment levels in the six counties and border region through targeted support for small businesses, education and training initiatives at community level, and the promotion of cross-border and cross-community social connections.

In 1987, the American-Irish Foundation, founded in 1963 by Presidents Kennedy and de Valera, was merged with Tony O'Reilly's Ireland Fund to form the new American Ireland Fund. By this time, O'Reilly's Ireland Fund, founded in 1976, had established a fund-raising network across many of America's major cities, and, on its merger with the American Irish Foundation, became the largest private organisation in the world raising donations for Ireland.

Following the 1987 restructuring, the American Ireland Fund established an international network throughout Europe, Australasia, South Africa and Japan. These networks, according to the Fund's own literature, are 'uniting the aspirations of the Irish diaspora, a global community of more than 70 million people'.[81] As with the governmental International Fund for Ireland, the American Ireland Fund is the diasporic leader in donations to the Ireland Funds, having established a programme of endowed funds and bequests as well as its more general fund-raising activities. The objectives of the American Ireland Fund are listed as being focused on specific areas. 'These are peace and reconciliation between the communities in Northern Ireland, culture and the arts, education and community development. The need in Ireland is great.'[82] In a more detailed discussion of the Fund's attempts to promote peace and community development, its literature explains:

> Whatever the daily headlines, this much at least will likely not change: In Northern Ireland, there are great numbers of Protestants and Catholics who seek reconciliation and promote tolerance. Men and women from Derry to Newry have begun working together, and they have come to share a vision of a common future ... Economic well-being, cross-community reconciliation, and cultural identity daily do battle with forces that ultimately may cause decline and marginalisation.[83]

The American Ireland Fund had, up to 2001, raised over $120 million towards the combined Ireland Fund's support of more than 300 separate organisations in Ireland, ranging from the Artane Boys Band in Dublin to the Northern Ireland Women's Aid Federation in Belfast.

By the early 1990s, the Irish-American Partnership had also begun raising substantial funds for economic and social development in Ireland. Their mission statement explains that 'Funds raised by the Partnership's programs support science and technology education in Ireland, North and South, job creation and entrepreneurial projects in Ireland, North and South, and the advancement of trustful business relations throughout the island and the United States.'[84]

The Partnership, though much less financially powerful than the American Ireland Fund, is now one of the larger Irish-American organisations, with more than 18,000 members across the United States. The Partnership regularly conducts opinion polls of members and states that, in a poll of the late 1990s, over 70 per cent of respondents 'showed greatest concern for "Peace and Reconciliation" issues', with over 60 per cent choosing '[j]obs in disadvantaged areas as their second choice for Partnership funds'.[85] The organisation raises money through a graded system of memberships, as well as through social activities; most notably through a sponsored competitive golf tournament across courses in the United States, culminating in a final championship in Ireland.

It can be seen from their activities and the style of their fundraising that the two major private Irish-American charitable organisations, the American Ireland Fund and the Irish-American Partnership, follow the same priorities as the inter-governmental International Fund for Ireland. In this, they stress the value and necessity of 'cross-community' social interaction and development, as well as a strong belief in the connections between economic prosperity and political peace.

In 1984, during the same era as the rapid development of the fund-raising groups, the MacBride Principles for fair employment were drawn up. The MacBride campaign focused on enforcing, through state legislation in America, 'ethical investment' in Northern Ireland. Companies, including the powerful state pension funds, who were registered in states which adopted the MacBride Principles, were allowed to invest and trade in Northern Ireland only under the condition of implementing equal employment practices.[86] The goal of the MacBride campaign was to alleviate the marked differences in unemployment figures between the Catholic and Protestant communities in Northern Ireland. Despite considerable opposition from the British government, the campaign was eventually successful, with California, in 1999, becoming the eighteenth state to enact MacBride legislation.[87] Paul Arthur has argued that part of the success of the MacBride Principles campaign rested in its ability to marry constitutional politics with relatively radical politics while avoiding damaging associations with the radical political organisations, suggesting that '[Sean MacBride] carried a certain cachet among the political establishment *and* among revolutionaries. The campaign itself was to be conducted in state legislatures and city halls across the country. It was, in essence, an appeal to small investors and to the hearts of middle America.'[88]

This emphasis upon approaching the political difficulties in Ireland through economic development, rather than vice versa, became a characterising feature of Irish-American interventions in Ireland from the late 1980s onwards. As such, it can be seen as an illustration of the twin political priorities of the international politics of the time: anti-terrorism and global capitalism. Just as, following the Second World War, Ireland had been unable to overcome the 'special relationship', based on opposition to communism, between Britain and the United States so, by the mid-1980s, that global polit- ical issue had been further complicated by Britain and America's combined commitment to combating 'international terrorism'. While the events of the hunger strikes had cast Irish political activism against Britain into a more favourable light with the American press and public, the continued IRA bombing campaigns of the 1980s had made them easy to categorise as 'terrorists'. As such, any overtly ideological campaigning by Irish-Americans risked being allied with Noraid's activities, which under Reagan's presi- dency had completed its journey to political isolation. Equally, the governments of the United States, Britain and the Republic of Ireland were all, by the mid-1980s, committed to the neo-liberal policies of global free trade, international investment and deregu- lated industries as the perceived path to social as well as economic success.

The 'parallel economies' of charitable and philanthropic organi- sations, which became the principal voice of Irish-American commitment to Ireland during the 1990s, and far outstripped the more overtly activist organisations such as Noraid in power and influence, thus echoed this supposedly non-ideological, predomi- nantly economic pattern of international politics. This appears to operate in two distinct ways. On the one hand, the increasingly influential charitable organisations seem to operate as genuinely 'parallel' economies to the dominant neo-liberal economic govern- mental policies of the 1980s onwards in their foundation on the belief that economic factors are a higher priority than ideological factors. Therefore, national governments in the United States and Ireland during this time increasingly operated on the principle that social and political requirements were subjugated to those of the economy, as demonstrated by their commitment to low inflation rather than low unemployment and a strong belief in non-governmental, profit-oriented management or even ownership of 'social' activities such as healthcare and education. Equally, the Irish-American philanthropic organisations mirrored this neo-liberalism in their concern with economic development and social 'management' of conflict and inequality in Northern Ireland, rather than with the concerns of more 'traditional' diasporic campaign groups such as Noraid, which put ideological and strictly political matters first. The emphasis, within such fund-raising, on issues such as 'community development', 'peace and reconciliation' and 'employment and education', rather than on overtly ideological factors such as nationalism, republicanism and colonialism, is therefore a reflection of the dominant neo-liberal values of the period.

An early example of this 'managerial' approach occurred in 1975, when the future United States Ambassador to Ireland, William V. Shannon, proposed a solution to the Troubles. This solution did include obtaining an acknowledgement from the British government that 'Ireland is one nation indivisible', but also suggested that Belfast should be given the status of a city-state under dual British and Irish control. Furthermore, Shannon argued:

> I know of no poetry praising the beauty of Belfast...Therefore, I propose that an entire new city be built elsewhere in Ireland and that those of the Catholic population of Belfast who wish to do so be strongly induced by guaranteed jobs, by housing grants, and by quality schools to relocate there...This would...be a constructive enterprise in which American knowledge and American financial help might also be expected to participate.[89]

An even more extreme example of this economically driven approach appeared in a proposal put forward by an Irish-American academic and economist, James B. Healy, in 1989. His book, *Northern Ireland Dilemma: An American Irish Imperative*, is in effect a detailed manifesto for the unification of Ireland, to be achieved through economic rather than political means. Following an argument similar to that of McCaffrey, Healy begins by arguing that contemporary Irish-Americans, due to suburbanisation and social changes, 'view their responsibility to their homeland as being like the problems in Poland, Afghanistan, and South Africa, as a homogenous, far-off, unprioritized demand'.[90] Going on to argue that Irish America should instead utilise the social and economic developments of the 1980s, and therefore make use of 'multinational and transnational interests' in order to achieve wider political gains, Healy insists that: 'The long espoused model for social justice [POLITICAL >ECONOMIC >SOCIAL] must be discarded as dysfunctional and rearranged as a more feasible methodology [ECONOMIC >POLITICAL >SOCIAL] for a more pragmatic approach to the solution of the Northern Ireland dilemma.'[91] Most of the rest of Healy's book is a detailed suggestion as to how, having accepted that 'neo-colonial business enterprise should be employed' in order to achieve unification, the diaspora might initiate this, through their access to multi-national capital.

In essence, Healy proposed that the Irish border area, extending both North and South, should be transformed into a delineated free trade development zone, owned and managed by a special authority reporting to, but essentially independent of, both governments on the island. This proposed administration, termed the United Ireland Development Authority, should, Healy argued, be based upon the Port Authority of New York and New Jersey, as a successful model of economic development in a marginalised area:

> Following the model of PA, UIDA would finance the border project by issuing bonds. A prominent international investment banker must be engaged to underwrite, syndicate and float the issue world-wide. The bonds must be secured to the extent the issue will be collateralized by UIDA's acquisition of property. Later bond issues may follow to defray the cost of plant and building leasebacks... If, of the sixty-five million Irish living outside Ireland, a mere five per cent purchased a $1,000 bond each, UIDA would realise $3.25 billion.[92]

In effect, then, Healy was suggesting that the diaspora 'buy' the Irish border as an economic development zone, thus neutralising its ideological meaning by making it a thriving area which would attract workers and investors from all ideological positions and therefore create unification by economic default. This would create, according to the UIDA's proposed corporate mission statement, 'a compatible social, political and economic arrangement that will defy segregation and the border dividing the peoples of the Republic of Ireland'.[93]

CONCLUSION

Although an extreme example of a neo-liberal ideological approach to Irish America's involvement in Ireland, the underlying system of thought in Healy's proposal is not essentially different from that of the 'parallel economies' of charitable organisations whose donations and interventions have been both influential and popular with the governments of Ireland, Britain and the United States. Both concentrate upon the issues of economic development and social 'reconciliation' rather than political issues such as British colonialism.

Healy's proposal, unlikely as it seems, also prefigures the administrative structures of the Good Friday Agreement in many respects, particularly with regard to the involvement of cross-border governmental organisations, non-governmental organisations and international observers and negotiators. The establishment of these organisations, along with the nature of American involvement with the peace negotiations, reveals the ways in which Irish-American political involvement with Ireland continued to be heavily contingent upon prevailing global concerns.

The neo-liberal economic policies pursued by both Reagan and Thatcher during the 1980s had also become the standard approach of Irish governments by the 1990s, meaning that a belief in the social and eventually political benefits of economic regeneration policies, pursued through the development of international capital investment, had become an approach to Northern Ireland accepted by all governments concerned. Equally, the ending of Cold War politics during the early 1990s meant that, although the British and American governments maintained close ties, their 'special relationship' was no longer so crucial to American foreign policy.

The development of economic intervention within Ireland through the 'parallel economies' of large-scale Irish-American fundraising had also helped to develop a powerful and politically well-connected diasporic community, whose principal commitment to economic development as a method of 'peace and reconciliation' enabled them to capitalise on the new political relationships forming between Ireland, Britain and the United States. As Conor O'Clery comments on the progression towards the IRA's 1994 ceasefire: 'The new thinking among the Irish and the Irish-Americans coincided with major changes in the world ... [there followed] the emergence of a new, dual set of special relationships – between the United States and both Britain and Ireland, and between Irish-Americans and both peoples on the island of Ireland.'[94]

The election of President Clinton in 1992 marked the arrival of the first United States president to claim both Irish ancestry and an active interest in the nation's political situation. Clinton was also able to act on this interest, due both to the global shifts of allegiance initiated by the end of the Cold War and to the transnational shifts of interest and power relationships between Irish and Irish-American activists and fund-raisers. The power of these new Irish-American groupings was demonstrated by their involvement in the declaration of the 1994 ceasefire when, it is widely believed, figures such as Niall O'Dowd of the *Irish Voice* and the billionaire philanthropist Chuck Feeney played an important role in early negotiations between the United States government and Sinn Féin.[95]

It could therefore be argued that the neo-liberal corporate style of the increasingly influential 'parallel economies' became the template for the Peace Process itself. This is reflected in a number of ways; the managerial style of the Northern Ireland Assembly, the trade-oriented nature of the newly established cross-border bodies, and the continuing emphasis upon economic regeneration in Northern Ireland itself as a solution to ideological differences. Bernadette Devlin McAliskey, commenting on the new institutions in 2001, has termed it a 'top-down' process, in which large governmental and corporate interests are presumed to coincide with those of the wider population through a 'trickle-down' democracy analogous to the 'trickle-down' wealth central to the monetarist capitalism of globalisation.[96] As such, of course, the involvement of Irish America (and the United States government) is no less 'ideological' than the more overt republican campaigning of the *Irish People* or even Noraid. Its ideology is, however, in keeping with the dominant global culture of foregrounding economic structures above social or political radicalism. As such, contemporary Irish-American involvement in Irish political issues continues what this chapter has shown to be a history of intertwinement with the national and, crucially, international concerns of the day, as well as being profoundly affected by the current geo-political concerns of the United States government. This pattern of internationally divided loyalties and preoccupations emphasises the extent to which diasporic political affections appear to be especially prone to influence by the complexities of international relations at any given time.

NOTES

1   Pre-Presidential Files, Speech Files, Box 895, Kennedy Library, cited in Arthur Mitchell, *JFK and his Irish Heritage* (Dublin: Moytura Press, 1993), p. 119.
2   Jolle Demmers, 'Diaspora and Conflict: Locality, Long-Distance Nationalism, and Delocalisation of Conflict Dynamics', in *Javnost – the Public: Journal of The European Institute for Communication and Culture*, 1 Diasporic Communication, Vol. IX (2002), p. 88.
3   Adrian Guelke, *Northern Ireland: The International Perspective* (Dublin: Gill and Macmillan, 1988), p. 128.
4   See <http://www.philanthropyroundtable.org>. Accessed January 2001.
5   John Killick, *The United States and European Reconstruction 1945–1960* (Keele: Keele University Press, 1997), p. 82.
6   Ibid., pp. 82–97.
7   See *The European Recovery Programme: Basic Documents and Background Information*, p. No. 8792 (Dublin, 1949). For a detailed study of Ireland's participation in the Marshall Plan see Killick, *The United States and European Reconstruction*, and John F. McCarthy, 'Ireland's Turnaround: Whitaker and the 1958 Plan for Economic Development', in John F. McCarthy (ed.), *Planning Ireland's Future: The Legacy of T.K. Whitaker* (Dublin: Glendale Press, 1990).
8   Sean Cronin, *Washington's Irish Policy 1916–1986: Independence, Partition, Neutrality* (Dublin: Anvil Books, 1987), p. 197.
9   Cronin, *Washington's Irish Policy*, p. 196, and Roy Foster, *Modern Ireland 1600–1972* (London: Penguin, 1989), pp. 560–2.
10   Cited in Cronin, *Washington's Irish Policy*, p. 197.
11   J.J. Lee, *Ireland 1912–1985: Politics and Society* (Cambridge: Cambridge University Press, 1989), p. 304.
12   Cited in Cronin, *Washington's Irish Policy*, p. 192.
13   Guelke, *Northern Ireland*, pp. 129–30.
14   Congressional Record, Vol. 97, Part 9, 27 September 1951, cited in Mitchell, *JFK and his Irish Heritage*, p. 115. Equally, in his vice-presidential campaign of 1952, Richard Nixon also proposed foreign aid restrictions on Britain in order to gain American influence over the issue of partition. See Guelke, *Northern Ireland*, p. 130.
15   Cronin, *Washington's Irish Policy*, pp. 219–20.
16   For a detailed discussion of the decline of Irish 'machine' politics in city municipalities, see Steven P. Erie, *Rainbow's End: Irish-Americans and the Dilemmas of Urban Machine Politics, 1840–1985* (Berkeley: University of California Press, 1988), as well as George E. Reedy, *From the Ward to the White House: The Irish in American Politics* (New York: Scribner's Sons, 1991).
17   Reedy, *From the Ward to the White House*, p. 171.
18   *Time Magazine*, 11 July 1960, p. 20.
19   Cited in Mitchell, *JFK and his Irish Heritage*, p. 48.
20   Reedy, *From the Ward to the White House*, p. 174.
21   Andrew J. Wilson, *Irish America and the Ulster Conflict 1968–1995* (Belfast: Blackstaff Press, 1995), pp. 15–16.
22   Kevin Kenny, *The American Irish: A History* (Harlow: Longman, 2000), p. 246.
23   T.J. Kiernan Oral History Transcript, Kennedy Library, cited in Mitchell, *JFK and his Irish Heritage*, p. 128.
24   *Irish Press*, 26 June 1963, p. 1.
25   Cited in the *Irish Independent*, 27 June 1963, p. 2.

26   See Fergal Tobin, *The Best of Decades: Ireland in the 1960s* (Dublin: Gill and Macmillan, 1984), pp. 94–5.

27   *Irish Press*, 28 June 1963, p. 6, in which Kennedy's address to the Dáil is reprinted in full.

28   *The New York Times*, 30 June 1963, p. 29.

29   Guelke, *Northern Ireland*, p. 130.

30   See Kenny, *The American Irish*, p. 249, and Wilson, *Irish America and the Ulster Conflict*, pp. 31–40, for a full discussion of the conflicts surrounding Devlin's visits to the United States.

31   Wilson, *Irish America and the Ulster Conflict*, p. 33, Kenny, *The American Irish*, p. 248 and Jack Holland, *The American Connection: US Guns, Money and Influence in Northern Ireland* (Boulder, CO: Roberts Rinehart, 1999) p. 238.

32   The lack of press coverage of Irish affairs in the United States prior to the outbreak of the Troubles in 1969 is reflected by the fact that the official Irish government news bureau, the Irish News Agency, was asked by the *New York Times* in the 1950s to stop sending their press releases to the newspaper's offices. By contrast, an article in *TV Guide*, on 26 September 1981, p. 14, acknowledges the strong influence in Northern Ireland of television pictures of US civil rights protesters during the 1960s.

33   Seamus Metress, 'The Irish-Americans: From the Frontier to the White House', in Larry L Taylor (ed.), *Cultural Diversity in the United States* (Westport, CT: Bergin and Garvey, 1997), p. 142.

34   Brian Dooley, *Black and Green: The Fight for Civil Rights in Northern Ireland and Black America* (London: Pluto Press, 1998), p. 76.

35   For detailed discussions of this long-running court case and the difficulties it has caused in estimating Noraid's true income, see Holland, *The American Connection*, pp. 43–8 and Guelke, *Northern Ireland*, pp. 131–2.

36   These figures are taken mainly from Jack Holland, 'Noraid's Untold Millions', *Magill*, April 1987, pp. 34–9, and Guelke, *Northern Ireland*, p. 132, as well as *Christian Science Monitor*, 21 January 1985. As this chapter argues, these figures are more useful as a guide to broad fluctuations in Noraid's donations than as a guide to specific income.

37   Holland, *Magill*, p. 36.

38   Cited in Guelke, *Northern Ireland*, p. 130.

39   *New York Times*, 3 February 1972, p. 17.

40   Holland, *The American Connection*, p. 198.

41   Ibid., p. 201.

42   *Time Magazine*, 10 June 1974, p. 26.

43   Ray O'Hanlon, *The New Irish-Americans* (Boulder, CO: Roberts Rinehart, 1998), p. 180, Wilson, *Irish America and the Ulster Conflict*, pp. 182–4, Holland, *The American Connection*, pp. 227–32.

44   Cited O'Hanlon, *The New Irish-Americans*, p. 180.

45   *Irish Edition* (June 1981), p. 1.

46   Tim Pat Coogan, *The Disillusioned Decades: Ireland 1966–87* (Dublin: Gill and Macmillan, 1987), p. 167.

47   Wilson, *Irish America and the Ulster Conflict*, pp. 126–34.

48   Lawrence J. McCaffrey, *Textures of Irish America* (Syracuse, NY: Syracuse University Press, 1992), p. 161, and William V. Shannon, 'Northern Ireland and America's Responsibility', *The Recorder* (The American Irish Historical Society), Vol. 36, 1975, p. 39.

49   McCaffrey, *Textures of Irish America*, p. 158.

50   Reedy, *From the Ward to the White House*, p. 172.

51 McCaffrey, *Textures of Irish America*, p. 161.
52 *Christian Science Monitor*, 21 January 1985, p. 17.
53 <http://www.irlfunds.org/ww_usa.html>. Accessed January 2001.
54 Ibid.
55 Coogan, *The Disillusioned Decades*, p. 164.
56 Wilson, *Irish America and the Ulster Conflict*, p. 122.
57 Ibid., pp. 123–4.
58 *New York Times*, 8 March 1998, p. 23.
59 Cronin, *Washington's Irish Policy*, p. 313.
60 Holland, *Magill*, pp. 36–8, and Wilson, *Irish America and the Ulster Conflict*, p. 195. Also see note 36 above.
61 *The Irish Edition*, Philadelphia, 1981, p. 1.
62 *TV Guide*, 26 September 1981, p. 14. For a discussion of the gendered representation of this and other aspects of the Troubles, see Chapter 4.
63 Holland, *Magill*, pp. 36–8.
64 *Irish People*, 23 May 1981, p. 5.
65 See Holland, *The American Connection*, pp. 55–6, and Guelke, *Northern Ireland*, p. 135.
66 Guelke, *Northern Ireland*, p. 135.
67 *An Phoblacht*, 7 November 1985, p. 7.
68 Ibid.
69 *Irish People*, 16 November 1985, pp. 8–9.
70 *An Phoblacht*, 5 September 1985, p. 5.
71 *Irish People*, 14 September 1985, p. 8.
72 Ibid., 16 November 1985, p. 8.
73 Ibid., 22 August 1981, p. 11.
74 Ibid., 8 August 1981, p. 11.
75 Ibid., 9 June 1984, p. 6.
76 *New York Times*, 30 October 1995, p. 16.
77 *Christian Science Monitor*, 21 January 1985, p. 17.
78 Ibid., 15 January 1985, p. 16.
79 Cited in Paul Arthur, 'Diasporan Intervention in International Affairs: Irish America as a Case Study', *Diaspora: A Journal of Transnational Studies*, Vol. 1, No. 2, 1991, p. 153.
80 <http://www.internationalfundforireland.com>. Accessed January 2001.
81 <http://www.irlfunds.org>. Accessed January 2001.
82 Ibid.
83 Ibid.
84 <http://www.irishamericanpartners.org>. Accessed January 2001.
85 Ibid.
86 For an outline of the MacBride Principles, see <http://www.irishnational caucus.org>. Accessed July 2006. This is the website of the Irish National Caucus, one of the main campaigners for the implementation of the Principles.
87 Ray O'Hanlon, 'The MacBride Principles: Vital Force or Spent Force?', *Irish Echo*, 3–9 November 1999, p. 25. Emphasis added.
88 Paul Arthur, *Diaspora: A Journal of Transnational Studies*, p. 157.
89 Shannon, 'Northern Ireland and America's Responsibility', pp. 39–40.
90 James B. Healy, *Northern Ireland Dilemma: An American Irish Imperative* (New York: Peter Lang, 1989), p. 34.
91 Ibid., p. 38.
92 Ibid., p. 87.
93 Ibid., p. 90.
94 Conor O'Clery, *Daring Diplomacy: Clinton's Secret Search for Peace in*

Ireland (Boulder, CO: Roberts Rinehart, 1997), p. 12.

95   O'Hanlon, *The New Irish-Americans*, p. 225 and O'Clery, *Daring Diplomacy*, p. 145.

96   Bernadette Devlin McAliskey, 'Where Are We Now in the Peace Process?', *Irish Reporter*, 21 February 1996, pp. 23–8.

2

Irish 'Roots': Memory and History in the Diaspora

INTRODUCTION: IRISH 'ROOTS'

IN THEIR insightful re-reading of the development of an Atlantic proletariat, *The Many-Headed Hydra: The Hidden History of the Revolutionary Atlantic*, Peter Linebaugh and Marcus Rediker frequently highlight the intertwined nature of the Irish- and African-American experience in Atlantic history. A particularly striking example of this interconnection occurs in their description of one of the formative moments in the history of both diasporas. Following the end of the English Civil War in 1649, the victorious Oliver Cromwell prepared for an invasion of Ireland which would result in many thousands of Irish leaving in exile or slavery, most commonly to the American colonies, where they would become some of the earliest forebears of contemporary Irish America. Meanwhile, Cromwell's most renowned Royalist adversary during the Revolution, Prince Rupert of the Rhine, embarked on a career as a privateer in the West African slave trade, the other major source of new arrivals to the Americas at that time, whose victims were the forebears to the majority of the contemporary African-American population.[1]

Noting that the River Gambia, where Prince Rupert arrived in 1651, was also the area to which Alex Haley traced his ancestor Kunta Kinte in *Roots: The Saga of An American Family*, Linebaugh and Rediker nevertheless insist that 'the tale we tell is not a family saga but one of class forces at the critical meeting of the sailor of the European deep-sea ship and the boatman of the African canoe'.[2] This chapter will argue, however, that the publication of *Roots*, and the surge of interest in family history for which it was both a catalyst and a significant symbol, is in fact a powerful example of a radical social development in the politics of individual and group memory and identity formation – particularly among ethnic diasporas in the United States, including the Irish-American community as well as the African-American population.

The social and cultural impact of *Roots* was enormous, and extended well beyond the African-American community for whom it had the most explicit appeal.[3] Chioni Moore describes how the book sold more than 1.5 million hardback copies in its first eighteen months, 'was translated into twenty-four languages, and sat atop *The New York Times* non-fiction best-seller list for more than five months beginning in late November 1976'. As a result of its television serialisation the following year, 'seven of the ten most-watched television shows in United States history were episodes of "Roots". Over the course of those nights, some 130 million Americans, or nearly three in five, and of all races and ethnicities – indeed more than 100 million of whom must statistically have been white – had seen some or all of the show.'[4]

One of the more obvious – and inter-ethnic – uses to which the book and television series were put was the huge increase in interest in genealogy and family history. While this was a rising trend which pre-dates *Roots*, and was clearly linked to other social changes within and beyond the United States, which will be discussed in greater detail below, the role of the novel as both a catalyst for and symbol of the 'genealogy industry' is clear. This was signalled early on by Haley himself, in an interview with the *New York Times*, in which he agreed that 'whites too may become interested in their genealogy. The book's theme is universal in terms of lineage, heritage and the common concern with oral history.' Going on to discuss his initially tentative communications with the contemporary descendants of the slave-owning Murray family discussed in *Roots*, Haley insisted that, eventually, 'there was a sense of acceptance, of realising that our pasts were intricately knotted with one anothers' ... it also points out the fact that there are very few of us who are ethnically pure'.[5]

An ambivalent response to the *Roots* phenomenon was already evident at this time among those previously engaged in family history research. The *Chicago Irish-American News*, in May 1977, printed a story headed 'Family Tree Group Searches Irish "Roots"', in which Bea McGuire, the founder of the Chicago Irish Ancestors genealogical group, established in 1975, pointed out to their reporter 'that, although there was a temporary flare-up nationally of interest in genealogy following the TV series "Roots", it had little impact on the CIA. "We are a stabilised group", states Bea.'[6] In July 1977, however, *Newsweek* reported on 'Everybody's Search for "Roots", and included reference to the Chicago Irish Ancestors group, specifically citing it as one among other ethnically based societies whose appeal had grown as a result of the popularity of *Roots*.[7] The particular appeal of the book to diasporic Americans, including Irish-Americans, was clearly understood and mobilised by the travel industry, which responded rapidly. In 1977, Continental Airlines had launched a discount fares promotion under the slogan 'Take Our Routes to Your Roots', and, by 1978, Aer Lingus were advertising in the Irish-American press, presenting a map of Ireland in which place-names had been replaced with local family names, under the heading 'This Is Your Ireland'.[8]

Following the phenomenal success of *Roots* in the mid-to-late 1970s, a number of other texts with particular significance to Irish-Americans appear to have taken on a specific meaning in terms of the diaspora's increased interest in their pre-emigration ancestry. Among the fiction and non-fiction reported as having been read and recalled by survey respondents questioned about their consumption of Irish-interest culture were Cecil Woodham Smith's *The Great Hunger*, Tim Severin's *The Brendan Voyage* and Thomas Flanagan's *The Tenants of Time*.[9] However, Leon Uris' novel *Trinity* is by far the most popular of these texts, with 50% of all informants in one study reporting that they had read it.[10]

Although, unlike *Roots* itself, *Trinity* is not explicitly concerned with the tracing of origins, and is strictly 'fiction', as opposed to Haley's controversial 'faction', the connections made between the two texts, at least within the Irish-American population, are striking.[11] *Trinity*, which details the effect of the Irish Troubles from the Famine to 1916 on several generations of a Catholic Ulster family, was also a success on a scale comparable to *Roots*, spending thirty-six weeks at the top of the *New York Times* best-seller lists.[12] The significance of this novel to the Irish-American community can be seen not only from its sales figures, but also from the nature of the spin-off events it spawned. In October 1977, for example, a 'Trinity Ireland Festival' was held at the Woodfield Shopping Mall in Schaumberg, Illinois. Organised around a promotion of both *Trinity* and *Ireland, A Terrible Beauty*, the book of photographs and text about Ireland jointly produced by Uris and his wife whilst he was writing the novel, this event was advertised as 'an arts, culture and entertainment festival'.[13] Previewing the festival, the *Chicago Irish-*

American News made a direct connection between the success of the book and its interconnections with the rising interest in family-based ethnic history inspired by the success of *Roots*, explaining: 'The "Trinity" consists of three families who represent the political elements that have fuelled the fires of Ireland's troubles for three centuries. Through successive generations of these families, Uris personifies the unending friction between these political elements, and the love and hatred among the people of a divided country.'[14]

The Irish-American diaspora had, of course, shown interest in tracing their genealogy back to 'the old country' prior to the mid-1970s. As in other social groups, this activity has precedents dating back at least to the end of the nineteenth century, some of which will be explored below. However, both the extent and the motivation for this practice began to change significantly following the end of the Second World War, evolving towards the cultural 'sensation' of *Roots*, after which the heightened levels of interest and actual research in genealogy became an accepted feature of the cultural landscape.

This chapter, in the process of exploring the construction of diasporic memory and identity within the Irish-American population, will explore that community's interest in origins and ancestry through the lens of a number of significant developments which have both affected and been affected by the establishment of a 'genealogy industry'. The first factor to be examined will be the changing conceptions of history itself during the period, and the ways in which the search for family origins has reflected that in a radical, rather than conservative, way. The chapter will then move on to examine, in the light of these changes, the role of narrative structures in both formal history and individual and collective memory constructions, particularly in the light of the popularity of reconstituting family narratives through genealogical research. Finally, following these broader social changes, the chapter will examine in detail the rise of new definitions of and emphases upon ethnicity among the Irish-American community, and the ways in which this contemporary reading of ethnic identity feeds into and is reflected by the more individual senses of identity provoked by family histories.

GENEALOGY AND HISTORICAL DISCOURSE

The implied criticism of *Roots* contained within Linebaugh and Rediker's statement is not unusual among responses to the novel, particularly from professional historians, who have long been suspicious of both its historical veracity and its apparently aspirational reading of the African-American experience. In one of the few scholarly articles to deal with the novel, David Chioni Moore, after commenting on the scarcity of academic engagement with it, proposes that the reasons for this critical silence are not only the discomfort of historians with Haley's use of 'faction', but also the unease of literary critics with 'the novel's decidedly middlebrow status'.[15] Chioni Moore goes on to argue:

> Yet another and partly connected reason for *Roots*'s critical non-existence may be that most scholars, particularly those many on the Left, have been uncomfortable with the unchallenging character of the book's politics: for though *Roots*'s white characters are almost without exception villainous, they are also, without *any* exception, dead. *Roots* situates American crimes of race all comfortably in the past, and when the family's narrative stops in about 1921, one is left with an American success story in the classic mold . . . [16]

Thus, while *Roots* was vilified upon its release by representatives of the political Right such as Nancy Reagan and David Duke for being inflammatory and vicious, it was also rejected by the Left as being middlebrow and politically unchallenging. It is within this vein of critical thought that Linebaugh and Rediker, engaged as they are upon the radical project of recuperating proletarian colonial history, implicitly reject the novel's ideological underpinnings.[17]

Significantly, the contemporary fascination with family history and its perceived relevance to personal and group identity has received attention which follows a similar pattern to that received by *Roots* itself. Frequently described (but rarely analysed) by newspapers and magazines, it is only occasionally remarked upon in more scholarly publications.[18] On those occasions, it often appears to be assumed that amateur genealogists, keen to discover their great-grandmother's place of birth, are, like the novel which was often their inspiration, pursuing an agenda alien to both the Left and Right of the contemporary history academy. The pattern of rejection for the family history phenomenon is generally that traditionalist historians are suspicious of the 'amateur' nature of these investigations, while more radical proponents of the discipline reject the implied ideology of an emphasis upon the 'family'.

The critical reception of *Trinity* has followed a similar pattern to that of *Roots*. The mainstream reviews it received on its publication (particularly those appearing in the Irish-American press) were highly enthusiastic, one reviewer even claiming, 'this is a classic. As a matter of fact, I would choose to call it a masterpiece, for it is truly a work of art.'[19] The book's 'middlebrow' success, however, has, like that of *Roots*, appeared to result in a lack of interest among more scholarly critics. And in the few cases where it has received scholarly attention, it has been attacked, again like *Roots*, for its fictionalisation of historical fact. The writer Eilís Dillon, speaking of Leon Uris and Thomas Flanagan in 1981, argued that they 'were so inaccurate in their facts that they have scarcely justified their incursion into the history of another country than their own. Taking liberties with history in fiction seems to me somewhat unprincipled but you will be told that Scott did it. One wonders if that justifies it.'[20] And James A. Cahalan, in his assessment of the Irish historical novel, reserves particular contempt for *Trinity*, again based upon its historical, social and literary inaccuracies. Reflecting Dillon's disapproval of Uris' nationality, Cahalan refers pointedly to *Trinity*'s obvious appeal to Irish-American (rather than Irish) readers, and then goes on to recount the fact that, during his fatal hunger strike inside Long Kesh Prison in 1981, Bobby Sands memorised the entire novel and recited it to fellow inmates over an eight-day period. Citing the partisan nature of the novel, he argues that:

> The Irish writer cannot escape the nightmare of history, nor could Bobby Sands escape *Trinity*. Thus has fiction pathetically influenced life: not only is history relived in the historical novel; the historical novel resounds in history... in its inaccurate, twisted view of history it is a very long way indeed from the moderate Sir Walter Scott or, for that matter, from the partisan but conscientious Irish writers.[21]

It is, however, the contention of this chapter that the sustained rise in interest in genealogy during the late twentieth century in fact reflects several genuinely radical shifts in both historical and social conceptions of memory and identity, and that these shifts have particular relevance for the Irish-American diaspora.

The suspicion with which family history is regarded, particularly by the Left, appears to stem from its historical origins rather than its current usage. Due to patterns of social organisation and their all-important perpetuation, as well as to the more pragmatic reasons of widespread illiteracy and lack of official record-keeping, the tracing of family history was traditionally an activity largely confined to social elites, or, perhaps more importantly, to those attempting to join the elite, based upon often spurious claims to aristocratic lineage. The connections made by professional scholars between the individual and group motivations for this traditional use of genealogy are evidenced by Eric Hobsbawm's description of 'a more familiar form of genealogy, that which seeks to buttress an uncertain self-esteem. Bourgeois parvenus seek pedigrees, new nations or movements annex examples of past greatness and achievement to their history in proportion as they feel their actual past to have been lacking in these things.'[22]

This formulation suggests a useful reading of the activities of many genealogy 'scholars' through Freud's analysis of the 'family romance', in which the subject rejects their actual lineage in favour of a fantasy parentage of greater status.[23] Family history, therefore, was already, by the beginning of the twentieth century, associated with nostalgia. This association has continued to the present, as illustrated by Raphael Samuel's reference to 'the child's rejection of real-life parents in favour of imaginary and more glamorous others – a recurring fantasy which seems very germane to the current enthusiasm for family history, and the discovery of "roots" '.[24]

Before discussing this formulation of the subject, however, it is worth remembering that genealogy as a prototype of professional history has a long lineage of its own in Ireland. The descent of the tribes and chieftains was traditionally memorised and recited by genealogists such as Dubhaltach MacFirbisigh, who, in 1650, proclaimed himself able to relate the 'branches of kinship and genealogy of every immigration that took possession of Ireland from now to Adam (excepting Fomorians, Norsemen and Saxon foreigners)'.[25] In its post-Enlightenment form, Irish genealogy became adapted to the political and social needs of the age. John G. Barry argues that 'one of the manifestations of the romantic revival in the early nineteenth century, with its emphasis on blood, race and, in consequence, roots was a marked revival in the interest in heraldry and genealogy'.[26]

Barry also noted that the particularly strong attachment to family history in Ireland may well have had its origins in the pre-Famine social structures of the country, particularly the Gaelic legal system's emphasis upon genealogy. The historical experience of colonisation and dispossession of inherited lands in Ireland also points towards another explanation for a cultural emphasis upon an ancestry only decipherable through narrative accounts of family history, rather than through personal experience. Barry describes the way in which, before the Famine, dispossessed peasant families many generations removed from the actual loss of lands and property frequently made wills which bequeathed these lost inheritances to their heirs.[27] This practice is also referred to in Cecil Woodham Smith's account of the Famine, in which she makes the assertion that 'that figure of fun in Victorian days, the Irish beggar who claimed to be descended from kings, was very often speaking the truth. "I am descended from perhaps as good a family as any I address, though now destitute of means", runs a letter imploring assistance in the Distress papers.'[28]

One of several Irish exponents of this revived interest was John O'Hart, who, in his 1881 *Irish Pedigrees; or, The Origin and Stem of The Irish Nation*, insisted on the importance of genealogy, 'on account of the intimate bearing it has upon the individual, together with the tribes, people, nation and family to which he belongs...Even our blessed Saviour would condescend to have his genealogy, according to the flesh, traced up and left on record.'[29] Clearly, enterprises such as O'Hart's attempt to trace the 'stem of the Irish nation', read through Freud's 'family romance' theory, have obvious connections to both individual and collective or national desires to break away from the flawed reality of one's 'family' and to derive a greater level of status and prestige from other, more impressive, origins. At an individual level, a few traces still remain today of such motivations for family history research. One of the quoted correspondents to Reginald Byron's 1999 sociological survey of the Irish-American community of Albany, NY, when asked of the extent of their genealogical knowledge, replied:

> And my mother, what little she knew, she told me. Mostly about her family...So her family [are] direct descendants of the O'Connor *dun*. And that's how I knew about the family history and as far back as the history of Ireland goes. I go back to the Druids and the Normans and the Spaniards and the English and the way they treated [the Irish].[30]

However, the use of genealogy in this way during O'Hart's time was clearly motivated by complex political and cultural concerns, partic10ipating as it did in the cultural nationalist project of separating Ireland from its British, and colonial, 'parent' by reconstituting a different lineage, which included ancient Greece and Persia as well as Milesius of Spain. The extent to which O'Hart's work, like all history, was a result of the context of its production is illustrated by a lengthy discussion in *Irish Pedigrees* of the religious implications of his work. O'Hart evidently feels the need to explain how 'the latest results of genealogical science', and its implications for a genealogy of 'Man', do not conflict with the story of Genesis and Adam's role as the origin of the human race. Going into some detail on theories of the difference between human and cosmic time, he reveals himself to be concerned with important contemporary debates provoked primarily by Darwin's theories of evolution and their apparent conflict with the religious teaching which was so crucial to the nationalist project of which O'Hart's own work was a part.[31]

If O'Hart's genealogical work was a reflection of the social concerns of the time, then so, it will be argued, is the current mass interest in the subject. In order to examine the specific interest of Irish America in their family origins, the particular circumstances of that interest need to be explored first.

For the Irish-American diaspora, rather than the Irish in Ireland, there is, in particular, the experience of emigration to consider in examining the motives behind genealogical interest. The trauma of loss and dislocated identity expressed by the writer of the letter cited by Woodham Smith was exacerbated for millions by the disjuncture of exile to the United States before, during and after the Famine. This process, whatever its ultimate material gains for many, was a further removal from a culturally significant narrative of connection between generations as well as their physical localities. This feature of the Irish diaspora's (among others') appetite for tracing distant ancestors back 'home' has been recognised by Lowenthal, who admits that 'quests for roots reflect this trauma; heritage is invoked to requite displacement'.[32]

There are a number of theories surrounding the recent growth in family history research by amateurs unconnected to the history academy. The most pragmatic of these is that it has only been within the last three or four decades that such research has been possible for non-elite social groups, particularly diasporic groups like the Irish-Americans. The particular problems of Irish-Americans researching into their family history were recognised by an American genealogical publication of 1962, which stated: 'Americans have previously had little hope of discovering the historical and genealogical records of their forbears, due to the lack of any comprehensive and detailed guide'.[33] These archival difficulties have decreased over recent decades, with a growth in comprehensive cataloguing, the use of computerised databases for cross-referencing and, more recently, the enormous impact of the internet on the retrieval and exchange of disparate and scattered information.

The Irish genealogy service of the National Library in Dublin, newly re-designed in 1998, received 10,000 visitors in its first year, 40 per cent of whom were from the United States. A professional researcher working for the National Library's service was quoted as saying that 'prosperous families in the US often want to know how their ancestors lived and are extremely pleased to hear they were famine emigrants living in extreme poverty with lots of children, because it shows how far they have come'.[34] In 1998, the *Irish Times* reported that 'the number of "roots tourists" has more than doubled in the last ten years and in 1996 over 70,000 visitors spent £30 million in Ireland while tracing their family history'.[35] Research on genealogy has also become one of the most popular uses of the internet, with a huge proliferation of dedicated sites and 160 million messages passing through RootsWeb, one of the more established websites, in just one month during 1999. Another indication of the level of enthusiasm for the subject has been the growth of specialist genealogical computer programmes available to researchers, including the highly complex *Master Genealogist* and the *Millennia Legacy Family Tree*, designed to complement the database of the Church of the Latter-day Saints, themselves major contributors to the increased levels of access to genealogical information.[36] David Hey, in his assessment of these developments, has argued that 'ordinary' people's increased free time, disposable income and access to information systems has been crucial to the family history phenomenon.[37]

It is clear, therefore, that the contemporary growth in family history research has been characterised not so much by the 'Irish beggar claiming descent from kings', as by the increasingly affluent Irish-American middle classes enthusiastically claiming descent from Irish peasants. While this does not in itself disprove allegations of nostalgia and romanticism, it does require a new approach in assessing the meaning of the practice as invoked by its practitioners. As David Hey has pointed out, 'knowledge of overcrowded houses, insufficient food, long and tedious hours of work and inadequate defences against disease soon shatters the myth of "the good old days"'.[38]

However, significant as they are, the greater accessibility of records relating to Irish-American (and other ethnicities') family history is not, in itself, a sufficient explanation for the scale and enthusiasm with which such research has been undertaken, particularly in the period following *Roots*. Just as significant, in fact, have been the major theoretical shifts which have occurred within the history itself, and which have both reflected and enabled not only practical developments such as the cataloguing of historical information, but also the re-evaluation of the entire process of 'making history'.

The publications of *Roots* and *Trinity* in the mid-1970s coincided with the institutionalisation of radical forms of historical practice pioneered during the 1960s. These included oral history, local history, history workshops and folk histories. These new practices varied according to context and ideology, but shared an intention to open up the parameters of historical knowledge to include those categories of information, experience and perspective which had not been sufficiently recognised by traditional and 'national' histories. This type of historical work has been characterised as wanting to 'democratize not just the content of history (adding the stories of African Americans, industrial workers, immigrants, women, and gays) but also its practice; they wanted to turn audiences into collaborators'.[39] Within the Irish context, Kevin Whelan has argued that these 'radical' forms of historical practice have offered an invaluable method of reassessing Irish national and, crucially for our purposes, international history, by offering an alternative to revisionist/nationalist arguments. 'With its diverse micro-narratives, local history acted as a defence mechanism against both the ruthless totalling claims of historical meta-narratives and against the rootless blandness of mainstream Anglo-American consumer culture.'[40]

It is within this development of a recognition of the value of micro-narratives that the surge of interest in family history must be understood; within this context, genealogy, performed largely by amateurs tracing their own ancestral origins, can be understood as, in effect, the smallest possible unit of such micro-narratives. The features and implications of the narrative element itself of these historical practices will be explored in greater detail below, but at this point it is useful to explore the particular meanings these developments in historical theory have for a diaspora population such as that of the Irish-Americans.

The importance of diaspora populations to the growth of genealogy has frequently been recognised. David Lowenthal has asserted that 'diaspora are notably heritage-hungry...Dublin is deluged with inquiries from Sons of Erin abroad, some seeking a long-lost legacy or an heir on whom to bestow one, others just hoping to find some-one who remembers Uncle Seamus',[41] and Whelan has noted that, in Ireland, 'family history has also undergone a marked metamorpho-sis in recent years. The initial momentum was driven by the diaspora but has increasingly gained local impetus.'[42] An explanation for this notable feature of diaspora relationships towards 'home' and their ancestral past, as well as for the increase of interest in pursuing this relationship from the 1960s onwards, may in fact lay in develop-ments similar to those which have occurred within the arena of professional history during the same period.

If the methods and values of 'traditional' history concentrated upon the activities and perspectives not only of elite social groups and individuals, but also upon the pursuit of a 'national' history, the majority of emigrants and their descendants were, in effect, doubly excluded from this narrative. Not only were the original emigrant founders of most diaspora families, for the most part, members of the largely undocumented and unconsidered working or peasant classes, but the fact of their migration meant that their life-histories could not (or would not) be encompassed within the framework of any one national history. This would appear to be particularly true in the Irish and American examples, as, from the late nineteenth century onwards, each nation, albeit for different reasons, placed a strong emphasis upon the establishment of a distinct and coherent national history which frequently sought to downplay the significance of outside influences in the interest of nation-building. This is not to claim that the narrative of emigration/immigration was not given attention in historical studies of either Ireland or the United States; rather that the twin processes were studied as discrete and uncon-nected events whose significance related largely to their impact upon the national body politic either left behind or entered into.

For the diasporic communities whose ancestors made these jour-neys, however, the process was a single and indivisible event, albeit one open to multiple meanings. Moreover, the experience of simul-taneously leaving one home and establishing a new one which characterises the beginnings of all diasporas was, in effect, a foun-dational narrative for the communities of the emigrants' descendants, and as such is of essential importance to the establish-ment and circulation of both individual and group memory and identity. This was precisely the kind of project which traditional historical practice was unable and unwilling to provide for such communities.

Given the importance, therefore, of tracing a coherent and unbroken trajectory between the old world and the new for a diasporic community such as the Irish-Americans, it is unsurprising that the development of new historical practices such as the recuperation of micro-narratives through the research of local and oral histories, as described above, should have been embraced with such enthusiasm by those diasporas. As Kevin Whelan argues in his discussion of the synergy between genealogy and local history, 'only if the meta-narratives by which intellectuals structure their concepts are in dialogue with the micro-narratives by which people understand their lives will there be fruitful co-operation'.[43] And, in assessing the kinds of micro-narratives by which Irish-Americans do 'understand their lives', as well as the structures by which these are generated and circulated, family histories and stories consistently appear as the most valued and meaningful.

HISTORICAL NARRATIVE AND NARRATIVE HISTORY

At this point, it is useful to consider the role played by narrative itself in the processes by which the Irish-American diaspora constructs and circulates its group memories and identities. It is here that the connections between history and narrative, as well as between narrative and collective memory, become clear; and here, also, that the crucial role of narrative construction within the pursuit of family history in particular is made apparent.

The use of narrative within historical discourse is a highly contested area. Theorists such as Hayden White have argued that historical narrative acts to 'subsume' individuals within the established system of social relations. Other commentators have suggested that narrative formulations allow for historical discourse to operate within the 'universal' patterns of story-telling, thus remaining tangible to non-professionals.[44]

Issues of narrative and story-telling are particularly pertinent in the arena of the 'new' forms of history which developed during and after the 1960s. Oral and folk histories, in particular, have a heavy reliance upon rediscovering and recuperating narratives 'from below', often through the use of individual and small-group story-telling. The construction of historical narrative requires a process of forgetting-through-selection, as well as remembrance; although the extent to which this was acknowledged within the traditional

historical academy is debatable at best. John Frow illustrates this
essential point in his discussion of 'repetition and forgetting', in
which he posits the metaphor of reversibility against the traditional
historical trope of retrieval. Within this model, therefore, it is recognised that, because the past itself does not exist, its reconstruction is
necessarily produced under the conditions of the present. Frow
argues that:

> rather than having a meaning and a truth determined once and for all
> by its status as an event, its meaning and its truth are constituted
> retroactively and repeatedly; if time is reversible then alternative
> stories are always possible ... Forgetting is thus an integral principle
> of this model, since the activity of compulsive interpretation that
> organises it involves at once selection and rejection ... memory has the
> orderliness and teleological drive of narrative. Its relation to the past
> is not that of truth but of desire.[45]

What this recognition suggests, therefore, is that the theoretical
contests over historical narrative described above are actually
discussing two very different kinds of narrative. The subsuming
narrative of mystification criticised by White appears recognisable as
the historical construction which does assume a 'meaning and truth
determined once and for all by its status as an event', as well as one
in which the crucial process of selection and rejection is not recognised, a deceptively ideological act, as White argues. With reference
to the memories of the Irish-American diaspora, the categories of
historical narrative which 'subsumed' individuals within its system
of social relationship creation were those of 'national narratives',
whether of Ireland or the United States, which sought to examine the
impact of emigration and immigration upon nation-building
projects, without reference to the levels of meaning such narratives
had within the lives of their main players, the diaspora themselves.

By contrast, the construction of micro-narratives which work
with and make room for the complex personal narratives of those
most affected by the creation of the diaspora seems more analogous
to those favoured by theorists anxious to allow a recognisable voice
to groups subsumed by traditional macro-narratives. It is important
to remember that these micro-narratives are not merely derived from
inviting different people to tell them, in effect, the masses rather than
the elite. Instead, they are the construction of different kinds of
narrative, with different concepts of time, space and events. In his

discussion of the concept of collective memory, Paul Connerton considers the issue of oral and folk histories, arguing that oral historians have discovered the difficulty of persuading interviewees to organise their life-histories into chronological narrative form. Connerton argues that this difficulty occurs because such an approach is primarily the form of an elite who are able, through their positions of public sphere privilege, to see their own histories as synonymous with the 'objective' history of institutions. In contrast, 'when oral historians listen carefully to what their informants have to say they discover a perception of time that is not linear but cyclical...The basic cycle is the day, then the week, the month, the season, the year, the generation.'[46] The connection Connerton makes here between the construction of micro-history narratives and the use of cyclical, rather than linear time is clearly reflected in the actual practices of those engaged in researching their family histories, and with far-reaching consequences which in many ways belie the critique of genealogy as being conservative and purely nostalgic.

The concept of a diasporic national 'home', with all the powerful nostalgic associations it contains, becomes particularly complex for a diaspora which has reached its second, third or even fourth generation since that home was left behind. Such is the case for the Irish-American diaspora by the period under discussion, that of the 1950s and beyond. While, of course, America was still receiving, and would continue to receive to the present day, many first-generation immigrants, by the end of the Second World War a substantial Irish-American population was established who had no first-hand experience of Ireland, and in particular no experience of post-independence Ireland. The negotiation of such Irish-Americans' relationship to Ireland therefore becomes one dominated by the concept of a 'home' nation which is not only elsewhere, but which is not directly and personally remembered. This negotiation, and all that it entails for the construction of Ireland within a global narrative, must also therefore take place primarily through the production and circulation of narratives and images. It is at this moment that Ireland becomes, for the majority of the world's population who identify themselves as Irish, a home understood through the consumption of narrativised images rather than first-hand memory or experience. It is therefore necessary to explore the effect that this imaginary Ireland had, not only on Irish-American expectations of the country, but also on the self-representation of Ireland itself. The principal vehicles for these representations, in the post-Second World War era, have been film and tourism.

Popular representations of Irish-American 'ethnic practice' in the later twentieth century also provide an important source of information about changing attitudes and experiences with regard to their relationship to their Irish origins. Since the end of the Second World War, the image of the Irish-American 'returning' to Ireland to trace their roots has been a recurrent one.

This theme of the Irish-American's 'return', most likely for the first time, was a central feature of many of the tourist promotional films produced by and for the Irish-American market during the 1950s and 1960s. One of the most striking features of these particular films is the extent to which, unlike travelogue films produced for other markets, they borrow their format so directly from the Hollywood fictional film tradition. This format includes the use of fictional characters, surprisingly detailed narratives and photography which make direct reference to mainstream feature films. This is in notable contrast to travelogue films about Ireland produced for the British market, which, although there are occasional narrative themes, generally tend to be 'informative' in a very functional fashion about the facilities and opportunities for holidays in Ireland.

The Irish In Me, made in 1959, deals explicitly with the subject of the Irish-American diaspora who have no direct knowledge of Ireland. It is heavily narrativised, centring on the story of Sheila, a 12-year-old Irish-American girl travelling to meet not only the grandfather she has never seen before, but also the nation to which she 'belongs'. The film, which is narrated by her grandfather, follows her from her arrival at Shannon Airport, through an exploration of Dublin alongside him, and then on a journey into the country to meet her extended family.

The film's narrative is used to explore the meaning this journey has for Sheila. She is shown making friends and exploring the countryside with Sean, a boy of similar age from her family's village. After a day of climbing trees and splashing in rivers, her now absent grandfather's voice-over declares:

> Deep in the heart of Ireland, Sheila becomes in spirit what she is in heritage – an Irish girl come home to the land of her forefathers. She cannot give a name to the thing she feels in her heart – it might be called pride, or a love of country. To Sheila it is a nameless joy – a feeling of belonging with the Irish boy Sean. There is deep

contentment...and then the summer is gone. It is time to return home...she takes Ireland with her.[47]

So, for Sheila, the experience of Ireland is one of spiritual home-coming, rather than 'mere' touristic pleasure. And indeed the narrative of the film itself almost obstructs the process of tourism which it is designed to promote, through its concentration upon the fictional characters and their relationships. *The Irish In Me*, in fact, through its engagement with Sheila's selective inheritance of Irish culture, is recognising and projecting the act of negotiation between diasporic memory and contemporary reality which is an essential part of the Irish-American visitor's experience of Ireland.

The same motivation would appear to be in evidence in *O'Hara's Holiday*, another 1950s promotional film aimed at Irish-Americans, when the eponymous hero, a New York policeman, visits Ireland for the first time, to have a 'damn good holiday', but also to trace his family. It is not made clear whether he has any particular knowledge of his family's place of origin, but he is shown near the beginning of the film, making enquiries in the Kenmare area – although to no immediate avail. Later on, however, after having enjoyed his holiday (and acquired a fiancée), O'Hara almost literally stumbles across his Irish family in a village he travels through on the way to Shannon Airport for his return flight. Making it clear that this development is the best possible end to his holiday, O'Hara promises to return again to Ireland in the future, bringing with him 'lots of little O'Hara's' to continue the family line.[48]

The distinctive use of narrative within material designed for the later-generation Irish-American diaspora, as well as the important place of family origins within that narrative, point again towards the role of collective memory and identity within such communities.

The nature of that collective memory, for a second- or third-generation Irish diaspora, is significant within the context in which it is created and reflected in their contact with Ireland itself. By the nature of cross-generational cultural transmission, much of the understanding and experience of Irish-Americans' Irish identity is necessarily through the medium of narrative, be it filmic or literary. This process is even more pronounced in the diasporic 'recollection' of Ireland (as distinct from their diasporic Irish identity within America) for those generations who have never previously been there. In the twentieth century and for Irish-Americans in particular, while a considerable amount of their cultural identification would have come from narratives within their community, such as family and other first-generation immigrants, they would also have acquired an extensive exposure to images of Ireland, primarily through the medium of film. Further, it is clear that this narrativised process of family and ethnic identification had become particularly central to the cultural practices of those later-generational Irish-Americans who had also experienced the impact of the enormous social changes in the United States following the Second World War.

FAMILY HISTORY AND ETHNIC HISTORY

It is outside the scope of this project to consider fully the social consequences of the Second World War within America. However, it is worth noting that, for the 'old-stock' European immigrant groups, many of whom were still the basis of America's inner-city, industrial working class in 1939, the war and its immediate aftermath brought a number of important new opportunities. Two of these changes worthy of particular note were the unprecedented levels of travel and wide social experience which occurred as a result of military service for both men and women, and the possibilities for higher education after the war offered under the terms of the GI Bill. Along with other social and economic developments throughout the 1950s, these events precipitated a very sudden opportunity for members of immigrant groups to move rapidly from ethnically-based urban and working-class environments into 'Americanised' suburban and nascently middle-class neighbourhoods. It has been argued that, of all these ethnic groups, the Irish-Americans were especially well placed to take advantage of the social mobility offered by the GI Bill in particular, and to engage in what has been termed 'generation-skipping' through education and economic success.[49] In describing the ways in which this affected his first-generation immigrant mother, Richard White argues that 'the war changed the country in ways that people would have resisted in peacetime but that in wartime seemed unavoidable and even welcome. Old categories broke down. The Army and war work mixed people who otherwise would have remained separate.'[50] And among the old categories which broke down were the relatively clear-cut categories of ethnic identification based upon neighbourhood, religion, marriage and occupation.

This reflects one of the principal points of discussion among later theorists of this subject: whether ethnic identification could survive the social movement of members of the group, from the predominantly working-class, communally organised ethnic 'ghettos', out into the middle-class suburbs. In the case of Irish-Americans, this question was explicitly raised by Lawrence J. McCaffrey in 1976, when he claimed that 'Irish America exists in a cultural nowhere. The trip from the old city neighbourhoods to the suburbs has been a journey from someplace to no place. It is probably too late to save the Irish, but their experience may help other ethnics to learn to cherish cultural heritages that are priceless and irreplaceable.'[51] By the end of the 1970s, however, it had become apparent that the Irish-Americans, like other diasporas, had not lost their sense of collective memory and identity in the way which McCaffrey suggested.

A number of primarily sociological surveys and studies of white ethnicities in the United States were carried out from the 1980s onwards, in an effort to discover the reason for such ethnic identities' persistent survival across several generations. These included the work of Richard Alba, Mary Waters, Roy Rosenzweig and David Thelen, and Reginald Byron, all of whose studies will be considered below.

A study conducted in 1984–85 by Richard Alba, on ethnic identification among white Americans, questioned 524 randomly selected residents of the 'Capital Region' of New York State; an area which consists of the towns of Albany, Schenectady and Troy. The principal white ethnicities of this area are Irish, German, Italian and Polish – all 'old-stock' European immigrant groups – who were studied both separately and jointly. Alba identified significant and interesting differences between these different groups' approaches to their ethnic identity, some of which will be explored below. With respect to interest in, and use of, family background as part of identity construction, however, Alba found, when asking respondents about the importance of their family's ethnic history, that 'noteworthy in this respect is the desire of many of my respondents to trace their genealogical roots. For them, the sense of their ethnic background does not really extend beyond the history of their own family. That history, however, is not ethnically exclusive; it is something that can be appreciated by others from different ethnic backgrounds.'[52]

Alba identifies in this phenomenon one of the crucial features of the population group of mainly later-generation European immigrants under study here: that their ancestry is, by the present day, likely to consist of at least two or more ethnic backgrounds. Noting that the Polish and Italian-American respondents were the most likely to assert that their ethnic backgrounds were of great importance to them, Alba goes on to state that 'the Irish seem to stand midway between the other old-stock groups and the Italians and Poles. Persons with an Irish identity are not more likely than their old-stock counterparts to view their ethnic background as very important, but they are less likely to deny it any role.'[53]

Alba highlights the issues of social mobility, intermarriage and geographical dispersion as having had a considerable effect on concepts of ethnic identity among later-generation white Americans; and he points out that the frequently identified process of suburbanisation may well be closely linked to the popularity of family history. As the 'zone of common experiences' in day-to-day life shared by members of an ethnic group are steadily diminished through their movement away from shared neighbourhoods and lifestyles, the specifics of family history may well become the only tangible link to ethnic cultural practices available to many people.[54] This is reflected in other studies particular to Irish-Americans in which respondents, when asked to identify cultural practices which they considered to be especially indicative of their ethnicity, often referred to relatively non-specifically Irish family rituals surrounding food and holiday celebrations, with the explanation that, because these were family rituals, and they considered their family to be Irish, the rituals by definition represented Irishness.[55]

Alba also discusses ethnic hybridity, which was to become a dominating feature of later studies. He noted that, with increasing intermarriage, many white Americans 'are largely free to identify themselves as they will'.[56] This process is particularly relevant to Irish-Americans, who, in Alba's own study, were some of the most ethnically mixed respondents.[57] Other studies conducted throughout the 1990s have paid great attention to this development, often allying it to Gans' theory of symbolic ethnicity, and it is in the reactions to this issue that deep-rooted and even unconscious attachments to the 'melting-pot' theory have often appeared.[58] Intermarriage and social mobility were the key components of melting-pot expectations of later-generation immigrant groups, and the dismissive attitude often displayed towards hybrid ethnic identities, whose 'symbolic' nature is therefore assumed to indicate a lesser degree of personal and social meaning, suggests that these expectations are still present.

The element of choice in the adoption of their ethnic identity by contemporary Irish-Americans was the central topic of another

major study conducted within this and other white European diasporas in the 1990s by Mary C. Waters. *Ethnic Options: Choosing
Identities in America* was a study deliberately designed to test the
individual and collective cultural identities of that now predominant
group of middle-class suburban diaspora members. It started from
the understanding that such respondents have made their ethnic
affiliations largely as a matter of choice, and it set out to examine
the ways in which this actually operates in terms of the transmission
and performance of cultural identities. Crucially, Waters examines
the differences between the 'ethnic choices' available to white
Americans and those available to African-Americans (whatever the
complexity of their ancestral origins), grounding her discussion in
the history of United States law on racial identification, as well as in
the politics of 'passing' as white or of giving recognition to white
ancestors who may have been slave-owners. This discussion not only
echoes Chioni Moore's examination of the selective genealogy of
Alex Haley's *Roots* (which largely ignores the author's white ethnic
heritage), but is also of great relevance to the issue of historical Irish-
American positioning in the social and racial hierarchies of
American society. The responses Waters received were very similar in
nature to those gathered in Alba's and Byron's study – considerable
emphasis was placed on family stories, family rituals and a strong
belief in inherited family characteristics which, within family lore,
are often related back to particular ethnic groups.[59] As with the
results of the other surveys, the social and economic conditions
which shape the lifestyles and cultural practices of this later-generation diaspora provide clear explanations for the strong intertwining
of family and ethnic identifications among these groups.

Among popular representations of the topic, a deliberately comic
example of the very real levels of conscious and unconscious 'choosing' of ethnicity by later-generation American immigrant groups is
provided in the 1997 feature film *The Matchmaker*. In the film,
Marcy, assistant to US Senator McGlory, is sent to Ireland to
discover his genealogy in order to attract the Irish-American vote for
his re-election in Boston. By the end of the film Marcy has failed,
despite her best efforts and the cheerfully fraudulent assistance of the
locals in the senator's 'home' village of Ballinagra, to find any of the
senator's ancestors. At this point, during a scene in which the
narrowly re-elected senator, wearing a plastic green hat, assures his
supporters that 'it's a great day for the Irish', his father admits to
Marcy that their family were originally from Hungary. 'The real

name was something like Mikelós... McGlory is an Ellis Island
name, you know the kind of thing, the US is full of them. And, er, as
a Democrat living in Boston, I may have played up the Irish thing
just a wee bit.'[60] *The Matchmaker*'s story of the expediency of Irish
ethnicity for American politicians may have derived some of its
inspiration from the rumours surrounding President Reagan's visit to
Ireland in 1984. During that trip, he was taken on a highly publi-
cised visit to his 'ancestral village' of Ballyporeen, in County
Tipperary. Ballyporeen had been selected as the birthplace of
Reagan's Irish ancestors on the basis of an entry in the parish register; a piece of genealogical documentation which came under
increasingly satirical scrutiny by the press. Gene Kerrigan, writing in
Magill during the visit, argued that:

> The whole thing rests on a name written in the local church register
> (Copyright: R.C. Parish of Ballyporeen 1981. All rights reserved)
> which says that Michael, son of Thomas Regan and Margaret
> Murphy of Doolis was baptized here on September 3 1829 ... A cynic
> might look at the scrawled 'Thomas Regan' and say that it looks
> mightily like Ryan to me, and might point out that there's an odd little
> squiggle there that looks like maybe someone did some post facto [sic]
> adjusting of history.[61]

1.   'It's a great day for the Irish', even if they're really Hungarian –
     a Boston politician 'chooses' his Irish-American identity in *The
     Matchmaker* (1997).

In *The Matchmaker*, the McGlory family's choices about their ethnic origins may not have begun deliberately, therefore, but, in their self-interested continuance, they are reflective of a long tradition not only of Hollywood representations of Irish family origins being mutable, but also of the very real opportunities for and advantages of ethnic 'choosing'. Many pre-Second World War Hollywood films (often comedies) dealt with the issue of immigrant attempts at social mobility and intermarriage between newly arrived immigrant groups, dramatising the difficulties an 'undesirable' ethnicity could cause. In perhaps the most celebrated of these, *Irene* (1926), Irene O'Dare's wealthy prospective mother-in-law engages a genealogist to discover her deliberately concealed Irish immigrant background. *Abie's Irish Rose* (1929) examines the sometimes tense relationship between New York's Irish and Jewish communities, and, in *His Family Tree* (1935), the plot revolves around immigrant Charles Murphy having changed his name to Murfree in order to achieve the political success his social-climbing wife craves.[62] What is most significant in *The Matchmaker's* examples of 'ethnic options', as well as in President Reagan's allegedly creative evidence of his own 'roots', is that, unlike in the pre-Second World War examples, it is deemed politically and socially expedient to adopt Irishness rather than disguise it.

Reginald Byron's study of *Irish-America* was conducted entirely in the Albany, NY area, among more than 700 randomly selected later-generation Irish-Americans, and is highly suspicious of the levels of cultural or personal meaning attached to ethnicity by respondents whose ancestry is mixed, and whose knowledge of Ireland or Irish history is not detailed. He goes so far as to produce statistical tables outlining the likely percentage of Irish ancestors belonging to the later-generation diaspora according to generation cohorts; therefore linking ethnic identity to 'blood-lines' in a manner suggestive of much earlier approaches to the subject.[63] The element of 'choice' regarding ethnicity for such Irish-Americans is then explicitly related to the rise of multicultural policies (particularly within the public school system) in contemporary American society. Byron argues:

> Nowadays, in the interests of even-handed, egalitarian multicultural-ism, American schoolteachers not uncommonly ask children to say what they 'are' (not merely to say what their immigrant ancestors' origins were a century ago), forcing them to identify with an *ethnie*, no matter how irrelevant such a question might be to the child's

circumstances. Teachers rely on manuals and textbooks to tell the children about 'their traditions' and 'their history' which they are presumed to have inherited along with their skin and hair colour, books which are authorised for use in publicly funded classrooms by state legislatures and local school boards.[64]

Overlooking the essential contradiction inherent in the fact that much of his attack on such enforced 'quasi-racial' identification is based on equally deterministic arguments about ethnic inheritance, Byron goes on to question the validity of diaspora-members' attachment to their ethnic heritage on the grounds of the lack of tangible evidence and information available to most of them.

Several of the questions Byron asked his respondents related to levels of interest in national history, family history, and actual genealogical research undertaken. Of the Albany-born (and therefore not first-generation immigrant) respondents, Byron found that 67.4 per cent said that they were 'very interested' in their Irish backgrounds, and 65.1 per cent had tried to learn about their family history. Byron, apparently following Alba's previous findings, appears to play down the significance of these figures, by highlighting the frequent paucity of information actually held by the respondents. He points out that most informants' genealogical information goes back one or two generations at the most, that only 37.6 per cent of those with any information could give the names, birthplace, occupation and religion of all four of their grandparents, and that 65.2 per cent of all respondents were unaware of any relatives currently in Ireland.[65]

The lack of results produced by an interest in family history among Irish-Americans, however, is hardly conclusive proof of the lack of meaning invested in the process by the individuals and families themselves. Byron himself points out the way in which documentation is easily dispersed between family members across only a couple of generations.[66] When this possibility is combined with the difficulties experienced by those attempting to trace ancestors who entered the United States through Ellis Island, for example, it becomes clear that, even with recent developments in databases and other searching techniques, success in tracing ancestors back to Ireland is not guaranteed by enthusiasm alone.[67] Byron, however, queries the validity of such a quest in the first place, basing his objections upon another reoccurrence of the 'melting-pot' theory:

> Our informants' parents and grandparents looked to the future, to the
> day their children and grandchildren would attain the American
> Dream. The dream may have turned to dust for some Americans, but
> for millions of descendants of European immigrants there was subur-
> ban middle-class respectability at the end of the rainbow and the
> melting-pot was, and is, most certainly *not* a myth but the everyday
> moral project of past and current generations. Multiculturalism has
> brought about a new kind of project and has opened up a bourgeon-
> ing [sic] market in politicised and manufactured heritage: both have
> produced essentialising myths.[68] [original emphasis]

A number of popular representations of Irish-American genealogical
interest within a multicultural American society have been produced
during the 1990s. *This Is My Father*, directed by Paul Quinn
in 1998, shows particular sensitivity towards the emotional
motivations for, and consequences of, the search for family lost
during the disjuncture of emigration, as well as suggesting a different reading from Byron's of multicultural recognitions of ethnicity
and genealogy in the classroom.[69] The story of history teacher Kieran
Johnston (played by James Caan) and of his journey from Illinois to
Ireland in search of the father his now dying emigrant mother never
told him of is triggered by the chance discovery of a photograph of
his mother and an unknown man. The film is divided between the
contemporary narrative of Johnston's search and the hidden narrative of his parent's tragic relationship in Ireland in 1939, which will
end with his father's suicide and his pregnant mother's emigration.
The film therefore takes place in three separate but irretrievably
intertwined locations of time and space: contemporary America,
contemporary Ireland, and a narratively reconstructed Ireland of the
past. In this way, the search for the central character's personal
history is framed not only within an explicit narrative, through the
reconstruction of his parents' story, but also through a narrative
which is cyclical and cross-generational in its shadowing and mirror-
ing of past and present events.

Particularly illuminating are the film's opening and closing
sections, respectively representing Johnston's motivations for his
quest 'back' to Ireland and the consequences of his discoveries for
his sense of personal and social identity. The film opens in his classroom in Aurora, Illinois, where a pupil is completing her
presentation to the group of a family history project set by Johnston.
Her implausible account of a self-aggrandising genealogy, which
makes unsubstantiated references to heroes of the American

2. The chance discovery of an unknown family photograph prompts a search for Irish 'roots' by an Irish-American history teacher in *This Is My Father* (1998).

Revolution, the King of Norway and 'Eric the Red', is a sharply drawn satire on the traditionally criticised 'family romance' fictional account of 'roots'. It acts as a catalyst for a bitter outburst from Johnston. He declares that: 'I'm not interested in your family tree, and I really *don't* want to know who you think you might be related to. I do want to know your family's history as it relates to the twentieth century.' He then goes on, after a mild confrontation with an African-American student regarding the 'relevance' of his teaching, to relate the statistically predicted life expectancies and demographic projections for the class as a whole. After listing what proportion of them can expect to go to college, as well as that which, statistically, will spend time in prison, he concludes with the projection that only two out of the class are likely to 'achieve some sort of financial stability'. The bleakness of these predictions is also reflective of the fractured social relationships among both the multicultural students and their teacher, and is immediately followed by scenes introducing

Johnston's lonely and fractured family life. Of this section of the film, Martin McLoone has commented that 'the framing story, set in the Chicago suburb of Aurora, is shot in muted browns, suggesting the lack of colour and excitement in the lives of these troubled and anxious Irish-Americans'.[70] Indeed, the opening scenes appear to reflect many of the concerns voiced during the 1970s regarding the loss of Irish-American identity within the 'lace curtain' suburbs of a city formerly characterised by inner-city Irish neighbourhoods.

Into this situation, however, *This Is My Father* also introduces the added complications of the multiculturalism of the contemporary United States: Johnston's history class is one of noticeably mixed ethnicity, and the African-American pupil who challenges the relevance of his teaching is clearly hinting at their ethnic differences as a source of this perceived lack of connection between them. The fact that these establishing scenes of contemporary American society among later-generation immigrants take place within a history classroom is in itself significant, as the national curricula of American history and social studies have been the embattled locus of ideological disputes concerning multiculturalism, often played out through the almost universal 'family tree' projects – directly inspired by *Roots* – set for schoolchildren.[71]

3. Tension in the history classroom between the Irish-American history teacher and his multi-ethnic students at the beginning of *This Is My Father* (1998).

At the end of the film, after Johnston has undertaken his journey to Ireland, the story returns to his history class. The camera pans back from a close-up on the photograph which prompted the search, to reveal that it is being passed from hand to hand by the now silent and attentive group of students as they listen to Johnston recount the story of his family history which the audience has just seen. McLoone suggests that, 'above all, the photograph symbolises an encounter between Ireland and America that is ambivalent and elliptical as it has resonated down the years'.[72] The clearly indicated change in the nature of the relationship between Johnston and his pupils, from distrust and alienation to sympathy and shared emotions, is obviously intended to suggest that the discovery of his origins has resulted in more than one kind of resolution. Not only, the film implies, has Johnston acquired a more secure sense of personal identity from the knowledge of his family history, but this factual and emotional knowledge has also allowed for a bridging of the social barriers of alienation between himself and his pupils; even those whose family and ethnic backgrounds are evidently very different from his own.

4. The teacher's recounting of his Irish 'roots' brings harmony into the multi-ethnic group at the close of *This Is My Father* (1998).

Another genre of increasing popularity which deals with Irish-American narratives of identity and communal memory is the 'memoir' of an individual Irish-American's search for the historical basis of their family background. These memoirs are often a hybrid form, part-autobiography, part-family history, part-travelogue, and they typically document an author's Irish-American childhood, often describing extended adulthood visits to Ireland to research the roots of their ethnic identity. Examples include Alice Carey's *I'll Know It When I See It: A Daughter's Search For Home in Ireland*, Joan Matieu's *Zulu: An Irish-American's Quest to Discover her Roots*, Maureen Waters' *Crossing Highbridge: A Memoir of Irish America*, and Richard White's *Remembering Ahanagran: Storytelling in a Family's Past*. These memoirs are very different in terms of both authorial position and style from the best-selling memoirs of aspirational re-emigration to the United States, as typified by Frank McCourt's *Angela's Ashes* and its sequel *'Tis*, as well as by his brother Malachy McCourt's *A Monk Swimming* and *Singing Him My Song*.[73] Writing of *Angela's Ashes*, George O'Brien has suggested that its positioning of the United States as the 'heroine' of the memoir, the only possible place in which the author may achieve the recuperation he requires from his Irish childhood, is indicative of its having been written

> at a time when not only has the old Ireland come to an end – Ireland, the emigrant factory – but when European emigration itself is a thing of the past. Those who participated in the various diasporas are now settled, are no longer a subject of public misgiving as they previously were . . . Perhaps part of the appeal of Angela's Ashes is that it marks the end of the psychological journey of all who booked their passage prompted by hunger and the deaths of innocents.[74]

The growth of this genre of 'family memoirs', however, would suggest that aspirational narratives culminating in the first-generation's arrival in the United States are far from being the 'end of the psychological journey' of diaspora formation. Instead, the second- or later-generation diaspora are increasingly showing a desire not only to trace their family narrative back to their ancestors' Irish homeland, but to position its multi-generational journey within the social and political context in which it has developed. As Maureen Waters argues at the end of her memoir *Crossing Highbridge*:

Historians of Irish America typically speak of 'progress'... Some would argue that we've all become 'white'. I have a lot of trouble with that concept. It's important to retain a sense of vulnerability, to remember where we came from, however disturbing that is. Sometimes, indeed, it's necessary to double back. The past, as Faulkner so well understood, is never really past.[75]

One of the most sensitively traced of these 'family memoirs', Richard White's *Remembering Ahanagran: Storytelling in a Family's Past*, is an exploration, by a professional historian, of the complex relationship between history and memory. White approaches this issue through a comparison of the congruencies and ellipses between the stories of Ahanagran in Co. Kerry, told by Sara, his first-generation immigrant mother, with the archival evidence and documentation of his family and their move to the United States.

White's project is one dedicated to a subtle exploration of the interdependent and revealing relationship between history and memory, rather than an attempt to discover a 'true' version of his mother's origins. At the end of what he describes as his 'anti-memoir', discussing the creative and selective nature of his mother's memories of her life, White asserts, 'my history needs to understand such memories, and other constructions of the past as well. History cannot afford to dismiss its rivals as simply fabricated or false, or history will weaken its own ability to understand the strange worlds we live in.'[76]

One of the most powerful uses of narrative history which White uncovers during his visits to Ahanagran is that of selectively cyclical narrative association, reminiscent of Connerton's arguments. Of particular relevance to White's experiences are Connerton's descriptions of the ways in which 'subordinate groups' adopt selection processes for the 'objective' historical narratives they recall. Connerton cites Carlo Levi's experience in a small Italian village in 1935, where he discovered that, despite a significant number of the residents having been killed serving in the First World War, there was no commemoration or remembrance of this conflict within village life. Instead, the inhabitants spoke vividly of the Brigand Wars in the area, despite the fact that these had ended in 1865; a time more or less prior to first-hand memory.[77] Similarly, White discovers in County Kerry the narrative of 'The Time of Troubles'. This cycle of local and family stories, which Sara has taken to the United States with her as one of the few sources of overtly historical memory circulated between her and her American-born descendants, deals with incidents in and around Ahanagran which relate directly to the Irish struggle for independence. White examines the first-hand accounts of, for example, Black and Tan raids on the homes of his extended Kerry family and their neighbours in the light of historical documentation of the same events, and discovers that the narrators could not, due to their ages, have actually witnessed these events – instead, they have become conflated with other stories relating to the Troubles, and merged into a cyclical and communal recounting among the group which relies upon a conception of time at odds with the linear approach of professional history. As White describes it: 'The Time of Troubles is less a narrative that seeks to chronicle than a matchmaker pairing past and present.'[78]

White also discovers other important differences between himself and his extended family in Ireland, ones which are based less upon his position as a professional historian, and more upon his own and his mother's positions as members of the diaspora 'returning' to the homeland which their relatives have never left. Recounting a fruit-less attempt by himself and Sara to persuade her brother Johnny to recall particular events in their past, he explains, 'for Johnny his card game is worth all the history in the world. The dead are of no concern to the living. He knows all he needs to know of the place in which he lives. He has lived here his whole life, and what he doesn't know he doesn't think has hurt him.'[79] However, such an organic and unstructured relationship to the past – even, or perhaps espe-cially, to one's own past and that of one's family – is unavailable to those who have the disjuncturing experience of emigration embed-ded in that past.

This suggests some interesting possible explanations for the strik-ing interest displayed by the Irish diaspora in their 'roots', an interest which is not always mirrored by their relatives who stayed in Ireland. The average amount of real, tangible knowledge held by most Irish people in Ireland about their extended family and ances-tors may not, in the main, be considerably greater than that held by diaspora members. Knowledge of families' maiden names, places of birth and memorable life-experiences is rarely likely to extend back further than three generations at best for those of 'ordinary' (and therefore little-documented) origins. An interesting aside to this kind of search for family information lies in the rise in popularity of 'Irish' names among Irish-Americans during the 1980s and 1990s. Taken in conjunction with the evidence of Irish-American interest in genealogy and ethnic identity, such a phenomenon is hardly surprising; what makes it more interesting is that the names chosen are not only the kind of Irish names popular in Ireland, such as Grainne, Aoife or Colm, often chosen in honour of Irish ancestors discovered through family history research. An article in the *Chicago Tribune*, commenting upon the increased popularity of Irish first names, also pointed out that Irish surnames, such as Flynn or Reilly, again perhaps belonging to other branches of an ethnically Irish family, are gaining in popularity as first names for Irish-American children of the 1990s. Even more interestingly, there is another set of 'Irish' names popular within Irish America, which would rarely if ever be found back in Ireland, such as Kerry, Shannon and Erin.[80] Such choices suggest the influence not only of specific family research, but also of a strong desire to locate the family's history within a specific geography as well as history.

What differs between Ireland and Irish America, therefore, is the *need* for the many and obvious gaps in this historical and geographical knowledge to be filled; this is the motivation which provokes Lowenthal's description of the diaspora as 'heritage hungry'. And the difference between the two groups is, predominantly, one of context. The disjuncture, and indeed trauma, experienced by the generation who left Ireland was most strikingly manifested in the removal of context for the knowledge and memories which they had of their group identities. By contrast, those who remain in the landscape and community which provides context to those memories have less 'hunger' for the inevitably missing details of their narratives. As Richard White noted of his uncle, 'for Johnny, what is forgotten remains forgotten and best left undisturbed. The past around him is past enough.'[81] For those whose personal history contains the rupture of emigration, however, the lack of context for the memories which do remain seems to provoke a need to fill in the gaps and elisions between those memories. The 'hunger' of which Lowenthal speaks, rather dismissively, is indeed a real hunger; but one which might be better characterised as being for a complete narrative whose unity of detail might provide a consolation for the lack of organic context in which to place it. Again, Freud's 'family romance' appears an appropriate metaphor for this process; rather than conjuring up a fantasy lineage, however, the diaspora seems more to desire an accurate and detailed lineage in order to compensate for the lack of a recognisable setting against which to place the group memories which constitute their identity.

The connections between genealogical investigations and the contributions of repetitive, cyclical narratives towards the formation of diasporic group identities are clear, therefore. In a closing chapter which reflects the final scenes of *This Is My Father* to a remarkable degree, White describes the assignment he habitually sets for his university history students:

> They are to take their family – a person, a generation, people from several generations – and explain how their lives intersected with major developments or trends in American history. When the assignment works, they see the lives of their ancestors and relatives as part of larger currents... The flaw in the assignment, I have gradually come to realise, is that I identify the past exclusively with history and history with the kind of work that I do: academic history... [82]

What White is arguing here is that, in contrast to his approach to the subject as a professional historian, his students, like his mother, have 'made memories where I seek history'; and he concedes that 'history has its own weaknesses that memory can uncover and probe'.[83]

In their study of 'popular uses of history in American life', conducted in the early 1990s, Roy Rosenzweig and David Thelen used in-depth telephone surveys with a total of 1,453 Americans in order to examine both the importance and the styles of engagement with history among non-historians. The motivations behind their study were, in themselves, an indication of the scale of change to the concept of 'history' over the previous two or three decades. Discussing their objectives, they state that, despite their long-standing commitment to 'people's history', 'as we contemplated reaching outside our professional circles, we realised how little we knew about the values and perspectives Americans were bringing from their personal experiences to these historical dialogues'.[84]

The results of this study, with respect to the importance of genealogy in respondents' lives, are revealing. Rosenzweig and Thelen's predominant finding is that the majority of white Americans contemplate 'history' almost entirely through the narrow lens of family history:

> In interviews with white Americans, 'we' most often centred on the family rather than other social groups – whether class, region, or ethnicity. The understanding of the past that white Americans get from their families is an enormously potent resource for living in the

present, a way of coming to terms with personal identity and of gaining personal autonomy. But white Americans, it seems to me, less
often use the past to reach beyond their families and recognise their
connections to wider groups of neighbours and fellow citizens...
they... seem to be writing their histories alone – or at least in small
familial groups.[85]

Rosenzweig and Thelen contrast this approach to the uses of history
with that of their special sample groups consisting of African-
Americans, Oglala Sioux and Mexican-Americans. Interviews with
these respondents showed that, although the levels of interest in
genealogical research were at least as high as among white
Americans, non-white groups showed a markedly greater tendency
to make connections between the historical experiences of their
family and the history of their class or ethnic group as a whole.
'Asked which area of the past (family, nation, community, or
ethnic/racial group) was most important to them, more than one
quarter of African American respondents chose ethnic or racial
history – a proportion almost seven times greater than among white
Americans.'[86] Such differences between the ethnic groups studied
would appear to offer support to those within the historical academy
who are suspicious of the motivations behind popular interest in
genealogy – at least among white Americans – on the grounds of its
perceived connection to a conservative and 'closed' social perspective. These findings, and the social structures and popular methods
of constructing meaning which they illustrate, may, however, be
usefully measured against the possibilities suggested by the final
scenes of *This Is My Father*. These scenes, in which the central character's relationship with his multicultural school history class is
rehabilitated through the use of his own family story, imply that,
within contemporary American society, family history may have
wider applications than merely the commemoration of narrow social
units.

Illuminating as these findings are, however, they are less instruc-
tive on the particular relevance of Irish-American interest in family
history than they might first appear to be, due to the authors' decision to categorise 'white Americans' as an undifferentiated group.
While it is clear from several interviewee quotations within the book
that at least a proportion of the white respondents identified themselves to interviewers as having specific ethnic backgrounds, no
effort was made within the methodology of the survey to isolate and

synthesise the results according to this information; despite the fact that considerable effort was made to produce 'comparative samples' of non-white ethnic groups. As well as raising far-reaching questions about the authors' assumptions regarding ethnicity as an area of study, this also fails to provide vital information about the specific uses of an Irish family history in the production and circulation of group identity within the United States.

Rosenzweig and Thelen's implicit assumptions about race and ethnicity in contemporary American society, and the rather more sensitive discussion of this issue (and the apparent lack of 'ethnic choosing' available to non-white citizens) in Waters' study, are unusually illustrated in the 1998 film *The Nephew*, directed by Eugene Brady.[87] The film concerns the arrival on an island off the west coast of Ireland of Chad, a black Irish-American teenager. Following the death of his emigrant mother in New York, he is coming 'home' to his mother's country to live with her estranged brother; the film's narrative centres around the revelation and resolution of the estrangement which caused Chad's mother to leave the island. *The Nephew*'s handling of its central plot device – the issue of Ireland's non-white diaspora – is indicative of how politically sensitive this topic still remains. Having placed race at the centre of its story, the film then appears to go to great lengths to avoid facing the contradictions inherent in its own subject matter; the few scenes in which Chad's race is mentioned are truncated, and the dialogue is often unconvincingly styled so as to discount this issue as a factor in plot developments.

In one of the most telling early scenes regarding Chad's cultural adaptation to island life, for example, he and his uncle attend a neighbour's funeral and wake. This is his first introduction to most of the local population, none of whom had known of Chad's ethnic origins before his arrival. Despite this, his race is not referred to by anyone present, and the one older woman who appears to be about to do so is cut off mid-sentence by another character; the film appears to be suggesting that the subject of non-white Irishness is literally unspeakable. Tellingly, the islanders, when referring to Chad in the third person, always describe him as 'the nephew', and, when he is introduced to Brenda, his mother's girlhood best friend, her first response is to assure him that he has his Irish mother's smile. Again, this suggests the unnameable nature of Chad's unusual 'ethnic choosing', and the expediency of using family characteristics to replace ethnic ones in such a situation. With the exception of

5. The unexpected 'return' of a black Irish-American to his Irish family village in *The Nephew* (1998).

Peter, the one character in the film who displays any overt racism to Chad (and this, it is implied, is largely due to romantic rivalry rather than genuine conviction), the islanders are shown giving communal sanction to Chad's Irishness at this funeral, during a scene in which he is prevailed upon to sing during the wake. To their surprise, he sings a mournful ballad in Irish, and, as he continues, the stunned silence gradually changes to a chorus of other voices joining in. When the song is finished, Patsy, the only character who will go on to demonstrate real and enthusiastic curiosity about Chad's African-American culture, demands to know: 'Who in the name of God taught you that?', to which Chad replies: 'You may find it hard to believe, Patsy, but I'm Irish.'

From this early point on in the film, Chad's ethnic 'choices' are rarely questioned again, an implausible narrative decision which neglects this sensitive issue in favour of foregrounding the resolution of a troubled romance blighted by a family-based feud. Leaving aside the effect this has upon the narrative coherence of the film itself, such decisions are highly revealing of the extent and limitations of ethnic identity representation for later-generation immigrant groups in the United States at the end of the twentieth century. Writing of the white (and partly Irish) ancestry more or less passed over in *Roots*, produced nearly twenty years earlier than *The Nephew*, Chioni Moore points out that:

> One would have been stunned, for example, to have found Haley's ancestral discursus beginning with a fully genealogically defensible sentence: 'Early in the spring of 1750, in the village of Ballyshannon on the upper end of Donegal Bay, a manchild was born to Paddy and Mary O'Reilly.' As a matter of day-to-day reality in the United States, the general dynamic of ethnic choice is divided very strictly by colour.[88]

The Nephew, despite its structural flaws as a text, usefully demonstrates both the changes and the consistencies in popular imaginings of such mixed ethnic and family history since its earlier representations in *The Irish In Me* in 1959, as well as in *Roots* in 1976.

CONCLUSION: ROOTS AND NETWORKS

It therefore appears that the growing interest in family origins and history among Irish-Americans over the second half of the twentieth century is a practice indicative of many more radical and socially significant projects than the middlebrow and conservative nostalgia it is predominantly associated with. Indeed, the genealogical 'industry' seems, on closer inspection, to be a symbolic practice which is a principal mode of popular engagement with the genuinely far-reaching social, cultural and ideological changes of the era.

Underlying the individual enthusiasms for discovering Irish personal origins and family stories is the highly contested ideological ground of personal and ethnic history and identity for later-generation Irish-Americans. The frequent dismissal of genealogical practice by commentators, ranged against the frequently unquestioning fervour of its practitioners, represents two deeply divided schools of thought on the place and role of ethnicity itself in American society.

As has been outlined above, the criticisms of the renewed interest in family history are most frequently contained in the work of social scientists engaged in investigations of the parallel interest in ethnic origins. These criticisms position such ethnic identification as being either a conservative attempt to disengage with wider social connections and movements,[89] or as being inherently 'inauthentic' due to its apparently symbolic nature among the largely middle-class and suburban exponents of the practice.[90]

With respect to the charges of conservatism, it is clear that many of these assumptions stem from genealogy's late nineteenth- and early twentieth-century formations, as opposed to its contemporary manifestations. And while it obviously cannot be denied that some individual motivations for undertaking family research may indeed still be conservatively nostalgic, professional genealogists note that most researchers are no longer hoping to discover elite ancestries, and are actively interested in the social conditions experienced by their forbears.[91] Equally importantly, as Alba discussed, many saw their activities as being inclusive rather than exclusive.[92]

The more prevalent charge of inauthenticity, in that most Irish-Americans expressing an interest in their backgrounds no longer lead lives necessarily structured by that cultural inheritance, requires a more detailed refutation.

As was outlined above, the historical development of contemporary interest in ethnic origins arose from the rejection of the melting-pot thesis of earlier social and political scientists studying immigrant groups' maturation in the United States. That thesis had supposed that the process of 'Americanisation' which was presumed to occur with the simultaneous passing of generations and achievement of upward social mobility would eradicate all interest in and practice of ethnically identifiable traits and histories. However, the evidently growing enthusiasm for 'roots' research among later-generational immigrant groups challenged this supposition. Those studies which have tended (to greater or lesser extents) to dismiss this trend for ethnic identification in American society have, following Gans' formulation of the concept of 'symbolic ethnicity', tended to do so on the continued assumption that later-generational immigrants, particularly those who are largely middle-class and suburbanised, cannot have a 'genuine' connection to their family's previous national or ethnic history because of their current social status.

This approach to contemporary genealogical research shows, through its own methodology, a continuing though often unstated reliance upon the basic tenets of the melting-pot thesis in its equation between economic or temporal change and formations of group identity and history. It also, crucially, relies upon dubious cultural concepts of 'authenticity' in determining which groups of Irish-Americans' ethnicities are 'authentic' and which are not. By its own methodological assumptions, this approach implies that only those who experienced the particular social and economic conditions of certain 'Irish neighbourhoods' in American cities during the late nineteenth and early twentieth centuries can claim 'authentic' Irish-American identities. The highly prescriptive definition implied here is clearly flawed in itself, but also fails to take into account the different patterns of later immigration.

For Irish immigration into the United States continued throughout the later twentieth century, albeit on a smaller scale than that of earlier decades, and therefore the creation of the later-generation Irish diaspora is an ongoing project; contemporary second- or even third-generation Irish-Americans may easily be descended from immigrants who arrived after the social impact of the Second World War on Irish inner-city neighbourhoods. It should also be remembered that contemporary first-generation Irish immigrants are arriving in the United States from a considerably more culturally and ethnically heterogeneous Ireland than previous generations of new arrivals. The ways in which their ethnicity structures and dictates their social and cultural practices is potentially 'symbolic' even before they left Ireland, let alone once they are a part of American society.[93] Critics of contemporary interest in family history (and the interest in ethnic history which it often indicates) are therefore, through the typically exclusive device of 'authenticity', potentially denying the 'Irishness' of even first-generation contemporary immigrants. It can therefore be argued that a much less prescriptive and predetermined perspective on the levels of meaning attached to ethnic and family identification needs to be brought to the analysis of survey respondents' assertions on this subject. Such a perspective would avoid the development of hierarchies of cultural authenticity determined according to social and economic positioning.

The ideological assumptions of the 'roots' industry, however, also need to be analysed with greater critical awareness. Without denying the very real meaning its practice represents to those involved, as well as the wider implications it has for the interrelationships of America's different ethnic groups, there seems to exist a largely unexplored contradiction at the heart of genealogical research.

Most later-generation Irish-Americans (including those investigating their family history) are of mixed ethnic origin, and are 'choosing' their researched ethnicity with full knowledge of, and often equal interest in, their other ancestry. This is reflected in their responses to surveys such as those cited above, in which recognition is given of their complex ethnic associations. It is clear that the 'choosing' of one predominantly cited background, such as Irishness, does not require, for the majority of the very large number of people involved, a rejection of their other ethnicities. Indeed, it is in this way that popular practice appears to have avoided some of the methodological exclusiveness expressed by scholarly researchers, as described above.

Precisely because of the inclusive and complex ethnic reality recognised in popular expressions of interest in Irish 'roots', however, it seems necessary to reassess the underlying ideology of 'rootedness', as manifested in genealogical research. This concept of the 'root' as a determining source for diverse but interrelated later developments is one profoundly embedded in many forms of cultural and scientific discourse – and is in many ways being further enforced by the presentation, if not the content, of recent developments in genetic knowledge. The limitations of such a metaphor have been highlighted previously, as in Chioni Moore's call for a discussion of Haley's work in terms 'not about *roots* but about *routes*; trajectories, paths, interactions, links', in which he goes on to call for the use of the rhizome rather than the root as the central metaphor of social and biological interconnections.[94] Such a theoretical position is compatible with the wider perspective of postcolonial and postmodern diaspora theory, recognising as it does the dangers of assumptions of 'purity' in cultural construction. It is also compatible with the theoretical explorations of Irishness within that postcolonial and postmodern discourse; these have tended to emphasise the difficulties of canons of 'authenticity' as linked to purity and monocultural origins.[95] However, as will be discussed in more detail in the final chapter, the rhizomic metaphor also carries with it a danger of essentialising doctrines, and might better be replaced with a non-botanical image of webs, or networks.[96]

The resulting challenge, in academic discourse, to concepts of cultural or genetic 'roots', in favour of webs or networks, is clearly in accord with the practical approaches of popular genealogy, in which diaspora groups such as mixed-descent Irish-Americans negotiate their hybrid identities and histories without, for the most part, cultural difficulty. As Catherine Nash has argued, 'genealogy, despite its easy co-optation in essentialist versions of identity, may provide a way of beginning the task of understanding the complexities of subjectivity and social location, and of rethinking identity as neither fixed and essential, nor endlessly fluid and freely self-fashioned, and an always incomplete inventory of the self'.[97]

What appears to have occurred, in fact, is a dislocation between practice and terminology in the pursuit of family history. While the language of genealogy remains anchored by the 'rooted' tradition of O'Hart's *Irish Pedigrees; or, The Origin and Stem of The Irish Nation*, the practice has, by necessity, accepted the inapplicability of concepts of 'rootedness', and has moved towards new, if largely unarticulated, models of webs and networks.

NOTES

1   Peter Linebaugh and Marcus Rediker, *The Many-Headed Hydra: The Hidden History of the Revolutionary Atlantic* (London: Verso, 2000), p. 123. Also see R.F. Foster, *Modern Ireland 1600–1972* (London: Penguin, 1988), p. 115.
2   Linebaugh and Rediker, *The Many-Headed Hydra*, p. 130.
3   Alex Haley, *Roots: The Saga of An American Family* (New York: Doubleday, 1976).
4   David Chioni Moore, 'Routes: Alex Haley's *Roots* and the rhetoric of genealogy', *Transition*, Issue 64, 1994, p. 6.
5   *New York Times*, 26 September 1976, p. 18.
6   *Chicago Irish-American News*, May 1977, p. 7.
7   *Newsweek*, 4 July 1977, p. 6.
8   *Chicago Irish-American News*, April 1978, p. 18.
9   Reginald Byron, *Irish America* (Oxford: Oxford University Press, 1999), pp. 117–8.
10 Ibid., p. 260.
11 Leon Uris, *Trinity* (London: André Deutsch, 1976).
12 *Chicago Irish-American News*, October 1977, p. 10.
13 Ibid., p. 1.
14 Ibid., p. 10.
15 Chioni Moore, 'Routes', p. 8.
16 Ibid. Original emphasis.
17 Ibid., p. 7.
18 A recent exception to this is Catherine Nash, 'Genealogical Identities', in *Environment and Planning D: Society and Space* 20 (2002), pp. 27–52. Nash's nuanced reading of popular genealogical practices usefully considers the specifically diasporic enthusiasm for family history research.
19 Tommy McGuigan in *The Irish World and American Industrial Liberator and Gaelic American*, 26 June, 1976, p. 13.
20 Cited in James M. Cahalan, *Great Hatred, Little Room: The Irish Historical Novel* (Dublin: Gill and Macmillan, 1983), p. 193.
21 Cahalan, *Great Hatred, Little Room*, p. 202.
22 Eric Hobsbawm, *On History* (London: Weidenfeld and Nicholson, 1997), p. 21.
23 In his essay 'Family Romances', first published in 1909, Freud describes how, once a child's initial worship of its parents is diminished by the reality of their individual flaws, 'the child's imagination becomes engaged in the task of getting free from the parents of whom he now has a low opinion and of replacing them by others, who, as a rule, are of a higher social standing'. See Sigmund Freud, 'Family Romances', in J. Strachey (ed.), *The Standard Edition*

of the Complete Works of Sigmund Freud (IX) (London: Hogarth Press, 1953), pp. 238–9.

24   Raphael Samuel, Theatres of Memory, Volume I: Past and Present in Contemporary Culture (London: Verso, 1994), p. 374.

25   Cited in John G. Barry, The Study of Family History in Ireland (Cork: Cork University Press, 1967), pp. 9–10.

26   Ibid., p. 18.

27   Ibid., p. 3.

28   Cecil Woodham Smith, The Great Hunger, Ireland 1845–9 (London: New English Library, 1984), p. 21.

29   John O'Hart, Irish Pedigrees; or, The Origin and Stem of the Irish Nation, preface to the 2nd edition (Dublin: Gill and Son, 1881), p. vii.

30   Byron, Irish America, p. 111.

31   O'Hart, Irish Pedigrees, pp. xxv–xxxi.

32   David Lowenthal, Possessed by the Past: The Heritage Crusade and the Spoils of History (New York: The Free Press, 1996), p. 9.

33   Margaret Dickson Falley, Irish and Scotch-Irish Ancestral Research: A Guide to the Genealogical Records, Methods and Sources in Ireland, Volume I: Repositories and Records (Dublin: Genealogical Publishing Co., 1962), p. iii. The difficulties of tracing earlier Irish emigration into the United States have also been commented upon in detail by Donald Harman Akenson, The Irish Diaspora: A Primer (Belfast: Institute of Irish Studies, 1996).

34   Irish Times, 29 June, 1999, p. 8.

35   Irish Times, 3 August, 1998, p. 6.

36   Time, 19 April 1999, pp. 58–9.

37   David Hey, Family History and Local History in England (London: Longman, 1987), pp. xi–xii.

38   Ibid., p. xi.

39   Roy Rosenzweig and David Thelen, The Presence of the Past: Popular Uses of History in American Life (New York: Columbia University Press, 1998), p. 4.

40   Kevin Whelan in David Hey (ed.), The Oxford Companion to Local and Family History (Oxford: Oxford University Press, 1996), p. 242.

41   David Lowenthal, Possessed by the Past, pp. 9–10.

42   Kevin Whelan in David Hey, The Oxford Companion to Local and Family History, p. 246.

43   Ibid.

44   For a detailed discussion of this debate, see Alex Callinicos, Theories and Narratives: Reflections on the Philosophy of History (Cambridge: Polity Press, 1995). Callinicos contrasts the condemnation of historical narrative by theorists such Hayden White with Alasdair MacIntyre's assertion that 'narrative history of a certain kind turns out to be the basic and essential genre for the characterisation of human actions' (cited p. 54).

45   John Frow, Time and Commodity Culture: Essays in Cultural Theory and Postmodernity (Oxford: Clarendon Press, 1997), p. 229.

46   Paul Connerton, How Societies Remember (Cambridge: Cambridge University Press, 1989), p. 20. Connerton draws extensively on the classic theories of collective memory formulated by Maurice Halbwachs. Halbwachs' work itself crucially emphasises the importance of family groups in the production of lasting collective memories, pointing out that, despite the individual differences of perspective within a family group, 'It is not because memories resemble each other that several can be called to mind at the same time. It is rather because the same group is interested in them and is able to call them to mind at the same time that they resemble each other.' Maurice Halbwachs, On Collective

Memory (Chicago: University of Chicago Press, 1992), p. 52.

47 *The Irish In Me*, dir. Herman Boxer (Universal International Colour/Dudley Pictures Corporation, 1959).

48 *O'Hara's Holiday*, dir. Peter Bryan (Tribune Films Inc., 1950s). Although the exact date of the film is unknown, the Irish Film Archive classifies it as dating from the 1950s, and the film's visual clues strongly support this classification.

49 Lawrence J. McCaffrey, *The Irish Diaspora in America* (Bloomington: Indiana University Press, 1976), pp. 158–9.

50 Richard White, *Remembering Ahanagran: Storytelling in a Family's Past* (Cork: Cork University Press, 1999), p. 217.

51 McCaffrey, *The Irish Diaspora in America*, p. 178.

52 Richard Alba, *Ethnic Identity: The Transformation of White America* (New Haven, CT: Yale University Press, 1990), p. 315.

53 Ibid., pp. 70–1.

54 Ibid., p. 300.

55 Byron, *Irish America*, pp. 125–7.

56 Alba, *Ethnic Identity*, p. 295.

57 Ibid., p. 47. Of the 'old-stock' European immigrants in Alba's study, 82 per cent of those with Irish ancestry were of mixed ethnicity, compared to 46 per cent Italians and 64 per cent Poles. Only the Germans and the Scots, at 88 per cent and 90 per cent respectively, were more likely than the Irish to be of mixed ancestry.

58 Herbert Gans, 'Symbolic Ethnicity: The Future of Ethnic Groups and Cultures in America', *Ethnic and Racial Studies*, 2, 1979, pp. 1–20.

59 The equation between ethnic group and individual personality or physical traits is one of the most common popular responses to questions about ethnic identification in several studies. A typical example of such associations is the perceived connection between red hair, a strong temper, and an Irish background. See Byron, *Irish America*, pp. 228–39, and Mary Waters, *Ethnic Options: Choosing Identities in America* (Berkeley: University of California Press, 1990), pp. 75–81.

60 *The Matchmaker*, dir. Mark Joffe (Polygram/Working Title, 1997).

61 Gene Kerrigan, 'Waiting For the Sheriff', *Magill*, May 1984.

62 See Kevin Rockett, *The Irish Filmography: Fiction Films 1896–1996* (Dublin: Red Mountain Media, 1996).

63 Byron, *Irish America*, p. 146.

64 Ibid., p. 290.

65 Ibid., pp. 127–8.

66 Ibid., p. 129.

67 See Akenson, *The Irish Diaspora*, pp. 225–32, for a thorough discussion of the limited value of United States' immigration and census material when attempting to determine the ethnic origins of the Irish-American diaspora. The main difficulties centre around the incomplete information gathered at entry points such as Ellis Island, as well as the inaccurate or omitted categories of information requested on census forms until late into the twentieth century.

68 Byron, *Irish America*, p. 295.

69 *This Is My Father*, dir. Paul Quinn (Filmline International/Hummingbird Communications, 1998).

70 Martin McLoone, *Irish Film: The Emergence of a Contemporary Cinema* (British Film Institute, 2000), p. 190.

71 The popularity of this classroom exercise in the United States' history curricula has been highlighted by respondents to a number of studies on ethnicity. See Byron, *Irish America*, p. 128, as well as Roy Rosenzweig and David

Thelen, *The Presence of the Past*, pp. 179–81.

72   McLoone, *Irish Film*, p. 194.

73   Alice Carey, *I'll Know It When I See It: A Daughter's Search For Home in Ireland* (New York: Clarkson Potter, 2002), Frank McCourt, *Angela's Ashes* (New York: Scribner, 1996), Frank McCourt, *'Tis* (New York: Scribner, 1999), Malachy McCourt, *A Monk Swimming* (New York: HarperCollins, 1998), Malachy McCourt, *Singing Him My Song* (New York: HarperCollins, 2000), Joan Matieu, *Zulu: An Irish-American's Quest to Discover her Roots* (Edinburgh: Mainstream, 1998), Maureen Waters, *Crossing Highbridge: A Memoir of Irish America* (Syracuse, NY: Syracuse University Press, 2001), Richard White, *Remembering Ahanagran: Storytelling in a Family's Past* (Cork: Cork University Press, 1999).

74   George O'Brien, 'The Last Word: Reflections on *Angela's Ashes*', in Charles Fanning (ed.), *New Perspectives on the Irish Diaspora* (Carbondale: Southern Illinois University Press, 2000), p. 247.

75   Waters, *Crossing Highbridge*, p. 119.

76   White, *Remembering Ahanagran*, p. 272.

77   Connerton, *How Societies Remember*, pp. 20–1.

78   White, *Remembering Ahanagran*, p. 31.

79   Ibid., p. 43.

80   *The Chicago Tribune*, 17 March 2000, p. 12.

81   White, *Remembering Ahanagran*, p. 44.

82   Ibid., p. 271.

83   Ibid., p. 272.

84   Rosenzweig and Thelen, *The Presence of the Past*, p. 4.

85   Ibid., pp. 186–7.

86   Ibid., p. 150.

87   *The Nephew*, dir. Eugene Brady (Irish DreamTime/World 2000 Entertainment, 1998).

88   Chioni Moore, 'Routes', p. 15.

89   See Rosenzweig and Thelen, *The Presence of the Past*.

90   See Alba, *Ethnic Identity*, and Byron, *Irish America*.

91   Hey, *Family History and Local History in England*, pp. xi–xii.

92   Alba, *Ethnic Identity*, p. 315.

93   For a useful discussion of the position of 1980s Irish immigrants in the United States, see Mary P. Corcoran, *Irish Illegals: Transients Between Two Societies* (London: Greenwood Press, 1993), as well as Ray O'Hanlon, *The New Irish-Americans* (Boulder, CO: Roberts Rinehart, 1998).

94   Chioni Moore, 'Routes', p. 21.

95   See Luke Gibbons, *Transformations in Irish Culture* (Cork: Cork University Press, 1996), David Lloyd, *Ireland After History* (Cork: Cork University Press, 1999), and Colin Graham and Richard Kirkland (eds), *Ireland and Cultural Theory: The Mechanics of Authenticity* (Dublin: Gill and Macmillan, 1999).

96   See Chapter 5 for a full discussion of diaspora theory's engagement with the botanical metaphors of roots and rhizomes.

97   Nash, 'Genealogical Identities', p. 46.

3

Heritage and Consumption: Irish-American Tourism and Material Culture

INTRODUCTION

AT THE IRISH FAIR held in New York in May 1897, one of the most popular attractions among Irish emigrants was a large map of Ireland, divided into the thirty-two counties, and filled with 'genuine' soil from each county. Visitors were invited, for a fee of ten cents, to walk again upon the soil of 'home'. Many did so, displaying great emotion in the process, which was duly reported by the Irish-American press.[1] The powerful associations held for the Irish diaspora by actual Irish soil was demonstrated again a few years later in 1914, when the Kalem Company's popular 1911 film production of *The Colleen Bawn* was reissued to cinemas. The nascent film industry's recognition of Ireland's appeal to first-generation immigrants was made evident by the marketing techniques used to publicise this reissue. These included the gathering of earth from around the Colleen Bawn Rock in County Kerry, its transportation to the United States and the distribution of samples to cinemas; thus offering audiences the opportunity to stand on genuine Irish soil before they watched the film.[2] The success of such a marketing technique indicates the extent to which the audience, a large percentage of whom would have been first-generation emigrants from Ireland, felt a strong and directly physical connection with 'home'.

What is striking about the Irish-American diaspora's response to 'genuine' Irish soil, however, is that it appears to have continued well beyond the first generation, whose direct and personal memories included the earth of their childhood home. During the 1970s and

1980s, when the majority of the Irish-American community was already second- or later-generation, Irish earth – this time still *in situ* – was still being used to appeal to consumers. In 1978, advertisements for Leprechaun Land Ltd, of Chicago, appeared in the Irish-American press, offering readers the chance to 'Become An Irish Landowner For Only $10'. Described as the 'best Irish souvenir of all', the Irish land in question consisted of one-foot-square plots of land on Howth Hill in County Dublin, advertised with the slogan 'And remember, wherever you go, and whatever you do, you'll always have one foot in Ireland'.[3] Equally, in 1981, Heritage Lands Ltd, of Virginia, offered customers the chance to 'Own A Piece of the "Ould Sod"' in the form of one-foot-square land plots in Cornarona Point Park, Connemara, for $25, using the slogan 'Keep the Irish Eyes Smiling with Ownership of a "Little Bit O'Heaven"'.[4]

Indeed, the historical tradition of selling Irish soil (in one form or another) to the diaspora was well known enough throughout the twentieth century to be the subject of artistic irony in an exhibition by John Byrne at the Temple Bar Gallery, Dublin, in January 2001. Byrne's show, *The Border Itself*, focused on both the Irish border and the Irish heritage industry through installations and the establishment and documentation of a satirical Border Interpretative Centre. The gallery exhibition featured glass-cased samples of Irish soil from different border counties, ranging from 'rugged Donegal and soft Derry earth, to the undulating territory of Tyrone and the curvaceous charms of Monaghan', as described in Byrne's heavily ironic artist's statement.[5] The Interpretative Centre, which existed for one month in a lay-by on the Dundalk to Newry road at the site of the border, 'sold sticks of border rock and held various exhibitions of border paraphernalia, including bags of soil and various examples of border litter – discarded crisp packets and the like'.[6]

The positioning of Ireland as a national home which was familiar and 'knowable' at a detailed, locally specific level for the Irish-American diaspora is also evident in some of the earliest American feature films using Irish narratives, most notably the Kalem Company's productions such as *The Lad From Old Ireland* and *The Colleen Bawn*. For example, *The Lad From Old Ireland*, shot in County Kerry in 1910, was the first American film made on location in the place in which the narrative was set. Prior to this development (which the Kalem Company were quick to exploit as a marketing technique), there had been little or no emphasis in feature film production on the synchronisation of the ostensible background of the film with its actual location. The 1911 production of *The Colleen Bawn* is a clear demonstration of the value placed on the concept of authenticity and place-specific narrative memory within representations of Ireland to its diaspora, both in terms of filmic images of Irish locations and of the highly locally-specific intertitles which seek to illuminate those images. These appeals to the Irish-American audience were clearly based upon an understanding both of their eagerness to see images of the home which many of them would have left relatively recently and of the familiarity which they were already likely to have with such adapted narratives as *The Colleen Bawn*. This familiarity therefore allowed for the interjections of a second, place-specific narrative, within the fictional narrative of the film.[7] The success of such films also pointed to the unusual nature of their appeal to the niche audience of Irish-Americans. While Hollywood films of the era were generally directed towards the nation-building project of the 'melting pot' (the most obvious example being D. W. Griffith's *Birth of a Nation*, made in 1915), narratives such as the Kalem Company's repeated use of the 1798 Rebellion served to emphasise the difference of the Irish in America from other immigrant groups through their identification with the historical and political issues of their home country.

However, by the end of the Second World War, the questions of home and authenticity had been further complicated. The American film industry's early emphasis upon Irish narratives and images had begun as a recognition of the large audience, particularly in the East, who had emigrated from Ireland and whose only likely chance to see again the home they remembered was through films located there. By the 1950s, however, such films were a source of identification for new generations with the home they had never been to, but, very significantly, would increasingly have the chance to visit as tourists. So, with the concurrent rise of the population of Irish-Americans who had never been to Ireland and the rapid growth in opportunities for foreign travel after the Second World War, filmic representations of Ireland changed from remembered personal histories (and, of course, geographies, under the form of location) which were lost to the emigrant who could rarely expect to return, to representing inherited collective histories to later-generation Irish-Americans who might well make the journey 'back' to Ireland.

And it is this concept, which recurs again and again within filmic and touristic representations of Ireland from the 1950s onwards, of going 'back' for the first time, of the possibility of a 'return' to a place which has not yet been visited, which illuminates the construction of Ireland by and for its diaspora through film imagery, and which is so vividly displayed in the development of the Irish tourist industry.

This chapter is an examination of the forms of material production of Irish heritage intended for consumption by later-generation Irish-Americans. While the exhibition or sale of Irish soil may be the most material example possible of material culture, many other examples will be discussed below, including, though not being limited to, souvenirs and memorabilia of diaspora travel to Ireland. This examination of material culture is also extended to allow for an exploration of the late twentieth-century phenomenon of 'global Irish culture', as exemplified by the success of Irish-themed pubs and the *Riverdance* show. The chapter also includes detailed discussion of the diasporic heritage tourism industry, from its marketing strategies to specific attractions, and documents the ways in which these developed between the end of the Second World War and the end of the twentieth century. The common factor which unites all of these practices is clearly the process of commodifying Irishness and its representations for diasporic consumption. Diane Negra has highlighted the long-standing positioning of Irishness as an available commodity in her analysis of, among others, the 'Irish Spring' soap advertisements on American television. She points out that 'In recent ads landscape becomes pre-eminent over the individual in an Ireland that here seems to be non-existent until it is commodified and given a commercial value.'[8] The following discussion is therefore an attempt to disentangle the complex and often competing narratives of commodification, ethnicity and belonging, as they both affect and effect Irish-American identities.

THE DIASPORIC 'RETURN' IN FILM AND TOURISM

Of the immigrant population of the United States, well into the twentieth century, the Irish had one of the lowest rates of return to their home country.[9] However, as has been noted above, after the Second World War the idea of 'the return' to Ireland became an increasingly prevalent theme in Irish-American culture, described in one assessment as 'the phase of reassessment of the myth of exile, the assumption that local life is insufficient and that real life is elsewhere... The conditions and terms of return or of remaining have therefore become more frequent themes in Irish writing since the 1950s'.[10] This theme was, significantly, mirrored by the rapid development of the modern Irish tourist industry, which enabled many Irish-Americans to consider the possibility of returning, or making a first visit to Ireland, if only in the temporary form of a holiday.

In 1952, at the time when international tourism was starting to become a realistic opportunity for significant numbers of Americans, there appeared one of the most popular and enduring representations of the journey home: John Ford's film *The Quiet Man*. The story of Sean Thornton's return to his ancestral home in the West of Ireland, and his process of adaptation to the local culture, an exercise which is eventually rewarded by a happy marriage to the Irish girl Mary Kate, *The Quiet Man* was an epic re-telling of the Irish-American journey of return.

In the film, Sean returns to the cottage in which he was born, White O'Morn, in the village of Inisfree, or 'another name for Heaven' in Sean's own explanation of his journey. The magnitude of the emotional journey he has undertaken is expressed in this phrase alone, as he attempts to return 'home', an act he explicitly equates with a return to Eden. In terms of the wider cultural theme of the diasporic journey back to the home country, the film's portrayal of Sean's initial contact with his family cottage is extremely significant. While it is the place in which he was born, thus making him, in literal terms, a first-generation emigrant, it is made clear within the film that he has no personal memories of either Inisfree or White O'Morn. Instead, as he is being driven into the village upon his arrival, and the cottage is pointed out to him, the narrative of memory is transferred to his mother, whose voice-over in the film, as she describes their family life there, takes the place of his own memory. She says, 'It was a lovely little house, Seaneen, and the roses! Your father used to tease me about them but he was that proud of them too!'[11] As Luke Gibbons comments on this crucial scene in the film:

> These words reverberate in the voice-over through Sean's mind when, early in the film, he first apprehends his ancestral cottage, bathed in sunlight in the midst of luxuriant verdure. Yet the fact that the cottage is revealed to us in a point-of-view shot through Sean's eyes, and that little effort is made at maintaining spatial continuity between Sean's position and the countryside surrounding the cottage, throws into relief the possible fictive status of his vision.[12]

6. 'Another name for Heaven' – Sean Thornton's first sighting of his mother's cottage in *The Quiet Man* (1952).

If Sean's vision of 'home' is potentially fictive, his memory of it certainly is, in that it is an inherited one, passed on to him by his mother, as indicated in her narrative interruption within the film. But the status of Inisfree, and by extension of Ireland itself, as the home to which the Irish diaspora is struggling to return, remains unchallenged by this admission of the collective and inherited nature of the diasporic imagination. *The Quiet Man* was heavily criticised from its initial release for its apparent romanticisation of Ireland and its lack of realism. In a contemporary review in the *New Yorker*, John McCarten complained that within the film the Irish are 'just as cute as a button. The people are not only cute but quaint, and the combination, stretched out for something more than two hours, approaches the formidable'.[13] And in its preview of the film, the *Irish Independent* commented, 'clearly Republic Pictures had their eye on the American market when they went to work in Co. Galway and perhaps that is the excuse for the exaggerations...American audiences should like all of it; we will like some of it very much.'[14]

However, contained within *The Quiet Man*'s representation of that attachment to memories and images of 'home' was a serious assessment of the diasporic experience. The film is a portrait of Sean's attempts to reconcile his Irish and American senses of identity. The strength of his identification with a home he has never known is demonstrated in his very decision to 'return' and to reject his American identity. The difficulties inherent in this action, however, are played out within the film's treatment of his developing relationship with Mary Kate. In that romantic relationship, which serves as a marker of Sean's emotional homecoming, lies the film's representation of his slow adaptation to Irish culture within Ireland, as distinct from the diasporic Irish cultural identification which he has maintained in America.

What is also made clear within the film, however, is that an understanding of this cultural difference between the diaspora and the homeland is always already an inherent part of diasporic Irishness. The Irish-American 'sentimentality' for Ireland, such a constant source of criticism from those seeking to propound a more 'realistic' Irishness, and a quality of which *The Quiet Man* itself was so vigorously accused, is shown in the film to contain already an understanding of the inherent division between the diasporic image and the reality of experience. So Sean's instinctive response to his first, Edenic vision of Mary Kate caught in the sunlight between the trees, 'Hey, is that real? She couldn't be', is described by Luke Gibbons as demonstrating

> the ability of certain strains in Irish romanticism to conduct a process of self-interrogation, to raise doubts at key moments about their own veracity, which cuts across any tendency to take romantic images as realistic accounts of Irish life. This suggests that it is not so much realism which offers a way out of the impasse of myth and romanticism, but rather a *questioning* of realism or any mode of representation which seeks to deny the gap between image and reality.[15]

Within the diasporic context of Sean's questioning of realism and representation in *The Quiet Man*, the film demonstrates the subtleties contained within the Irish-American negotiation of cultural contact with Ireland, which the harsh criticism of its 'sentimentality' unsubtly overlooks. As Sean reveals in his reaction to

Mary Kate's appearance, he already recognises that his understanding of Ireland, informed as it is by his mother's memories and other received images, is an unreliable source in terms of realism. What he is also recognising, however, in his very decision to return to Inisfree, is that, however 'unrealistic' his connection to Ireland is, it remains nevertheless a powerful force in his Irish-American identity, and is therefore no less culturally valid in its meaning for him as a member of the Irish diaspora.

7.   'Hey, is that real? She couldn't be' – Sean Thornton's first sighting of Mary Kate in *The Quiet Man* (1952).

As was discussed in the previous chapter, narratives of later-generation Irish-Americans' 'return' to Ireland became increasingly prevalent in popular culture from the 1950s onwards, and this was also reflected in the tourist narratives produced for the Irish-American market. The influence of already-circulating narratives and representations, predominantly those produced in Hollywood, upon the promotion of tourism to Ireland has also been discussed in the previous chapter, with particular focus upon the popularity of fictional plot-lines and characters. In this, tourism texts aimed at Irish-Americans differed noticeably from those produced for other markets, suggesting an explicit attempt by the industry to capitalise upon the specific features of diasporic memory and identity transmission.

There is little archival information now available regarding the production and distribution policies behind the travelogues of this era. What is known, however, is that Bord Fáilte had a conception of the United States market as being divisible into three distinct niches: the Irish-born, their Irish-American descendants, and the non-Irish. The content of the films (which will be discussed in detail below) suggests that they were overwhelmingly aimed at the first two of these groups. The distribution of the films appears to have been controlled by Bord Fáilte and other 'traffic operators' such as airlines and major tour operators. Not only were they shown at conventions and trade fairs run or attended in the United States by these organisations, they were also loaned out to interested groups through Bord Fáilte's lending-libraries of travel information. These groups could include diverse social organisations in the United States (such as sporting or musical associations), who were considering taking a tour group to Ireland. One such group known to have been a regular user of these films (along with other promotional material), and a frequent organiser of visits to Ireland, were the Irish-American 'parish associations'. The centrality of the Catholic Church to the Irish-American diaspora, and the large number of Irish clergy working in their parishes, appears to have created a definable audience for the travelogue films.

It is also known that some of the films had limited releases in United States cinemas – presumably those based in Irish-American areas and which would have been practised in actively promoting Irish-themed feature films through the use of other Irish material.[16] Although some of the films may also have been broadcast on United States television, it appears that the gradual decline in production of travelogues coincided with the increasing number of network-produced television travel programmes, which would have superseded the use of pre-produced films, as well as with the rise of more sophisticated media marketing by tour operators, replacing the *ad hoc* connections between Irish-American organisations and the tourism industry.[17]

One of the American-produced promotional films, *Honeymoon In Ireland*, made in 1963, adopts a narrative tour around Ireland, thus highlighting the country's attractions to foreign tourists. However, the highly developed narrative and fictional characters around which the film is constructed appear to obscure its explicit marketing techniques, pointing to an understanding of visits by Irish-Americans as being more complexly motivated than those by non-Irish tourists. The film follows Mary, a fairly recent emigrant from Cork, and Bill, her American husband, on their honeymoon in Ireland. The voice-over consists of their conversation as they travel around the country. Delivered in the past tense, the story gives the impression of a joint re-telling of their trip to friends back in the United States, with the images serving in place of holiday photographs. This format, combined with the content of their narra-tive, means that, within the film, Mary explains Ireland to Bill, and Bill 're-interprets' this for a non-Irish audience. The relationship which the film establishes between the Irishwoman and her new American husband points to a complex understanding of the posi-tioning of Irish-Americans within wider American society, and of the implications of this for the international 'meaning' of Ireland itself.

The film opens with a scene of the newlyweds on board an Irish International Airlines plane, bound for Dublin Airport. Bill is openly distracted by the attentions of a glamorous Irish air hostess, musing on the voice-over about the attractions of Irish girls, until Mary is forced, in order to regain his attention, to remind him that she too is Irish. The underlying point of this exchange within the narrative is soon made clear to be not so much Bill's susceptibility to the erotic charms of Irish women, even on his honeymoon, but instead the question of the pair's ethnic and emotional origins, both as a couple and as individuals. Immediately after this incident, while still on the plane, Mary begins a sentence with the words 'We Irish . . . ', only to be cut off by Bill's insistence, 'You're American now', to which she responds forcefully, 'Oh, don't be ridiculous.' It is not clear, at this stage of the film, whether her identity is seen as questionable because of her emigration or because of her marriage to a non-Irishman. Mary's sense of loss at leaving Ireland is made clear later on when the film's jocular tone is disrupted upon their arrival in Cork, her home town. She says, 'I felt terribly sentimental in Cork, and we didn't talk very much. I little guessed when I was here last, that when I came back I would be on my honeymoon. I so hoped Bill wouldn't laugh at me for being so solemn.'[18]

Mary's anxiety that her American husband will not understand her feelings for 'home' is therefore a continuation of the debate begun on the plane about her identity and the challenge to it posed by a non-Irish husband. The resolution within the film of this painful barrier between the couple, however, suggests significant implications for Ireland itself, as well as for individual Irish emigrants. This resolution occurs at the very end of the film, as the couple are preparing to board another plane to leave Ireland. Mary again expresses sadness at leaving 'home', and this time, Bill too shares this feeling of loss, to the extent of delivering double-edged praise for the advent of modern travel to Ireland, when he declares that at least air travel makes leaving easier, because it removes the painful experience of having to watch the shoreline disappearing. With this statement, Bill, as a departing tourist, is positioning himself firmly within the historical experience of colonial emigrants for whom the act of departure from Ireland to the United States was one of leaving home, rather than returning to it. He is, therefore, eliding the apparently profound division between the migrant exile and the tourist, as his own ostensible act of return becomes his point of departure.

What this narrative resolution of the film appears to suggest, therefore, is that, rather than Mary's marriage to Bill having made her an American, Bill has instead become Irish, not due to the legalistic fact of marriage, but through the emotional and cultural experience of his visit. This claim for the effects on tourists of a visit to Ireland is another sharp negation of the classic interpretation of the tourist experience as being empty and lacking in authentic meaning. It also suggests, by implication, that if his apparent return is actually his departure, then his arrival was itself an act of return, again reinforcing the concept of Ireland as an archetypal 'home', to which even the first visit is a return. What is most significant about the representation of this theme within *Honeymoon In Ireland* is the extent to which it engages with serious questions regarding diasporic identity and Ireland's own relationship to such identities. While, unsurprisingly for a tourism text, the film provides few answers to such questions, it does raise the issue not only of the divided affections of Irish emigrants, but also of the further complications of identity created by those emigrants' formation of a multi-ethnic diaspora in the United States. Both Mary, as a first-generation immigrant, and Bill, as a non-Irish-American who has married into the diaspora, are seen to be actively questioning and exploring such issues of ethnicity and identity; a process apparently provoked and heightened by their visit to Ireland, despite its occurence within the commodified form of tourism.

This representation within *Honeymoon In Ireland* of Ireland as an archetypal home is similarly reflected in other tourist material, in which the nation is depicted primarily in terms of its hospitality, warmth, and maternal nurturing of the visitor. In *Glimpses of Erin*, a much earlier American film promoting Ireland, the narration states that 'here a stranger needs no introduction, for he is always a welcome guest', suggesting that the visitor is always already 'at home' in his lack of need for an introduction, even on first arrival. The film then goes on to make a more explicit connection to the idea of Ireland as a home to which the diaspora may return. During scenes from a market day in Galway, shots of old, shawled women are accompanied by the narration:

> The native mothers of any country always inspire a certain sentiment. But the older Irish mothers as we see them in the little towns today appeal most to our emotions. For we know there is hardly one among them who has not a son who left her to seek his fortune in some faraway country – especially the United States.[19]

The connection between the Irish emigrant's journey to America and the American tourist's visit to Ireland is thus made circular by implication in this film, as in *Honeymoon In Ireland*. And the dynamic driving this circular movement is that sense of loss and nostalgia for 'home' contained within the Irish experience of emigration. The implication within the tourist films aimed at the Irish-American market is of Ireland as a home (and mother) which they were forced to leave, and the tourist experience is presented primarily as their opportunity to satisfy the craving to return which that painful loss of home has created, even several generations on from the original departure.

MODERNITY AND TRADITION IN IRISH-AMERICAN HERITAGE

This cross-generational possibility of closing the circle of emigration by completing the journey 'home' through tourism again raises interesting questions about the nature of the concept of time and memory under the colonial experience of emigration, exile and diaspora. The understanding that, for the Irish diaspora, even a first visit to Ireland is a return, contains within it the clear implication that under these conditions time is not to be understood purely in linear terms, and that memory is of more than personal, first-hand experiences. This implication complicates the classic touristic trope of depicting the journey through space to the tourist destination as also being a journey back through time. Such a representation of the destination is typical of tourist imagery, and certainly has been particularly striking in Irish tourism, no matter which category of tourists have been the target market.[20] The depiction of Ireland in terms of a pre-modern idyll for visitors (and, by implication, for the Irish too) is one of the most consistently recurring themes of the nation's tourist imagery. This process has its roots within colonial imaginings of Ireland, in which the land and its people were co-opted into the Romantic vision of unspoilt landscapes and equally unspoilt inhabitants, whose culture had not been fractured by the 'civilisation' of modernity. Thus Ireland, for the imperial visitor, represented the possibility of cultural renewal, even while this positioning of the Irish and their land also provided justification for the continuation of the imperial project. The leisurely pace of Irish life, and its promise to the visitor of the opportunity to escape from the pressures of modern, work-dominated life, is also a central feature of Irish tourism's ongoing representation of the country. So, the 1966 film *Ireland Invites You*, produced by Bord Fáilte, begins with the statement: 'This is Ireland, a green island set in the seas like a gem of a rare beauty, a haven of undisturbed peace in a restless world, a land of infinite variety of scenes, an ageless, timeless place where old beliefs and customs live on beside the spreading tide of human progress.'[21]

Such images, of a country apparently cut off from the instability and loss of cultural authenticity which is associated with the modern world, are typical of the tourist advertising of many countries. As MacCannell has argued, it is precisely this possibility of recapturing the lost 'authenticity' which the West believes to have existed in its own 'golden age' of Edenic innocence, before the onset of modernity, which inspires many tourists in their choice of destination. MacCannell asserts:

> The progress of modernity ('modernization') depends on its very sense of instability and inauthenticity. For moderns, reality and authenticity are thought to be elsewhere: in other historical periods and other cultures, in purer, simpler lifestyles. In other words, the concern of moderns for 'naturalness', their nostalgia and their search for authenticity are not merely casual and somewhat decadent, though harmless,

attachments to the souvenirs of destroyed cultures and dead epochs. They are also components of the conquering spirit of modernity – the grounds of its unifying consciousness.[22]

If one of the principal motivations of tourists is an attempt to step back across the historical divide between themselves and the time which they perceive as having been more 'authentic', and more particularly as having possessed a cultural coherence, then it is obvious that potential destinations will seek to market themselves as still existing in this mythical past. Therefore the descriptions of Ireland as 'a haven of undisturbed peace in a restless world', and the accompanying images of undeveloped landscapes and such indicators of pre-modern lifestyles as thatched cottages and horse-drawn transport are consistent with the attempts to commodify a nation's history which are common within the tourist industry across the world.

However, when the audience for these images of Ireland is the Irish diaspora, it would seem that there is more to this process than the 'inauthentic' commodification of the past. If that diaspora's identity is understood to be collective and cross-generational, then the images of Ireland as 'traditional' and pre-modern are not necessarily anachronistic within the terms of their process of memory and recovery. While the Ireland described by *Ireland Invites You*'s voice-over may not be 'timeless', it was perhaps not unreasonable to recognise that, for diasporic tourists, their contact with Ireland, constructed as it was as an 'original' return, was primarily governed by the events of a previous era, and therefore a recovery of memory which was simultaneously personal and historically collective. As discussed earlier, this process is a result of the non-linear narrative of images and memories created by the cultural dislocation of emigration.

Such a touristic act, therefore, cannot be so easily dismissed as to characterise it in terms of an uninformed and romanticised consumption of 'heritage' without context or meaning, as critics of tourism often attempt to do.[23] An indication of the greater complexity of the experience of diasporic tourists can be seen in representations of modernity within the very tourist texts which also contain such 'traditional' images of Ireland. Despite the emphasis upon the country's apparently 'timeless' qualities, the process of modernisation is not only discussed by the promotional tourist films, it is actively eulogised, and often in contexts which have no obvious relevance to the practice of tourism.

Honeymoon In Ireland, for example, actively plays with the image of Ireland as a pre-modern idyll of peasant life. When Bill and Mary, the honeymoon couple, first arrive at Dublin Airport, it is explained that Mary has already arranged for a hire car to be waiting for them. This information is immediately followed by a shot of a 'vintage' 1930s car waiting outside the terminal building as the couple emerge. After lingering on this car for a moment, the camera then follows Bill and Mary past it, to the brand-new open-top red sports car which is to be their hire car. In this visual joke, the film simultaneously acknowledges and challenges the currency of the 'thatched cottage' image of Ireland presumed to be familiar to the American visitor.

This blending of the modern and the traditional in the representation of Ireland to its diaspora points towards the need for a more careful interpretation of the description in *Ireland Invites You* of the country as 'an ageless, timeless place where old beliefs and customs live on beside the spreading tide of human progress'. The crucial wording in this description therefore appears to be the use of the term 'beside', suggesting parallel and simultaneous time within the visitor's experience of the nation. This in turn appears to reflect the complex experience of time and memory of the 'returning' Irish-American, in which the Ireland they encounter is both their own present and the past of their collective diasporic memory.

The nature of that collective memory, for later-generation Irish-Americans, is significant within the context in which it is generated and reflected in their contact with Ireland itself. By the nature of cross-generational cultural transmission, much of the understanding and experience of Irish-American Irish identity is necessarily through the medium of the image, be it filmic or photographic. This process is even more pronounced in the diasporic 'recollection' of Ireland for those generations who have never previously been there. In the twentieth century and for Irish-Americans in particular, while a considerable amount of their cultural identification would have come from narratives within their community such as family and other first-generation immigrants, they would also have acquired an extensive exposure to images of Ireland, primarily through the medium of film.

As described earlier, the use of fictional characters, strong narrative and even flash-back sequences in the promotional films which were designed to appeal to the growing market of Irish-American visitors to Ireland indicates a recognition by the industry of the importance within that diasporic group of filmic images as a source of community identity formation. The use of these devices within promotional films for the industry's advertising to Americans appears to be predicated on an explicit understanding that, for later-generation Irish-Americans, the principal source of their images of the 'home' country had been that of Hollywood films, and as such their concept of that home was already structured by narratives and fictional characterisation. A particularly striking example of the 'cross-fertilisation' between the feature film industry and the tourist industry in Ireland is an American-produced tourist film of the mid-1950s, *The Spell of Ireland*.[24] Narrated principally by the actor Jack McCarthy, the film, which at fifty-eight minutes was uncharacteristically long for a tourist promotion, is structured in the form of a tour around Ireland, highlighting not only the major tourist attractions of different regions, but also facets of Irish life which are clearly considered to be of interest to the audience even though they do not have obvious connections to tourist activity.

The narrator, who does not appear within the film, acts as a guide for the audience through the travelogue. It is noticeable that the film's journey around Ireland is geographically disjointed; rather than constructing its movement in the form of a tour which visiting tourists might follow, it jumps from location to location and doubles back on itself. This is unusual for tourist films, and suggests that, rather than providing practical information for visitors to Ireland, it has instead constructed the nation as a location in a filmic sense, in which geographical positionings are secondary to the events being shown in them.

The Spell of Ireland is not constructed around a narrative in the same way as films such as *Honeymoon In Ireland* are. The narrator (Jack McCarthy, a well-known member of the Irish Players theatre group in the United States) not only does not appear within the film, but he also is not narrating for the viewer the 'story' of a particular journey to Ireland, as those other films did. Instead, *The Spell of Ireland* follows a format similar to that of television documentaries. There is a scene of traditional Irish dancing at a crossroads, for example, which has anthropological overtones in its lengthy and unnarrated camera shots. There is also a lengthy episode of the film shot at a Croagh Patrick pilgrimage. This section of the film is dramatically untouristic in its focus on the dedication, devotion and physical suffering of the pilgrims in appalling weather conditions, showing them collapsing, encountering accidents on the mountain due to exhaustion, and being rescued by medical teams. The musical score and the tone of Jack McCarthy's voice changes significantly during this section of the film to one of sombre respect and awe for the devotion of the pilgrims. The pilgrimage is not portrayed as being accessible to tourists as a potential source of entertainment or pleasure, and is instead treated as a serious religious experience. This reinforces the documentary nature of *The Spell of Ireland* and its apparent aim of informing its audience about the culture of Ireland.

However, in the latter section of the film, the 'tour' of Ireland reaches Donegal, which the narrator describes as his home county, therefore one which has special memories and associations for him. At this point, not only the tone but the entire structure of the film changes abruptly. Unintroduced, Helena Carroll (another member of the Irish Players group) takes over the narrative in the guise of Jack McCarthy's mother, reminding him of his childhood and family home. In a direct reference to the scene in *The Quiet Man* in which Sean Thornton returns to Inisfree and first sees his family cottage, the narration of *The Spell of Ireland* continues: 'Ah yes, Seaneen, you've been gone a long time, but your roots are still in Ireland. You were born in that little cottage and it was your sister who kept the cottage going for all you wains...'

The film then continues for the next ten minutes to portray the narrator's childhood, in the form of a flashback using staged footage of scenes from village life in Ireland, still narrated by his 'mother', who, like McCarthy himself, remains unseen on screen. This flashback sequence takes the form of childhood 'memories' of gathering hay in the fields, village festivals and specific individuals, such as a young man whom the narration informs us is now a policeman in New York. The flashback sequence (and his mother's narration) ends with the words, 'Ah, Seaneen, those were your happy, carefree days in Ireland', and the film then continues its documentary tone, moving on immediately to scenes of the horse-show at the Royal Dublin Showground, including shots of President O'Kelly's attendance, before showing an interview with Eamon de Valera about his continuing aspirations for a united Ireland.

This departure from the documentary style of the preceding sections of the film indicates a number of manoeuvres within the text. First, there is the sudden introduction of a fictional narrative at the point at which the narrator announces that within the film he has returned to his home, as opposed to the documentary tone of the earlier sections. Second, there is the expectation that the audience will be so familiar with *The Quiet Man* that the film's scriptual and visual references to it remain unexplained; this presumption on the part of the filmmakers is so strong that, at the very moment at which the narrator drops the role of objective and informative guide to facts of Irish life in order to adopt a more personal and evocative narration of his own history, not only is his voice displaced by that of his (fictional) mother in order to effect such a transformation, but without explanation she refers to him as Seaneen, rather than Jack. This introduction of a clearly fictional and narrativised section into the film at the very point at which the subject of individual history and memory is raised points to the centrality within that diasporic memory of the fictional narratives of films such as *The Quiet Man*. And, within both *The Quiet Man* and travel films such as *The Spell of Ireland*, there is a significant manoeuvre by which diasporic memory is delineated as non-individual and always already fictionalised through the inherited, second-hand processes by which it is acquired.

Another, more recent, example of the influence of such processes of diasporic memory construction occurs in Alice Carey's 2002 'family memoir', *I'll Know It When I See It: A Daughter's Search for Home in Ireland*. It is an account of her New York childhood as the daughter of unhappily married first-generation Irish immigrants, of her escape from this life into a career in show business, and finally of the cathartic decision by herself and her husband Geoffrey to buy and restore an old house in County Cork. Carey uses the memoir largely as an attempt to resolve her difficult relationship with her mother. Near the end of the book, Carey describes a remarkable imaginative moment, in which, as in *The Spell of Ireland*, both *The Quiet Man* and the voice of her absent mother construct her emotional experience of being 'back' in Ireland. Walking along Bantry Bay on a summer's evening, Carey sees a woman who looks strikingly like her own mother, a sighting which prompts a fierce inner dialogue concerning her diasporic need to 'return' to the Ireland her mother was so determined to leave. This argument with her dead mother is accompanied by the musical theme from *The Quiet Man* drifting out from a local shop, and intertwining with Carey's struggle to explain her feeling of being 'at home' in Ireland. The internal dialogue finishes with the following exchange between mother and daughter:

> 'I didn't want ye to know a thing about old Ireland. I wanted ye to be a real New Yorker.'

'And I am, Mammie. I am. I'm a real New Yorker living in Ireland.'
O'Brien's shop starts playing the theme from *The Quiet Man*, and
Mammie, my mammie, looks both wondrous and different. Yet she is
the same. On the other side of the square I see my Geoffrey buying a
bunch of sunflowers.

And when the moonlight creeps across the rooftops
Of this great city, wondrous though it be ...

'Alice M'rie, ye're here in Ireland. I can't get over it. Ye've come
Home. Haven't ye?'
'Mammie, I'm not Alice M'rie anymore.'
'But you are, girl. To me.'
With that, she's gone. Gone without a shower of fairy dust.
Geoffrey crosses the square toward me. He's holding out the sun-
flowers.
The music continues.

And though they say the streets are paved with gold dust,
I long to be back home in Innisfree.

'Geoffrey,' I say, 'let's go home.'[25]

This imagined exchange, remarkably similar to that of *The Spell of
Ireland* in both its structure and influences, again indicates the
extent to which later-generation Irish-American identities and even
personal memories continue to be structured around and through
the powerful imagery of popular narratives and inherited memory.

IRISH-AMERICAN HERITAGE CULTURE

Heritage tourism was a relatively small aspect of global tourism
prior to the 1980s. Nevertheless, Ireland's heritage was a feature of
many earlier promotional films. What is interesting about this early
version of Irish cultural tourism, however, is the selection process by
which certain heritage attractions are highlighted again and again
within the films, and others, which in many cases have since become
significant features of the tourist industry in Ireland, rarely if ever
appear.

Ireland's built heritage, in the form of castles, houses and other
types of architectural history, is largely restricted within the films to

8.   The illustrated cover of the *The Isle of Innisfree*, the theme song from *The Quiet Man* (1952).

one or two examples which are almost universally promoted. While some of the films were produced in order to promote specific cities or regions of Ireland, many more take the form of a brief tour of the country, and include the major national attractions. The most prominent of these is Blarney Castle, which is shown in almost every film that includes a visit to County Cork.

Bunratty Castle and Folk Park is also a frequent subject of the films, often as a contrast to the modernity of the nearby Shannon Airport, as in *O'Hara's Holiday*.[26] This example of the inclusion of modernity within tourist narratives does at least have obvious connections to the practice of tourism, in which the industry was required, in its construction of national representation, to balance the advantages of promoting pastoral and pre-modern images of Ireland against the need to reassure visitors (particularly, perhaps, those from America) that their holiday will not be marred by a lack of 'modern conveniences'. This motivation would appear to be in evidence in *O'Hara's Holiday*, when the eponymous central character, a New York policeman visiting Ireland for the first time, begins an extended eulogy to Shannon Airport. His explanation of the principles of duty-free shopping as being a modern Irish invention – and one of great benefit to the world – appears at first to be located purely within the internal logic of tourist promotion. O'Hara himself, as the narrator, explains the principles of duty-free shopping at Shannon Airport in great detail for his American audience, accompanied by shots of the various consumer goods available in the airport shops. However, after explaining that 'Shannon isn't just an airport – it's an idea', O'Hara goes on to describe some of the finer points of the tax incentives for foreign companies setting up and investing in the airport complex, a narrative which is accompanied by a number of distinctly unpastoral shots of modern industrial development at Shannon. Following this, *O'Hara's Holiday* then easily returns to images of nearby Bunratty Castle, with its pastoral and historical associations.

The emphasis on Gaelic and Roman Catholic, rather than colonial, heritage is noticeable in earlier promotions of built heritage. Blarney Castle's Gaelic history and its role in resisting British rule are highlighted through the retelling of the legend of the Blarney Stone, while neatly avoiding the fact that the castle had for many years been the family seat of an Anglo-Irish family, the Colthursts. Indeed, the absence of colonial architecture, in its most common form, the Big House, is striking. None of the promotional films concentrates upon this aspect of Irish heritage, and Georgian architecture in general, which has since become a central feature of tourism in the country, is largely ignored. In *Green For Ireland*, a castle which has been converted into a country hotel is commended – ostensibly for its recognition of the importance of providing good facilities for tourists, but also, perhaps, for its appropriation of a colonial building.[27]

The avoidance of colonial heritage in Ireland leads to a particular difficulty in the promotion of Dublin, which is a largely Georgian, and therefore colonial, city. The films which visit Dublin, even those which are solely centred around the city, such as *See You At The Pillar* and *Autumn in Dublin*, give very little time to its colonial architecture or history. Instead, they tend to concentrate on the city's contribution to the struggle for national independence and on its contemporary everyday life.[28] *No More Yesterdays*, for example, describes Dublin as 'once a city of violence, now a city of culture', and the plaques on the city's statues of national leaders are described in *Green for Ireland* as being 'lively with insurrection'.[29] Dublin Castle is never featured in the films, and even Trinity College is only occasionally shown.

Irish cultural heritage, as portrayed in the films, tends to be concentrated on traditional crafts and music. Tourists' incidental encounters with villagers dancing at a crossroads are a common feature, occurring for example in *Honeymoon in Ireland*. Traditional Irish music also features strongly in the films, not only in the soundtracks but also on the screen, as visitors are assured that they will encounter it regularly as they travel around the country. *Ireland in Spring*, for example, features a traditional music festival in Ennis, and a demonstration of uileann pipes.[30] The use of such cultural activities to bridge the sometimes wide gap between visitors and their Irish hosts is demonstrated with startling clarity by *Green for Ireland*, which includes a scene shot in the Abbey Tavern, where there are, the narrator announces, 'English tourists applauding the rebel songs of 1916 while delighted Americans croon sad emigrant songs'. The presentation of Irish heritage in the tourism films therefore reflected the delicate negotiation within Ireland in the years following Independence of a selection of history which could express the Irish experience in a way which was both appealing to tourists and appropriate to the contemporary Irish national narrative.

In the later decades of the twentieth century, however, the presentation of Irish heritage to its diaspora changed considerably in both tone and content. From the end of the 1970s onwards, there has been a significant growth in the provision of heritage and interpretative centres across Ireland, reaching a proliferation during the 1990s. While many of these are aimed at a general audience, including local visitors, there is a recognisable subset of heritage and interpretation centres which have clearly identified Irish America as a target audience. These include the Cobh Heritage Centre's

'Queenstown Story', an interpretative presentation of emigration to America, the 1798 Centre in Enniscorthy, Co. Wexford, which is an exploration and celebration of the development of republican ideals and rebellions in both Ireland and the United States, and Strokestown Famine Museum, Co. Roscommon, a commemorative site dealing with both the death and the emigration caused by the Famine. There is also, albeit with a differently delineated audience, the Ulster-American Folk Park, Omagh, Co. Tyrone, a celebration of the Protestant Irish emigration to the United States.[31]

Where subjects such as colonial rule, the Famine, emigration and its consequences had previously been absent from tourist representations of Ireland, they have since become one of its major strands; at least partly due to the interest of the diaspora in exploring these aspects of their own history. One of the earliest signals of this change of direction can be seen in the comments of Chris Lockwood, then the editorial director of *Travel Agent Magazine, USA*, at a seminar hosted by the National Tourism Council of Ireland in 1977. Discussing the tourist marketing of Ireland at the time, Lockwood argued that there had been too great an emphasis on presenting Ireland as sophisticated and, in effect, less 'Irish', resulting in 'an impression of diluted Hibernians or Emerald Englishmen'. Instead, he suggested, with particular reference to Irish-American tourists:

> Let us entice tourists with images of what they expect to find and allow them to discover the real Ireland once they're here. One of the major things going for Ireland is the pre-established image of a rural, slow-moving, witty country of characters which has been established in American's minds through a wealth of Irish mythology from the myth mills of Hollywood... Such a suggestion may sound like blasphemy to a nation pre-occupied with the notion that it should show itself to be the antithesis of the stage Irish 'top O' the Mornin' shore and begor-rah how's yer leprechaun' image which, like it or not, still persists. This image, in its worst form in America, is what we have come to call the 'Irish Spring' syndrome, named after a particularly distasteful, corny and insulting TV commercial. However, it does sell soap![32]

Lockwood closes his address to the Irish tourist industry with an interestingly reversed metaphor of Irish-American tourism to Ireland, 'above all, don't let success and sophistication change the ways of Ireland. They are a consistent and universal appeal to all the tired, huddled masses across the Atlantic yearning to breathe a drop of Irish air.'[33]

This characterisation of an Irish-American visit to Ireland as an inverse of their ancestors' emigration (through the use of the 'tired, huddled masses' imagery) corresponds to that used in actual tourist advertising, including *Honeymoon in Ireland*, as discussed earlier. There continued to be strong references to the diaspora's ancestral connections in Irish tourist advertising in the United States throughout the 1980s. A particularly striking example of this is shown in an article in the *Chicago Irish-American News* in 1978, in which, announcing the opening of the Irish Tourist Board's Chicago office, it is stated that, 'whereas Ireland's greatest commodity traditionally was grandmothers for many decades, today the greatest commodity that Ireland has to sell is trips and tours to Ireland to see from whence these beloved grandmothers came'.[34]

This representation of Ireland clearly echoes Irish-American constructions shown in earlier promotional material, such as that of *Glimpses of Erin*. These recurring images of Irish-American heritage, both completing the circle of emigration and always already enacted within the circuit of commodity exchange, are signals of the ways in which the diaspora has little room for manoeuvre beyond the limits of commodification. Their separation in both time and distance from their original homeland positions them, historically and geographically, outside any of the (relatively) non-commodified circuits of cultural exchange available to the Irish within Ireland. As such, their only opportunity to engage with their ethnic heritage and material culture is through the external routes of an increasingly global capitalism.

A similar schema of representation of Ireland as a tourist destination for Irish America can be seen in Bord Fáilte's marketing techniques during the 1990s. Beginning in 1993, a television campaign centred on the strongly Irish areas of New York and Boston was produced by the advertising firm of Agnotti, Thomas, Hedge on behalf of the Irish Tourist Authority. Two separate advertisements, entitled 'Invaders' and 'Humor', were produced, both concentrating on the luxury and hospitality lavished on American tourists visiting Ireland. In her detailed analysis of this campaign, Diane Negra has commented:

> In what is perhaps the campaign's most intangible, but crucial effect, the feel of dusk that pervades these ads works strongly to inscribe a feeling of absence – which the arrival of the tourist will undoubtedly correct. This, coupled with the depiction of Ireland as unchanging,

serves to present Ireland as a static place activated only by the arrival of the tourist.[35]

As Negra also highlights, there are strong references within this campaign to the tourist's position within a history of 'visitors' to Ireland, all of whom except the tourist were invaders. As such, the representation of Ireland as empty and 'in need' of the visitors' arrival as a corrective fits disturbingly into the country's colonial history. In the case of diasporic tourists, however, the implications are rather different, again suggesting that their arrival may correct the genuine 'absence' created in the landscape by their ancestors' emigration.

SOUVENIRS AND MATERIAL CULTURE

Along with the experience of visiting sites (and sights) of heritage interest, the other significant tourist practice of the diaspora is the purchasing of souvenirs, mementos and other forms of Irish material culture. While most of the aspects of this material culture consumption discussed below relate to the purchase of goods in Ireland during a tourist visit, another important aspect of Irish-American engagement with Irish consumer goods involves the business of Irish import stores in the United States, typically based in and around areas such as New York, Boston and Chicago, which have a high density of Irish-American populations. While such commercial enterprises have been in operation throughout the period covered by this research, the advent of internet shopping has had a considerable impact upon the sale of 'ethnic goods' to all diasporas in the United States, and will be specifically addressed later on.

The cultural meaning and value of souvenirs, in their broadest definition, has, like other aspects of tourism, long been contested. As with other tourist practices, the central issue of debate has tended to be one of authenticity, or lack of it. One of the earliest theoretical analyses of souvenirs was that of Walter Benjamin, who commented several times upon the levels of meaning embedded in travel mementos. Typically, Benjamin's reading of souvenirs is complex. He criticises souvenirs as agents of a packaged and intentional memory, rather than catalysts of the unintentional memory he privileges; however, Benjamin also recognises that souvenirs, like other fetishised commodities, can become interrogative instruments of the relations of production and exchange.[36]

This issue of fetishisation, as it relates to concepts of authenticity, has particular relevance to diasporic consumption of material goods symbolically related to the 'homeland'. In one of the few scholarly assessments of Irish-American consumption of such commodities, David Lloyd has argued that not only are the material symbols of any nationalism fated to acquire the properties of kitsch, but this is particularly true of nationally or ethnically symbolic objects circulated within the diaspora. This occurs, he argues, because by its very nature nationalism requires its material objects, which are themselves most likely to be associated with non-standardised folk production, to become standardised and 'familiar' precisely in order to perform their nationalist function of 'represent[ing] a whole that is often yet to be constituted'. Therefore, he continues, 'a considerable degree of stylistic uniformity, a simulacrum of the anonymity of 'folk' artefacts, is indispensable to the project; stylistic idiosyncrasy would be counter-productive; stylisation is of the essence.'[37]

When this nineteenth-century process of stylisation evolves into twentieth-century mass production and, crucially for the diaspora, global distribution, it therefore becomes linked to the indexes of kitsch and inauthenticity most commonly associated with tourist objects. As Lloyd points out, 'not for nothing is the object that springs to mind so often a souvenir, a green Connemara marble cross or an ashtray embossed with a harp: kitsch is congealed memory that expresses simultaneously the impossible desire to realise a relation to a culture only available in the form of recreation *and* the failure to transmit the past'.[38] Following on from Lloyd's position, therefore, it can be argued that the extent to which the Irish material culture consumed by Irish America does indeed constitute kitsch, and the implications this may have for its 'authenticity', is not the significant debate. Rather, what is required is a more sensitive analysis of the contexts in which kitsch manifests itself, both in the objects themselves and in the processes by which they are consumed.

In an analysis of precisely these processes by which kitsch is produced and recognised within the circulation of material culture, Jukka Gronow has argued that 'the impression of kitsch is, however, often simply created by the fact that the models in question have been removed from their original context...it is only relatively few products that act as status symbols at any given time'.[39] For diasporic consumers of homeland culture, not only are the objects in question likely to be out of time, but also, crucially, out of place. What this recognition points towards, then, for Irish-American consumption of

Irish material, is a double exclusion from the status of 'authenticity', manifested through both the objects themselves and the context in which they are produced.

First, the objects require the levels of familiarity and stylisation described by Lloyd. Just as nineteenth-century nationalist objects required this process of standardisation in order to represent an as yet unconstituted nation, so twentieth-century tourist and diaspora objects require the same high degree of stylisation in order to function as representative figurations of a culture that is otherwise distant or unknown. If they are to operate as markers of ethnic identity in a multi-ethnic society, as well as, in the case of tourist objects, embody fully the touristic memory of a visit to Ireland, they must display their markers of both ethnicity and experience vividly and in such a way that they will be recognisable with a minimum of cultural 'work' or prior knowledge on the part of consumers. And it is through this process of the standardised representation of Irish ethnicity that these objects become situated as kitsch according to standard rules of taste and aesthetics.

Second, for diasporic consumption of Irish material goods, the very context in which they are consumed contributes to their marking as kitsch and inauthentic. Following Gronow's argument that kitsch is created through the consumption of goods out of their original or suggested context, the consumption of Irish culture outside of Ireland, as the diaspora must do, is always already an act of kitsch-consumption or even creation.

Further evidence that it is the mobility of the material culture consumed by the diaspora which renders it inauthentic according to the aesthetic hierarchies of more fixed cultures is indicated in more general theorising about tourist art and objects. Much of the work produced about tourist objects has emerged from the discipline of anthropology, and frequently concentrates upon the movement of non-Western objects into the West, whether in the form of tourist souvenirs or as higher-status museum pieces. Little specific attention has so far been paid to the movement and cultural evaluation of tourist objects within the West itself. However, some more general theories of tourist objects have been produced, from which it is possible to extrapolate some useful approaches to Irish-American consumption of Irish culture in the form of tourist arts. Celia Lury, discussing the objects of travel, attempts a schema of such materials in which they may be approximately assigned to one of three categories: the traveller-object, the tourist-object and the tripper-object.

Within this schema, traveller-objects retain the highest level of cultural status, predominantly through their 'ability to signify their meaning immanently, most commonly by an indexical reference to their 'original' dwelling... Significantly, traveller-objects do not necessarily have to move to acquire their status as such – indeed, typically, they stay still, although their images frequently move.' By contrast, tripper-objects are those of the lowest cultural status, where, 'while the object may have 'personal', 'sentimental' meaning in its final resting place, this is a meaning which is not deemed intrinsic to the object and, thus, is not publicly valued'. Between these two extremes lies the tourist-object, which 'may be identified as such by their (putative) place of origin, by their medium of distribution, or by their marketing – in each case, what is important is their self-conscious location in mobility'.[40]

While Lury points out that this schema must not be applied too deterministically to specific objects of travel, it nevertheless provides a useful method by which to assess diasporic consumption of such objects. For by its very nature, diasporic material culture must, above all else, be mobile. This therefore involves its consumption not only 'out of context', thus increasing the likelihood of its classification as kitsch, but also in highly standardised forms, given its 'self-conscious location in mobility', and the need to identify its cultural meanings across wide geographical and social areas.

Discussing national origin as part of the object-biography of commodities in general as well as tourist objects in particular, Lury assesses the ways in which marketing strategies in the global economy of late capitalism rely upon already-formed consumer opinions about particular ethnic 'characteristics'. Describing the way in which ethnicity is mobilised in order to provide objects with culturised features, she argues that, 'more generally, country-of-origin surveys seek to measure perceptions of "risk" and "trustworthiness" associated with the cultural dimensions of national identity, and, in the process, allow the national identity of specific countries to be disembedded from specific places and mobilized as cultural resources, or properties of objects'.[41]

This process of 'disembedding' cultural properties from specific places and their utilisation in the marketing of objects also has clear relevance to the consumption of Irish material culture by Irish America. One of the most important aspects of contemporary diaspora consumption of such material is its relationship to the largely non-commodified consumption patterns of previous generations. As will become clear below, many of the objects most commonly acquired by the late-twentieth-century diaspora mirror those which would previously have been transferred through inheritance practices; most frequently, these are domestic items which, in the 'original', would now be classified as Irish heirlooms within an Irish-American family. Reginald Byron, in his sociological surveying of a large Irish-American population in Albany, New York, noted that the possession of material objects brought from Ireland by first-generation ancestors was statistically unlikely for most later-generation Irish-Americans, due simply to the ratio of such objects to ever-increasing families. He explained that:

> Thirty per cent of our sample of Albany-born informants possessed objects passed down from a grandparent or still-earlier generation; in most cases, however, it was doubtful that these objects had come with an emigrant from Ireland; more likely they had been acquired in America by someone in the second or third generation and handed down to the fourth, fifth, or sixth. About half this number, 15 per cent, possessed undated and unmarked heirlooms which were thought to be quite old . . . which might, possibly, have belonged to an ancestor who emigrated between 1847 and 1854.[42]

Byron noted, however, that the majority of those he surveyed who had visited Ireland (approximately 60 per cent of the sample group) had brought back souvenirs with 'specific associations' with Ireland, and he describes these as:

> More than just trinkets casually acquired on a vacation, these objects were often regarded as special treasures, symbolizing their connection with the land of their ancestors. These objects, seen and handled, are the material mnemonics of past generations, though they might not be more than a few years old and might have been bought in a Dublin department store, the duty-free shop at Shannon, or even in an Irish curio shop in Albany.[43]

Byron goes on to list, in exhaustive detail, the types and categories of such objects the respondents possessed. The list, in full, is:

> paintings and watercolours; sculptures in silver, bronze and porcelain; rosaries, crucifixes, and statues of the Virgin; crystal, china, and pottery; jewellery; linen tablecloths, runners, napkins, mats, doilies, antimacassars, and handkerchiefs; woollen blankets, hats, sweaters, coats, suits, skirts, socks, scarves, ties, and tartans; blessings to hang

on the wall, doorknockers, shillelaghs, coats of arms, crests, banners and flags; framed maps, coffee-table books of photographs, volumes of history and poetry; musical instruments, dancing costumes and shoes; CDs, records and tapes of Irish music.[44]

A striking feature of many of the categories of souvenir he mentions is their origin in older craft or folk production processes such as linen and other fabrics, pottery and glass, and traditional sporting or musical artefacts.

The underlying representations of Ireland favoured by Irish-Americans in their acquisition of material culture are therefore interestingly revealed by an analysis of these categories of object, as well as by the ways in which they are marketed to this sector. Indeed, despite the fact that Ireland's national 'characteristics' in the global marketplace of ethnic markers, as described above by Lury, might not generally be thought to include luxury or opulence, particularly in terms of consumer goods, food and drink, it is noticeable that these are precisely the terms on which Irishness is often embedded in the diaspora's material culture consumption of their ethnicity. While there is a scarcity of evidence regarding the differences in taste between those sections of the Irish-American diaspora with differing amounts of cultural capital, the above list is notable for the fact that it ranges across a wide spectrum of taste and expense, from luxury and high-status goods such as linen, to cheaper and lower-status goods such as reproduction prints. This implies that the market caters to consumers with a wide range of cultural as well as economic capital.

Consumption, in the form of food, drink and shopping, has always occupied a central position in the global tourist industry, and the promotion of Ireland has proved no exception. One of the earliest examples of consumption-oriented promotion of Ireland is *Crystal Clear*, which is framed as an informative film about the Waterford Glass factory, and narrated by Eamonn Andrews. Made in 1959, it adopts a documentary tone, following the lengthy production process of the glass from beginning to end, accompanied by shots of the foundry workers and the furnaces. The voice-over, however, not only includes information regarding the process of glass production, but also stresses the unique qualities of the Waterford products in terms which are revealing of the market position Irish consumer goods as a whole were attempting to occupy in the tourist industry. After explaining the Waterford factory's long history, and its trading connections with 'Philadelphia and Stamboul', the narration goes on to emphasise the difference between these Irish glass products and those the consumer might find in other locations. After a detailed representation of the long-established and complex glass-making process, the film describes the finished product as being 'not a spurious antique, but it is an ancient tradition which is outside of the machine but suited to modern life ... [and] has an atmosphere of timelessness and dignity'. Describing the glass-makers as craftsmen rather than factory workers, and comparing their skill to that of the craftsmen of Rome and Venice, the film states: 'For these are not utility items, following each other in monotonous succession on the conveyor-belt – each is unique and different in the way that mass-produced and machine-built articles can never be unique and different.'[45]

Such description of the Waterford factory and its glass, in effect, deliberately positions both the workers and the product as being outside of the exchange and labour relations which are likely to be the common experience of the tourist at home, both as a worker and a customer. And it is precisely through this positioning of Irish craft products as being essentially outside the market, and therefore 'authentic', that their market was and is firmly established.

In later marketing to the diaspora, Waterford Crystal has continued to position itself as producing luxury consumer goods whose role within the circuit of other objects works outside of the relations of capitalist mass production. For visitors to their Waterford site, the company provides a factory tour combined with a visit to their main customer showrooms. The brochure accompanying this tour states that, 'during your fascinating visit to our factory, you will witness generations of design experience worked into pieces as individual as the people that make them. We have designed the Waterford Crystal factory tour so that you can see the process close up, almost through the eyes of the artisans.'[46] Throughout all Waterford promotional literature, factory workers are referred to as either artisans or craftsmen, and the company's historical background and continuation of traditional working practices are stressed, despite the fact that it is now part of the Waterford Wedgwood multinational conglomerate, with annual sales of more than €678.6m.[47] This intention to identify Waterford products with both tradition and luxury is also evident in their design categories, such as the Romance of Ireland collection. The same approach is taken in many respects by Belleek China, who also stress the

historical background of their company, and the luxurious crafts-
manship which creates them.

Another of the principal forms of consumption shown in Irish
tourist promotion is that of food and drink. Guinness, whiskey and,
in particular, Irish coffee feature strongly in many promotional films,
with the recipe for Irish coffee, often in the form of a rhyme,
frequently being given. Irish coffee is generally promoted as a luxury
and high-status item, and therefore something which the tourist can
purchase as a tangible sign that they are on holiday, and enjoying a
higher standard of living than they might normally have. The prominence of the recipe and technique of making the coffee, however,
which is particularly noticeable in promotional films made for the
American market, such as *O'Hara's Holiday* and *Honeymoon in
Ireland*, also suggests that tourists to Ireland were being encouraged
to consider this product as something which they could reproduce
for their friends and family back at home as an ongoing souvenir of
their holiday, in the particularly covetable form of a skill. This
would also, presumably, boost the sales of Irish whiskey both at the
tourists' points of departure from Ireland and in the overseas
markets. In fact *Honeymoon in Ireland* goes to such lengths to
emphasise the strength and potency of Irish coffee that it appears to
endanger its own marketing of Ireland as a romantic honeymoon
destination. After giving the recipe for the coffee, Bill, one of the
honeymoon couple, admits that two of these drinks in the evening
had made him 'sleep like a log – I'll never hear the end of it!'.

Beer, particularly Guinness, appears mainly in the films' representations of Irish pub life, and is positioned largely as a marker of the
conviviality of social encounters which tourists can expect to enjoy
in Ireland. In *Ireland Invites You*, for example, it is claimed that 'in
a pub conversations run as freely as the Guinness where no one is a
stranger for very long'. Food in general is positioned in a similar way,
and the high quality of the food tourists can expect to find in Ireland
is regularly emphasised.

Touristic representation of consumption, both of consumer goods
and of food and drink, therefore works to reinforce the portrayal of
the tourist experience in Ireland as being one based on authenticity
and the possibility of sharing the 'real' culture of the country. Both
the shopping and food consumption available to tourists in Ireland fit
into the pattern of tourist consumption described by Curtis and
Pajaczkowska as 'transactions of incorporation', in which visitors
attempt to create the sensation of belonging to the culture they are

visiting. As they argue, material culture consumption is a method of allaying feelings of marginalisation as it allows a sense of participation in the local culture, and 'shopping always activates the fantasy of acquisition and thus of "incorporation" of a fragment of the Other. The goods "abroad" can be sampled without concern for utilitarian constraints which may be in operation at home.'[48]

If this process is important for all tourists' negotiation of the experience of temporarily visiting a different culture, it is clearly of even greater importance for diasporic tourists, whose relationship with the local culture is simultaneously one of connection and distanciation. This complex and frequently fraught relationship, when placed within the framework of the global tourist industry, may help to explain the extent and type of Irish material culture acquisition that Irish-Americans engage in. For, while diasporic visitors to Ireland are clearly justified in feeling that they do have connections to the local culture which go beyond those of more typical touristic relationships, in most cases they have very few ways of actually marking or demonstrating these connections outside of the typical touristic relations of production and consumption in the form of souvenirs and heritage networks.

This process throws into extreme relief the fault-lines running through both the cultural performance embodied in the objects themselves and the process of performativity contained within their consumption by Irish-Americans. It also highlights some important reasons for the emphasis upon luxury and authenticity in the market positioning of such objects; as well as the considerable censure they and their consumers receive for the inevitable failure of a commodity exchange fully to escape the conditions of commodification.

One of the ways in which this process is most in evidence is in the material construction of the tourist objects themselves which are popular with Irish-Americans. One of their most frequent design characteristics is a heavy reliance upon overtly kitsch markers of Irishness such as shamrocks, harps, leprechauns and generalised 'Celtic' images. As was discussed earlier, one of the functions of such design for a diasporic market is its overtness and 'over-performance' of ethnic identity. It is this very 'over-performance' of ethnicity – the catalyst for the censure received by the objects and their consumers – that is in fact necessary for the function of such material culture. As David Lloyd has argued: 'Nowhere are the deracinating and alienating effects of capitalism felt more powerfully than in communities whose histories are determined by domination, displacement and immigration . . . kitsch becomes, in such spheres, the congealed memory of traumas too intimate and too profound to be lived over without stylisation and attitude.'[49] Not only are the shamrock designs and leprechaun models – so decried as 'inauthentic' – functioning as 'congealed memory', but also as concentrated identity markers, necessary for the performance of attenuated ethnicity within a circuit of capitalist exchange.

The extent to which these material cultural markers have become 'disembedded' by the operations of the market has been further accentuated by the rapid growth of internet shopping during the 1990s. It is important to acknowledge that, even prior to this development, Irish America was able to purchase Irish consumer goods without the need for a trip to Ireland, through the use of 'Irish import stores'.[50] In 1981, for example, there was considerable participation by such businesses in a Giftwares Trade Show, which toured the United States. As import stores, such as All Things Irish, of Chicago, were at that time the principal outlet in the United States for 'nationally branded' Irish goods such as Waterford Crystal and Belleek China, this trade show was also attended by the Irish Export Board.[51]

Most Irish import stores were traditionally located, for obvious demographic reasons, in densely populated Irish-American areas. However, the growth of internet shopping during the 1990s allowed them to extend their markets, as well as allowing Irish-based businesses to reach the Irish-American consumer directly. The result has been a proliferation of Irish material culture available on the internet from specialised sites. These include Irishshop and Carroll's Irish Gifts, among many others including major brand-names, such as Waterford Crystal, which are now able to market their goods directly to diasporic consumers.[52] The effect of the availability of Irish material culture via e-commerce has been to further remove it from its original context as well as disembedding its national 'characteristics', heightening the impression of kitsch already conveyed by the objects themselves. Indeed, the very methods of presentation employed to market Irish goods on the internet often contributes to this process, as there is inevitably an even stronger emphasis upon the visual excess of many of the goods.

GLOBAL IRISHNESS

The issue of the commodified circulation of culture and the accusations of 'inauthenticity' associated with it became all the more identifiable and urgent in the last decade of the twentieth century. The 1990s were characterised by an unprecedented surge of interest in Irish culture around the world, from both the diaspora and beyond. Coinciding with dramatic levels of economic growth in Ireland itself, which fuelled an increasing amount of cultural production, almost all aspects of Irishness became marketable on a global scale. From pop and more traditional music, as well as theatre, dance, literature, film, heritage and tourism attractions and consumer goods, Irish or Irish-themed cultural products became best-sellers around the world.

Within this phenomenon, the United States – and specifically the Irish-American – market was crucial as the prime site of the popularity of Irishness. Coinciding with the marked increase of interest in ethnic identity among almost all groups within the United States, Irish America's consumption of Irish culture during this period nevertheless showed some distinct characteristics. It would be beyond the scope of this chapter to provide a full survey of all the commercial successes of Irish culture in Irish-American markets. Rather, it is revealing to examine the more common characteristics of what is meant by 'global' Irishness, while analysing in detail one or two representative examples. These will include the spectacular success of the *Riverdance* shows, and the spread of Irish-themed pubs.

Riverdance began as an interval entertainment during the 1994 Eurovision Song Contest, held in Dublin. An instant and unprecedented success with Irish audiences and critics alike, its updating of traditional Irish dance was rapidly developed into a full-scale 'Broadway' narrative, retaining its original principal performers. Crucially, both of these dancers – Michael Flatley and Jean Butler – were Irish-Americans, and the show's groundbreaking style and techniques were often attributed to the hybrid amalgam of Irish tradition with American innovation. As Lance Pettitt has noted, 'much comment was made about the fact that Ireland was embracing the talents of the diaspora in Flatley and Butler to produce strong, vibrant culture'.[53] Many of the analyses of the show – not all of them complimentary – have concentrated upon the eclecticism of its cultural references, but the single most common critical approach taken to the show, and one which is strongly reflected in its own marketing, is that its success is largely due to its very diasporic hybridity. The *Washington Post*, in 1997, asserted that, 'in the 1990s, Irish and Irish-American culture have burst into full song –

inventing fresh ideas of Irishness, cross-pollinating across the ocean, eliciting critical interest and, in the process, enjoying commercial success'.[54] Not only does *Riverdance* reflect this celebratory diasporic hybridity in its marketing and stylistic references, but crucially this theme was also highlighted when the original show was translated into a full-length narrative. The experiences of Irish-American emigration, settlement and ethnic identity formation are central to *Riverdance*'s on-stage story and its climactic final scenes in particular. In the twelfth scene, 'The Harbour of the New World', for example, the programme text explains that: 'The music and dance that forged a sense of identity are now exposed to new and unfamiliar cultures. Ultimately, in the blending and fusion that follows, the emigrants find that the totality of human experience and expression is greater even than the sum of its many diverse parts.'[55]

Following this evocation of the assimilation experience of first-generation Irish-Americans, the thirteenth and last scene before the finale, entitled 'Home and Heartland', presents the later-generation desire to return 'home', annotated in the programme notes as:

> Always the child of the emigrant feels the tug of the homeplace; always that child feels the urge to return. What she or he brings there is a sustaining knowledge: we are who we once were, we are who we have become. With newfound confidence and pride, the child of the emigrant carries treasured memories home to their birthplace. A long journey ends under a native sky, a new and richer journey has taken its place.[56]

This narrative construction therefore engages directly with the issues of ethnicity and diasporic identity reflected in other aspects of global Irishness, such as the collection of material culture. As was mentioned earlier, *Riverdance* has received considerable unfavourable criticism as well as approbation. These criticisms have tended, perhaps predictably, to concentrate upon its 'kitsch' content and presentation. In 1997, for example, the *Boston Globe* published a review entitled '*Riverdance* – More Glitz Than Green', which commented that: ' "Riverdance" is supposed to journey from Dublin to New York, but it overshoots and lands in Las Vegas. The hugely popular dance show billed as a celebration of Irish culture drowns in glitz, flashing lights, skimpy costumes, postcard projections of lurid sunsets, a ludicrous narration.'[57]

It is no coincidence, perhaps, that such fierce criticism should include an evocation of tourism in its use of the word 'postcard'. In discussions of authenticity, an association with tourism always connotes the inauthentic, and *Riverdance*'s displays of kitsch – and glitz – inevitably give it such associations. Barbara O'Connor has outlined, in a discussion of *Riverdance*'s adaptation of traditional dancing styles, 'a discourse which sees culture as becoming increasingly commodified. Within this scenario, local cultural expression is appropriated by cultural entrepreneurs for the global marketplace and in the process loses its authenticity.'[58] Such discourses specifically equate the success of cultural products such as *Riverdance* with the postmodern experience of local practices and products becoming global through a process of cultural hybridity and intense commodification.

One of the most widespread aspects of the development of 'global Irishness' during the 1990s has been the proliferation of 'Irish-themed' pubs, which have been established, to great commercial success, in parts of the world as diverse as Miami and St Petersburg. These themed pubs have been particularly popular in the United States, despite the prior existence of 'Irish-American' bars, many of which have been trading for a century or more. Such bars, although they are usually owned, staffed and often frequented almost exclusively by people of Irish origin, are nevertheless fundamentally American in their design and ambience. By contrast, the successful introduction of Irish-themed pubs has been based upon a conscious attempt to reproduce a simulacrum of Irish pubs supposedly as they are (or were) in Ireland. They are often designed, equipped and fitted by developers who trade in their knowledge of how to produce and display 'Irishness'. One such organisation is the Irish Pub Company, established in Dublin but with an American subsidiary based (perhaps appropriately) in Las Vegas. Their promotional literature is highly revealing of undercurrents in the larger phenomenon of 'global Irishness'. There is, it claims,

> nothing to equal the ambience of an Irish pub, nothing to match its casual and attractive sociability. The Irish have always known that. Now, other nationalities have come to the same conclusion. Irish pubs allow people to relax and be themselves. To take pleasure in company and enjoy the art of conversation ... The authenticity of the Irish pub stands up to scrutiny – the deeper you dig, the more interesting and attractive it becomes.[59]

The social and cultural qualities listed here, such as sociability, relaxation and authenticity (of both the pub and its customers) are considered not only highly desirable but intrinsically Irish.

Although Irish-themed pubs have successfully opened in cities and countries with no significant ethnically Irish populations, the majority – particularly in the United States – are located in areas such as Boston, New York and Chicago, which do have large Irish-American populations. The promotional literature of the companies responsible for designing and installing the pubs often makes specific reference to their heightened chances of success among diaspora populations, such as the Irish Pub Company's assertion that 'the Irish diaspora of millions worldwide certainly does add to this allure'.[60]

In order to produce this 'authenticity', companies such as the Irish Pub Company or Celtic Dragon Pub Company offer a range of different 'design packages' which encompass everything, from the structural and technical layout of the pub to its interior design and menus. The Celtic Dragon Pub Company, for instance, offers designs from the 'Village and Town Pub', the 'City Pub' or the 'Castle Restaurant and Pub', on an ascending scale of luxury and size.[61] Like other similar companies, it also offers full interior design packages for each of these designs; meaning that each pub is in effect constructed from an *à la carte* 'kit', right down to the pictures on the walls. It is in these decorative features, including furniture, that many similarities can be seen with the souvenir qualities of Irish material culture. The overwhelming majority of Irish-themed pubs are 'antiqued' replicas of a perceived style, usually nineteenth-century, from the Irish past. Consequently, their fixtures and fittings are mass-produced copies of old drinks advertisements, agricultural and sporting equipment and domestic artefacts, frequently 'aged' in order to further the illusion of antiquity and therefore authenticity.

One of the most striking features of these theme pub fixtures is not only their material redundancy – they are often utility items now redesignated as decoration – an effect heightened by the sheer volume of display in most cases, but also their emphasis upon anachronistic commodification. One of the most often recurring themes among the disparate objects chosen for display is that of old advertising and prominently shown old brand-names. Late nineteenth and early twentieth-century advertising signs, and branded artefacts for alcohol, food, domestic and farming equipment, mass-produced with customized patinas of age, are the staple format of Irish-themed pubs of almost all designs. In his analysis of such decorations, Eamonn Slater has suggested that this commodification is also redundant, and that 'they, as "aestheticised" objects, still maintain a sense of desirability, not now for consumption but for a flight of fantasy'.[62]

I would suggest instead, however, that this process reveals some intriguing manoeuvres around the questions of authenticity and commodification which are so central to diasporic engagements with Irish culture. Following Lury's arguments about the 'disembedding' of widely perceived national cultural characteristics in the interest of mobilising them for global marketing purposes, it is clear that, in the case of global 'Irishness', authenticity and pre-modern style are two principal aspects of this 'disembedding' in the form of Irish-themed pubs. As such, the decorative styles of these pubs (and products served, such as recognisably Irish drinks) are the vehicles of this 'mobilisation' of a distinctively Irish authenticity. It is therefore significant that so much of what creates this self-evidently simulated authenticity is in fact the undisguised material of commodification from a different era, in the form of advertising and branding; often for long-vanished products. Echoing David Lloyd again, this cross-generational commodification suggests that a simplistic challenging of the authenticity of Irish-American consumption is insufficient to analyse the complex processes it is engaged in. It is indeed suggestive of the 'deracinating' effects of global capitalism – an experience familiar to diaspora cultures well before the late twentieth century – that even recourse to the grammar of 'heritage' in the form of period reconstructions must operate through the syntax of commodification itself.

It could be argued that Irish-American consumption of products such as *Riverdance* and Irish-themed pubs could be construed in terms of a postmodern irony – with particular reference, perhaps, to the concept of the 'post-tourist' and their self-aware engagement with inauthenticity. Urry argues, for example, that 'Post-tourists find pleasure in the multiplicity of tourist games. They know that there is no authentic tourist experience, that there are merely a series of games or texts that can be played.'[63] Undoubtedly a proportion of such large-scale consumption does fit this characterisation. However, the clear sincerity with which much of it is consumed suggests that, on its own, or even as a principal argument, this again seems an insufficient explanation of the phenomenal success of both these products and other aspects of 'global Irishness'.

It is through this detailed mapping of the consumption process of Irish America that the fundamentally contradictory nature of many claims made about it are revealed. If, as so many commentators claim, the diaspora is now thoroughly assimilated into the supposedly 'non-ethnic' white-collar middle class of the United States, the kitsch material and heritage culture described here would not find the ready market it so clearly does.[64] After all, the very nature of 'kitsch', as described by critics from Veblen onwards, is that it is necessarily defined by its exclusion from middle-class categories of taste, on the basis of its perceived embodiment of excess and vulgarity.[65] While contemporary categorisations of taste are more complex than those described by Veblen, and further complicated by the existence of a postmodern ironic taste, the majority of Irish-American consumption of Irish culture severely contravenes the edicts of discrimination governing kitsch as a category.

This would suggest that, despite being economically part of the white-collar, educated middle class, the Irish-American diaspora is demonstrating other allegiances in their acts of ethnic consumption. Rather than demonstrating either postmodern irony or a naïve sentimentality in their purchase of kitsch material culture and apparently inauthentic heritage experiences, it seems clear that Irish-Americans are instead attempting to express a diasporic commemoration of their ancestral culture; a commemoration which is, crucially, conducted within the circuit of postmodern global economics.

CONCLUSION

In conclusion, I would suggest that the Irish-American diaspora's engagement with Ireland is not indicative of an anti-modern romanticism that is to be compared with a realistic and modern Irishness. Rather, in this context, the nostalgia evident within the diasporic gaze should be seen as the self-interrogating framework through which the diaspora negotiates a reconciliation between its narrativised collective history and its engagement with contemporary Ireland.

I would also suggest that the act of tourism, as well as its associated texts, particularly the material ones, forms an essential and inherently meaningful aspect of this reconciliation. As this chapter has described, the convergence between widely available international tourism for many United States citizens in the aftermath of the Second World War and the rapid expansion of the American-born Irish population created an important new dynamic in the relationship between Ireland and its largest diaspora. Where, prior to this era, that diaspora's understanding of their cultural relationship to the 'old country' had been predominantly constructed through the use of narratives (fictional or historical), the advent of mass tourism provided the opportunity for those narratives to be experienced within the context of contemporary Ireland. This experience appears to have had a significant impact both upon the structures of the Irish tourism industry itself and upon the diasporic relationship to the country. On the one hand, the centrality of narrative themes and forms to the currently dominant cultural and heritage attractions of the present-day tourism industry could be argued to have many of its roots in the highly specific needs of diaspora tourists. These tourists' contact with Ireland was preceded by and predicated on a circulation of collective narratives, and this has perhaps influenced the contemporary reliance upon narrativised cultural attractions. On the other hand, the modern relationships and identity constructions negotiated between Ireland and its diaspora may be attributed, at least in part, to processes of tourism. That process of diasporic tourism to the 'home' country has allowed for an exploration of the complex temporal and spatial connections between Irish and Irish-American culture. The structures of material culture appear to function as another form of narrativisation of these complex connections, through their 'overperformance' of ethnicity and touristic memory through kitsch stylisation.

One of the most significant features of diasporic commemorative consumption is, in fact, its lack of opportunity to escape from the commodification process. Geographically and historically removed from the source of 'authentic' Irish culture, Irish America can only gain access to it in the United States through the channels of commerce. Curtis and Pajaczkowska, in their discussion of tourist objects, point out that:

> The predicament of refugees and diasporic cultures is compounded of poverty and marginalization and the insidious appropriations of a kind of 'static' tourism in which they experience fundamental components of 'home' transferred into leisure commodities – jazz or soul music; Indian, Greek and Chinese food; Jewish humour; Irish sentiment; and increasingly the idyll of nineteenth-century values and fantasies of pre-colonial primitivism.[66]

It can thus be seen that discussions centring around the issue of the diaspora's cultural 'authenticity' or lack of it are not sufficient to the situation, as well as operating from a position of considerable privilege. As David Lloyd has remarked: 'Is it not the experience of virtually every migrant community to be articulated around icons that are despised by the culture from which we come as no longer authentic (as if its own icons ever were!) and by that to which we come as vulgar, sentimental, gaudy – as signs of underdevelopment and inadequate assimilation?'[67]

The contemporary, later-generation Irish-American diaspora, while in the main no longer subject to the pressures of poverty and marginalisation it once experienced, is, ironically, subjected instead to the pressures of highly commodified global cultural marketing. In a further ironic twist, not only does this occur in the form of 'static' tourism described by Curtis and Pajaczkowska, but in the more mobile form of actual tourist marketing from the official institutions of their original homeland, such as Bord Fáilte. This process is illustrated by the language used in the promotion of Irish tourism. In the announcement of the Irish Tourist Board's opening of an office in Chicago, for example, it was asserted that 'Yes, Ireland is for sale – one trip at a time!'[68] More than twenty years later, one of the slogans used by Tourism Ireland Limited, the new all-Ireland tourism promotion body created in November 2001, is 'Island of Memories'.[69] The unambiguously commercial title of this new tourist authority combines revealingly with its invocation of memory to highlight the extent to which 'global Irishness' is in fact an appropriation of Irish culture *from*, rather than by, Irish America. In order to draw on Irish culture at all, the diaspora is now obliged to purchase it as a commodity, in an exchange in which the vendor is frequently Ireland itself.

NOTES

1   For a full description of this exhibit, see Fintan O'Toole, *The Ex-Isle of Erin: Images of a Global Ireland* (Dublin: New Island Books, 1997), pp. 129–30.
2   Anthony Slide, *The Cinema and Ireland* (London: McFarland & Company, 1988), pp. 42–3.
3   *Chicago Irish-American News*, April 1978, p. 9.
4   *Chicago Irish-American News*, January 1981, p. 8.
5   John Byrne, 'Artist's Statement' (Dublin: Temple Bar Gallery, 2001).
6   *Observer*, 18 March 2001, p. 15.
7   For more information on Hollywood films containing Irish themes, see Kevin Rockett, *Still Irish: A Century of the Irish in Film* (Dublin: Red Mountain Press, 1995).

8   Diane Negra, 'Consuming Ireland: Lucky Charms Cereal, Irish Spring Soap and 1–800–Shamrock', *Cultural Studies*, Vol. 15, No. 1, January 2001, p. 86.
9   David Fitzpatrick, *Irish Emigration 1801–1921* (Dublin: Economic and Social History Society of Ireland, 1984), p. 7.
10   Thomas Bartlett, Chris Curtin, Riana O'Dwyer and Gearód Ó Tuathaigh (eds), *Irish Studies: A General Introduction* (Dublin: Gill and Macmillan, 1988), p. 84.
11   *The Quiet Man*, dir. John Ford (Republic Studios, 1952).
12   Luke Gibbons, 'Romanticism, Realism and Irish Cinema', in Kevin Rockett, Luke Gibbons and John Hill (eds), *Cinema and Ireland* (London: Croom Helm, 1987), pp. 199–200.
13   John McCarten, *New Yorker*, 23 August 1952.
14   *The Irish Independent*, 19 May 1952, p. 8.
15   Gibbons, 'Romanticism, Realism and Irish Cinema', p. 200 (original emphasis).
16   See Marian Casey, 'Ireland, New York and the Irish Image in American Popular Culture, 1890–1960', D.Phil. thesis (New York: New York University, 1998). Casey includes a detailed discussion of the use, from the 1920s, of 'ballyhoo' (the creation of interest around a new film through the use of themed events and merchandising) as a marketing device by local cinemas. She also demonstrates the particular relevance and effectiveness of this form of promotion for Irish-themed films in Irish-American areas.
17   For the above information on the production and distribution policies regarding the tourism films of this period, the author is grateful for the assistance of both Bill Morrison and Derek Cullen of Bord Fáilte.
18   *Honeymoon In Ireland* (Bord Fáilte, 1963).
19   *Glimpses of Erin*, dir. James A. Fitzpatrick (Fitzpatrick Travel Talk, 1934).
20   See Barbara O'Connor, 'Myths and Mirrors: Tourist Images and National Identity', in Barbara O'Connor and Michael Cronin (eds), *Tourism in Ireland: A Critical Analysis* (Cork: Cork University Press, 1997), pp. 75–6.
21   *Ireland Invites You*, dir. Colm O'Laoghaire (Colm O'Laoghaire Productions, 1966).
22   Dean MacCannell, *The Tourist: A New Theory of the Leisure Class* (New York: Schocken Books, 1989), p. 3.
23   See Robert Hewison, *The Heritage Industry* (London: Methuen, 1987), and David Lowenthal, *The Past Is A Foreign Country* (Cambridge: Cambridge University Press, 1985).
24   *The Spell of Ireland*, dir. Danny Devlin (Celtic Films, 1950s). The exact date of the film is unknown. Its United States distributors advertise it as 'a visit to the Ireland of the 1940s', and indeed some of its sequences may well be from that period. However, the visual clues of other sections, along with the film's few historical references, suggest that the film was completed and released in the 1950s, most probably during the administration of de Valera's 1951–54 government.
25   Alice Carey, *I'll Know It When I See It: A Daughter's Search For Home in Ireland* (New York: Clarkson Potter, 2002), p. 280.
26   *O'Hara's Holiday*, dir. Peter Bryan (Tribune Films Incorporated, 1960).
27   *Green For Ireland*, dir. Arthur Wooster (Arthur Wooster, 1968).
28   *See You At the Pillar*, dir. Peter Bayliss (Associated British Pathé, 1967) and *Autumn in Dublin*, dir. Terry Wogan (1962).
29   *No More Yesterdays*, dir. Martin Rolfe (Associated British Pathé, 1967).
30   *Ireland In Spring*, dir. Colm O'Laoghaire (Colm O'Laoghaire Productions, 1956).

31   For a detailed analysis of both the Strokestown Famine Museum and the Ulster-American Folk Park, see David Brett, *The Construction of Heritage* (Cork: Cork University Press, 1996). Brett pays particular attention to the ways in which different narrative approaches in heritage attractions affect their presentation of historical events. Also see Niall Ó Ciosáin, 'Hungry Grass', in *Circa*, Summer 1994, and Luke Dodd, 'Sleeping With The Past: Collecting and Ireland', in *Circa* September/October 1991 for discussions of the politics of Irish heritage displays, and R.F. Foster, *The Irish Story: Telling Tales and Making It Up in Ireland* (London: Allen Lane, 2001), pp. 211–34 for a discussion of the 1798 Centre in Enniscorthy.

32   Chris Lockwood, 'Who Are the Customers – What Do They Want?', in *Come Back For Erin?* (Dublin: National Tourism Council of Ireland, 1977), p. 52.

33   Ibid., p. 54.

34   *Chicago Irish-American News*, May 1978, p. 7.

35   Diane Negra, 'Consuming Ireland', p. 90.

36   Cited in Esther Leslie, 'Souvenirs and Forgetting: Walter Benjamin's Memory-work', in Marcus Kwint, Christopher Breward and Jeremy Aynsley (eds), *Material Memories* (Oxford: Berg Press, 1999), pp. 116–19.

37   David Lloyd, *Ireland After History* (Cork: Cork University Press/Field Day, 1999), pp. 89–90.

38   Ibid., p. 91.

39   Jukka Gronow, *The Sociology of Taste* (London: Routledge, 1997), p. 43.

40   Celia Lury, 'The Objects of Travel', in Chris Rojek and John Urry (eds), *Touring Cultures: Transformations of Travel and Theory* (London: Routledge, 1997), pp. 78–80.

41   Ibid., p. 87.

42   Reginald Byron, *Irish America* (Oxford: Clarendon Press, 1999), pp. 132–3.

43   Ibid., p. 131.

44   Ibid., pp. 131–2.

45   *Crystal Clear*, dir. Brendan J. Stafford (Eamonn Andrews Studios, 1959).

46   Waterford Crystal Visitor Centre brochure, 2000.

47   Waterford Wedgwood Company Accounts, 2005, published on <http://www,waterfordwedgwood.com>. Accessed July 2006.

48   Barry Curtis and Claire Pajaczkowska, 'Getting There: Travel, Time and Narrative', in George Robertson et al. (eds), *Travellers' Tales: Narratives of Home and Displacement* (London: Routledge, 1994), p. 208.

49   David Lloyd, *Ireland After History*, p. 92.

50   See Marilyn Lavin, 'Consumer Goods: Reinforcers of Irish and Irish-American Identities in the United States', paper delivered at *The Scattering, Ireland and the Irish Diaspora: A Comparative Perspective*, Irish Centre for Migration Studies, University College Cork, Cork, 24–27 September 1997. Lavin provides survey data on the marketing and sales of Irish consumer goods through the Irish-American press during the 1980s and 1990s. For a detailed discussion of the sales of Irish-American goods through both import stores and the internet, also see Natasha Casey, 'The Best Kept Secret in Retail: Selling Irishness in Contemporary America', in Diane Negra (ed.), *The Irish In Us: Irishness, Performativity, and Popular Culture* (Durham, NC: Duke University Press, 2006), pp. 84–109.

51   *Chicago Irish-American News*, September 1981, p. 8.

52   See <http://www.irishshop. com> and <http://www.carrollsirishgifts.com>, as well as <http://www.waterford.com>. All accessed June 2002.

53   Lance Pettitt, *Screening Ireland: Film and Television Representation* (Manchester: Manchester University Press, 2000), p. 178.

54 *Washington Post*, 29 June 1997, p. 1.
55 See< http://www.riverdance.com>. Accessed June 2002.
56 Ibid.
57 *Boston Globe*, 13 January 1997, p. 7.
58 Barbara O'Connor, '*Riverdance*', in Michel Peillon and Eamonn Slater (eds), *Encounters with Modern Ireland: A Sociological Chronicle 1995–1996* (Dublin: Institute of Public Administration, 1998), p. 52.
59 <http://www.irishpubcompany.com>. Accessed July 2006.
60 Ibid.
61 <http://www.celticdragonpubco.com>. Accessed July 2006.
62 Eamonn Slater, 'When the Local Goes Global', in Eamonn Slater and Michel Peillon (eds), *Memories of the Present: A Sociological Chronicle of Ireland 1997–1998* (Dublin: Institute of Public Administration, 2000), p. 252.
63 See John Urry, *The Tourist Gaze* (London: Sage, 1990), p. 11 for a fuller discussion of this concept.
64 For a full discussion of this debate about Irish-American ethnic assimilation, see Chapter 2 above.
65 Thorstein Veblen, *The Theory of the Leisure Class* (London: Dover Publications, 1994).
66 Curtis and Pajaczkowska, 'Getting There', pp. 214–5.
67 David Lloyd, *Ireland After History*, p. 92.
68 *Chicago Irish-American News*, May 1978, p. 8.
69 <http://www.tourismireland.com/corporate>. Accessed July 2006.

4

Fiery Colleens and Fighting Irishmen: Representations of Gender within Irish America

INTRODUCTION

THIS CHAPTER seeks to analyse the ways in which the Irish-American diaspora constructs and represents gender within the boundaries of their ethnic identity. In so doing, it will approach two distinct but interconnected questions associated with gender and ethnicity. First, the chapter will discuss the centrality of gendering to the construction of national and ethnic identity itself, and examine the ways in which this is complicated within the diasporic experience of Irish America. Second, the chapter will analyse the specific representations of gender – as it impacts on the Irish ethnicity of Irish-Americans – produced and circulating within diasporic popular culture since the end of the Second World War. This dual analysis will, it is hoped, untangle some of the complex webs of representation surrounding the relationships between Irish gender and ethnicity in the diasporic context. The chapter is structured chronologically, in order to examine the shifting patterns of ethnic gendering within their historical context.

Analysis is concentrated upon the representational forms of film, television and, to a lesser degree, news media, as well as, where relevant, upon the development of Hollywood star personae, given that a strongly gendered ethnicity has been central to the external logic which a number of stars have brought to their films. These texts have been the predominant vehicles for the articulation of the norms, ideals and anxieties concerning gendered ethnicities within both Irish America and wider American culture. This process has also developed in a circular, self-perpetuating fashion, as representations of gender roles and identities have also been the predominant vehicles by which these cultural forms have approached their wider subject matters. John Hill, among others, has pointed to the importance of Hollywood's forms of representation, based upon 'classic narrative' conventions, in focusing attention and emphasis upon individual actions and relationships, rather than upon wider social or ideological concerns. He argues that this will 'almost inevitably encourage the explanation of events and actions in terms of individual psychology rather than more general social, political and economic relations. The conventions of 'classic realism', with their dependence on observable realities, will similarly privilege interpersonal relationships at the expense of social and political structures.'[1] Accepting this analysis of Hollywood representational conventions, it is therefore clear that, where interpersonal relationships are the privileged bearers of narrative, the presentation and development of gender roles and sexual politics will be among the most significant aspects of such narratives, thus placing the representations of gender and sexuality at the forefront of cultural exchanges produced within these conventions and forms.

GENDERING NATIONALISM

The foundational beliefs of ethnic identification are, in fact, profoundly gendered constructions, and the intertwining of contemporary notions of a diasporic ethnicity within Irish America with those of idealised gender roles and behaviour is therefore hardly surprising. Indeed, as this chapter will argue, the diaspora experience of ethnicity construction appears particularly focused on gender representations and symbolism.

The reasons for this emphasis on a gendered and heavily symbolised ethnicity within the Irish-American community are rooted in the construction of Irish national identity – mainly during the nineteenth century – and the later reconstruction of diasporic identity within the United States during the twentieth century.

In his seminal discussion of the development of nationalism, Benedict Anderson highlights the extent to which the language of national or ethnic group affiliation reflects its conceptual grounding in blood relations. In effect, he argues, the nation is perceived and projected as an inevitable extension of family networks and ties of loyalty and affection. The extent to which this process of extension is made material through symbols, both verbal and material, is emphasised by Anderson when he argues that 'something of the nature of this political love can be deciphered from the ways in which language describes its object: either in the vocabulary of kinship (motherland, *vaterland*, *patria*) or that of home (*heimat* or *tanah air* ...). Both idioms denote something to which one is naturally tied.'[2] This naturalisation of national or ethnic connections through associations with family relationships, Anderson goes on to argue, is the means by which the 'imagined community' is persuaded to display selfless or even sacrificial loyalty and affection for the entity of the nation.

As Andrew Parker has pointed out, however, Anderson does not develop this discussion to take sufficient account of the influence of familial imagery on the subsequent gendering of national identity. It is clear that a symbolic, idealised family group, as mobilised for the purpose of national affiliations, consists of a set of specific and highly charged gender roles – the most basic of which would at the very least consist of the tropes of mother, father, son and daughter. The relationships of such tropes with both each other and the national group as a whole must, then, rely upon the construction of identities based primarily on gender and sexuality.

In a further extension of this process, Parker points to Anderson's failure to highlight 'how deeply ingrained has been the depiction of the homeland as a female body whose violation by foreigners requires its citizens and allies to rush to her defense'. He goes on to assert that 'this trope of the nation-as-woman of course depends for its representational efficacy on a particular image of woman as chaste, dutiful, daughterly or maternal. If Britannia and Germania can thus be gendered feminine, this iconography operates despite or rather *because* of the actual experiences of their female populations.'[3]

What Parker is suggesting here, then, is that the use of this type of symbolic imagery – particularly that centring on women – to represent national or ethnic identity results in a highly gendered set of relationships to the national body politic for its citizens or members. In effect, while men gain access to a 'brotherhood' of equal access and rights (at least in theory), women receive only a symbolic access to the nation or group for whom they stand as idealised figureheads. Parker also points out that 'this idealisation of motherhood by the virile fraternity would seem to entail the exclusion of all non-reproductively-orientated sexualities from the discourse of the nation',[4] an issue which of course becomes important for the consideration of sexuality as well as gender in its connections to ethnic identity. Non-maternal women, as well as non-heterosexual men, therefore become excluded from nation-building narratives.

As Parker has intimated, the most frequently referenced symbolically gendered figurehead for nationalism is that of the mother-figure. This has also been recognised by Nira Yuval-Davis, who has pointed out that the 'figure of a woman, often a mother, symbolizes in many cultures the spirit of the collectivity, whether it is Mother Ireland, Mother Russia or Mother India'.[5] In the case of Ireland, the figure of Mother Ireland – as well as the 'daughter' figure of Erin – were well established in nationalist representation by the end of the nineteenth century, and would therefore also have been recognised and re-circulated within the Irish-American first- and later-generation diaspora.

As many commentators on anti-colonial nationalist movements have remarked, the figuring of the nation as female, with its embodiment taking the form of the Mother, was part of a complex process of masculinisation on the part of native cultures. This was seen as a necessary corrective to the emasculation of the colonial experience. Under colonial rule, native men experienced loss of agency and, to a large extent, their patriarchal roles. Simultaneously, they were also frequently represented as feminised by the colonising system, as one of a number of justifying strategies for retaining imperial rule.

Thus the process of nationalist masculinisation followed an imperial model in representing the native land as female and the native woman as a symbolic figurehead for a nationalist reclaiming of the land's 'honour'. It was through this process that native women's movements became secondary to the cause of national liberation, as their aims and methods of gender-liberation were often seen as directly contradictory to those of the nationalist agenda. In particular, throughout the late nineteenth century and the first half of the twentieth century, the intensely masculinist nature of nationalism's forms and objectives has been extensively commented upon by many critics.[6] Anne McClintock has suggested of national-liberation movements that 'women are represented as the atavistic and authentic body of national tradition (inert, backward-looking, and natural), embodying nationalism's conservative principle of continuity. Men, by contrast, represent the progressive agent of national modernity (forward-thrusting, potent, and historic), embodying nationalism's progressive, or revolutionary, principle of discontinuity.'[7]

The nationalist agendas which the first-generation emigrants from

Ireland to the United States would have taken with them during this period would, therefore, have been suffused with these gendered understandings of national identity. The nationalist agendas which they would have encountered in the United States would have been unlikely to challenge such concepts. The practices of a white European settler nation such as the United States, during the nation-building era of the nineteenth century, had been equally based in the gendering of both the land and the body politic. In such constructions, the settlement of land (and even the act of immigration itself) is frequently figured as an act of penetration, whether consensual or otherwise. David Savran, commenting on the 'manifest destiny' thesis first propounded by John L. Sullivan in 1845, has argued that 'O'Sullivan's perorations leave little doubt not only that the nation is a masculine construction (in relation both to the land and to other North American states) but also that Manifest Destiny represents an imperialist fulfilment of the heterosexual imperative'.[8]

GENDERING THE DIASPORA

The Irish-American diaspora, then, was formed within the context of a masculinised settler group penetrating the feminised American landscape and creating a new nation through an act of consummation. As Savran points out, the 'manifest destiny' theory is an example of the extent to which the settlement of the United States was thought of in these terms. Following the annexation of Texas, O'Sullivan urged the use of force to take control of other states, which, he predicted, would 'begin to thrill' for 'consummation' with the union.[9] In the gendering of the diaspora, the key aspect of this process is that it figures the act of migration itself as one of masculinisation – for both men and women. This was perhaps particularly true for the Irish, as opposed to other immigrant groups, because their emigration constituted a shift in status from being colonial subjects to one of becoming full citizens. This process, engaged as it was in a particularly self-conscious enactment of a nationalism based upon 'a deep, horizontal comradeship', as described by Anderson,[10] inevitably took place within a discourse of rationalism, self-determination and acculturation, all of which were perceived as being predominantly masculine qualities. This therefore placed immigrant women in an ambiguous position within the nation-building narrative of the United States. On the one hand, they could be seen to embody their new nation, and as symbolic bearers and protectors of national culture in exactly the same way as women were positioned within Irish and wider European nationalism. On the other hand, the act of migration for first-generation women, and the inheritance of liberal citizenship for later-generation women, figured them as always already masculinised by comparison to their European counterparts. The ways in which this was to affect the representation of Irish-American and, even more notably, Irish women, will be examined in detail below.

By the beginning of the twentieth century, the original settlement of the United States had developed into the officially sanctioned 'melting-pot' policy of citizenship creation.[11] Under this thesis, first-generation ethnicity was effectively erased in favour of a non-ethnically specific 'Americanness'. Ideally, this occurred at the moment of immigration, but more realistically was assumed to manifest itself in the second generation, whose upbringing in the United States was thought to remove any residual affections for ancestral cultures.

The important role played by gender in the representation of this assimilation process during the early twentieth century, particularly in film and fiction, has been extensively documented. Kevin Rockett, analysing the representation of Irishness during Hollywood's silent era, has cited numerous examples of unambiguously assimilationist dramas which figured their social concerns through the use of inter-ethnic (and frequently inter-class) romantic narratives. Any depiction of national identity which is developed through personal relationships is inevitably gendered in the process, but the representation of the Irish in early Hollywood films is particularly structured around gender roles, based upon the perception of Irish women's greater assimilation abilities. This was evident in the 'marrying up' and 'marrying out' stories of films such as *Irene* (1926), and the many Irish-Jewish narratives, including *Abie's Irish Rose* (1929) and *The Cohens and the Kellys* (1926).[12]

Probably the most successful of the silent era 'marrying up' films featuring Irish characters, *Irene* starred Colleen Moore, whose star persona was constructed around her role as an Irish 'flapper'. Moore's importance as a cipher for Irish-American female assimilation and social aspiration during the 1920s has been revealingly analysed by Diane Negra, who argues convincingly that Moore's Irish ethnicity was mobilised by Hollywood in order to counteract the influence of the New Woman and the 'vamp'. The essential difference between the vamp and Irish flapper, Negra suggests, is that of transformative potential, 'with the vamp announcing herself as finished product of her own labour in a way that foreclosed the shaping influence of patriarchy and the Irish girl as a raw resource to be acted upon by patriarchal and capitalist influences'.[13]

In *Irene* as in other films and in the pattern of her own career, Moore was typically presented as a non-threateningly modern girl who could be deflected into assimilation and consumerism through the device of a socially aspirant marriage. This deflection into traditional femininity, Negra argues, was largely constructed through Moore's Irishness:

> The promotion of Moore as Irish enabled the transformational energies associated with Irishness to be hijacked to stand for a reversion to dependent, passive femininity. This positioning of Moore as disqualified from taking part in the modernization process is crucially connected to her ethnic status as an Irish woman with the message being that women (or colonized, traditional cultures) need men's (or dominant, modern cultures) help to transform themselves.[14]

The Irish man was much less frequently or positively represented within American popular culture. He was likely to be presented as less socially mobile than the Irish woman, and his overt masculinity was largely connected to lawlessness and violence, particularly during the 1930s era of gangster films. James Cagney, among other stars, was a vehicle for such representations of urban, modern Irish-American masculinity. The novelist Peter Quinn, in an extended essay on the evolution of the Irish-American male persona, has argued that the first-generation Irish man was typified in nineteenth-century American popular representation as 'Paddy', who suggested the 'nightmare vision of Molly Maguires and their wild-eyed cousins'. The post-First World War, second-generation, city-born Irish-American, however, he characterises as 'Jimmy', taking his collective name from Cagney's on-screen characters.[15]

As Rockett has pointed out, however, the on-screen Irish-American gangster was, for all his violence and ruthlessness, almost always closely associated with a matriarchal family structure. In *The Public Enemy* (1931), the most influential of these films, Cagney's character, Tom Powers, is positioned as the product of an over-bearing Irish mother. Significantly, Powers is shown as a man not only outside the law in terms of his professional activity, but also one incapable of forming a satisfactory, non-violent sexual relationship, as demonstrated in scenes of his violence towards his girlfriend. This representation of the Irish-American male's inability to form productive romantic or sexual relationships, by implication due to the unhealthy influence of an Irish mother, was reprised in Cagney's role in *Shake Hands With the Devil* (1959), as will be discussed below.

During this pre-Second World War era, then, second-generation Irish-American men and women were frequently figured within the context of their first-generation, traditional family structures, most importantly influenced by the matriarchal, powerful figure of their Irish mothers. If this is considered through the construction of Irish nationalist and ethnic identity around the symbolically tragic figure of Mother Ireland, its underlying commentary upon the gendered nature of Irish adaptation to American life becomes clearer. In the case of young Irish-American women, such as Colleen Moore and the film characters she played, their acceptable femininity was in fact constructed from the 'purity' created by their mothers' teachings combined with the 'transformational' nature of their romantic relationships with American men. Bronwen Walter has also commented upon the ways in which, during this era, Irish women were seen as 'agents of "Americanization", as "civilizers" of their families'.[16] Young Irish-American men, however, were presented as developing a violent, socially unacceptable machismo which is so frequently mirrored by an extreme closeness to their Irish-accented mothers that the implication is unmistakeable. Irish-American men's masculinity was continually called into question through their intimacy with their mothers and, by extension, with a feminised notion of Ireland itself. Unlike their female counterparts, they were unable to transform themselves into acceptable, 'unhyphenated' Americans through the dual processes of capitalism and patriarchy.

MATERNAL NARRATIVES

The historical, social and cultural impact of the Second World War on the configurations of gendered identities within Irish America became clear before the end of the 1940s. The relationships suggested between Ireland and Irish America by their representations in popular culture after the end of the war show a number of very distinct changes from those of the 1920s and 1930s, all of which are clearly gendered.

One of the most obvious changes which occur after the end of the Second World War is in the cultural representation of the Irish-American man. The role of Irish-American servicemen during America's participation in the war, as well as the dramatic rise in social mobility of those men after 1945, due to developments such as the GI Bill, changed the ways in which their previously unruly or uncertain masculinity was represented. Peter Quinn argues that 'by the time of World War II, the association of Irish and fighting, once so basic to Paddy's disruptive image, had become a rallying cry for American patriotism. The 1944 movie *The Fighting Sullivans* … [was] the apotheosis of loyalty and sacrifice.'[17] Quinn goes on to suggest that where, in popular representation, the nineteenth-century 'Paddy' had been replaced during the Depression by the gangster-like 'Jimmy', he in turn was replaced after 1945 by 'good-natured, hard-working, decent Pat'.[18] While this generational development of Irish male archetypes obviously runs the risk of being overly schematic, it does point towards the essential shift in representations of Irish-American masculinity which are evident in post-war popular culture. As patriotic heroes, returned from the war to an almost assured place in the rapidly developing suburbia of middle-class America, Irish-American men became frequent signifiers of assertive but trustworthy American male strength.

A high proportion of these newly positive characterisations of Irish America were placed within the historical narrative of westerns, most particularly those made by John Ford, and often starring John Wayne as the archetypal Irish-American hero. The conflation between the Irish-American role in the armed forces during the war and their re-writing into American history can be seen most clearly in Wayne's prodigious output during this period. His Irish-American cowboy persona in films such as *The Fighting Kentuckian* (1949), through to *McLintock!* (1963), was interwoven with his roles as an Irish-American serviceman in war films such as *They Were Expendable* (1945) and *The Sands of Iwo Jima* (1949).

At the height of his fame and signifying power for an idealised Irish-American masculinity, Wayne starred in *The Quiet Man* (1952). His character in the film, Sean Thornton, continues the developing trope of this time, that of the hardened yet decent Irish-American man. While the date of *The Quiet Man*'s production indicates that its character development would have been heavily influenced by the Irish-American war experience, within the film itself Thornton's traumatisation has occurred in the modern urban environments of the industrial city and professional boxing in Pittsburgh; both features of a particularly American form of modernity. Upon his arrival in Ireland, when asked what they feed the Irish on in Pittsburgh, Thornton replies: 'Steel, Micheal Og, steel and pig-iron furnaces so hot a man forgets his fear of hell. When you're hard enough, tough enough, other things – other things, Michaeleen...'[19] This exchange, occurring at the outset of the film's narrative, establishes Wayne's character as an Irish-American who, having proven his masculinity within the United States, has arrived in Ireland in search of a recuperative experience. In his guide to the film, McHale cites background character information on Thornton in the production notes, which comment 'now to Ireland he is returning, a quiet man seeking forgetfulness of all wars of the human spirit'.[20] During his violent confrontation with Red Will Danaher near the end of the film, Thornton experiences flashbacks of the moment when he killed a man in the boxing ring, and Gibbons has argued of this device that 'the first fully-fledged use of unmotivated flashbacks... is generally considered to be Alan Resnais's *Hiroshima Mon Amour* (1959), a disorientating and harrowing re-staging of the long-term consequences of the trauma of the Second World War... Sean's flashback in *The Quiet Man* is of this variety, and is not unlike the first remarkable flash-cut in *Hiroshima Mon Amour* ....'[21] *The Quiet Man*, then, fits into the development of post-Second World War films which specifically reference the ongoing trauma of war for heroically constructed male characters. The 1940s and 1950s saw several films produced in Hollywood in which a traumatised or at least unfulfilled hero experiences a recuperative visit to Ireland.

Although this central element of *The Quiet Man*'s plot is played out in a number of narrative strategies, the principal form it takes is through the development of his relationship with Mary Kate Danaher, played by Maureen O'Hara. In this, *The Quiet Man* is in keeping with other films of the same period, focusing on a romantic relationship between an Irish-American man and an Irish woman. The Irish heroines of this era differ notably from their Irish-American counterparts of the 1920s and 1930s.

First, there is the fact of their nationality. Where the ethnically Irish heroines of the silent era were generally second-generation Irish-American women, depicted as socially mobile within American society due to their capacity for adaptation and transformation through marriage, the post-Second World War Irish heroine was to be found back in Ireland itself.

Second, the Irish heroine of this era, largely, it is suggested, because of her Irishness, was less girlish and already a more maternal figure, even before the plot denouement of marriage. As such, she was usually figured as pretty but natural, outgoing but traditional, and passionate but sensible. After the rigours of war, it appears, the Irish-American hero had earned the reward of nurture from a more profoundly domestic sexual partner than the flapper brides of previous generations. Maureen O'Hara, in *The Quiet Man*, is archetypal of this salvational mode of representing Irish women during the post-war period. The film's dispute between the newly married couple over Mary Kate's dowry is the most frequently rehearsed aspect of its treatment of gender relations, and critical opinions have been extremely divided. Luke Gibbons, for example, discussing the resolution of this dispute, argues that O'Hara's character is attempting to

> graft onto tradition newly emerging ideas of women's independence in the early 1950s. It is tempting, given the dichotomies available at the time, to construe her sense of self-worth in terms of a clash between the loveless matches of traditional arranged marriages, and liberal ideas of choice extolled by Hollywood depictions of romantic love – and this is indeed as Sean sees it. But Mary Kate, for all her dreaming, resists the Hollywood fantasy as well, and is more interested in establishing a material basis and communal recognition for equality within marriage.[22]

By contrast, Elizabeth Butler-Cullingford, analysing the basis for Sean and Mary-Kate's marriage, insists that:

> Her momentary possession of her 'rights' restores her self-respect, but the only use she makes of her liberation is to return home as 'the woman of the house' and cook Thornton's supper...O'Hara's fiery persona is allowed to hold centre stage for just long enough to surprise and please an audience accustomed to quieter women, but by the conclusion she is firmly re-enclosed in the domestic family hierarchy...[23]

While Butler-Cullingford may be under-reading the extent to which Mary-Kate's insistence upon her dowry gives her communal standing within Inisfree, the film's overall insistence upon O'Hara's role as an icon of domesticity seems its most powerful characteristic as a representation of Irish womanhood in the Irish-American imagination.

Precisely because of the death of her mother, whose possessions form the basis of the disputed dowry, Mary Kate is already positioned as a matriarchal figure within the film's opening story, due to her role as housekeeper for her brother. Even as an unmarried girl available to be 'courted', then, her capabilities as a future wife and mother are demonstrated to both Thornton and the audience. This is a representation conspicuously different from that of the girlish and unfettered characters of Irish-themed films of the 1920s and 1930s, such as those played by Colleen Moore. In *The Quiet Man*, whatever transformations of perspective the Irish-American male may have to make to adjust to life in an Irish village, he will not, unlike the heroes of Moore's films, have to expend effort and energy 'transforming' the Irish woman into a suitable model of feminine domesticity. The maternal nature of O'Hara's position as the object of Irish-American male desire is further emphasised by the powerful absent presence of Thornton's mother in *The Quiet Man*'s narrative. As a figure of psychologically scarred American manhood, Thornton, the film makes clear, is retreating to an Ireland previously

9. The maternal heroine – Mary Kate serving dinner in her brother's house at the beginning of *The Quiet Man* (1952).

known to him only through his mother's accounts of it, which replay in his memory at formative moments of the film. As such, it represents a therapy of maternal nurturing, in which his developing relationship with Mary Kate figures strongly. By marrying him and rejuvenating White O'Morn, the cottage of his birth which materially represents his mother in Thornton's memory, Mary Kate's Irish woman is enacting a narrative of maternal recuperation for Thornton's weary Irish-American man.

Although it is by far the best-known film of this era in which the Irish woman performs a recuperative function within the Hollywood imagination, *The Quiet Man* was not the only such narrative. In 1947, *The Luck of the Irish*, starring Tyrone Power, was the story of Stephen Fitzgerald, an acclaimed American war reporter briefly and unexpectedly stranded in Ireland while on his way to take up a lucrative career as a speech-writer for a corrupt media mogul and right-wing politician in New York. While there, he meets both a local girl and a leprechaun. The Irish girl, Nora, played by Anne Baxter, is, like Mary Kate in *The Quiet Man*, an embodiment of naturalness and chaste innocence, a point emphasised by direct comparison to the mogul's society-belle daughter, whom Fitzgerald is intended to marry in New York. As the narrative switches between Ireland and New York, it follows the battle for Fitzgerald's integrity, as both Nora and the leprechaun attempt to save him from the corruption of his new career and persuade him to maintain his true calling as a writer. As Gibbons has said of the film: 'Nora, with a little help from Horace the leprechaun, finally convinces Stephen that it is precisely the trappings of American capitalism which are preventing him from realising his true potential, the self which is expressed through his mastery of language.'[24] Leaving on one side the peculiarity of a leprechaun's intervention in an ethical dilemma, the film's playing out of an Irish-American man's rescue from the soul-destroying aspects of modern American life by an Irish girl is strikingly similar to that of *The Quiet Man*. Like Mary Kate, Nora is a maternal figure, acting as a housekeeper to her father following her mother's death – and, as in *The Quiet Man*, when Stephen is 'rescued' by her integrity, the film closes with him installed in that family cottage in Ireland.

The 1949 Bing Crosby vehicle *Top O' the Morning* also repeats the positioning of an Irish woman as the object of desire to an Irish-American man, albeit within an intensely confused narrative. Crosby plays an Irish-American insurance investigator who is sent to Ireland to investigate the theft of the Blarney Stone. Teaming up with the local police sergeant, played by Barry Fitzgerald, Crosby is rapidly recognised by Fitzgerald's daughter Conn as the suitor predicted for her by an ancient prophesy, and throughout the rest of the film their relationship is played out through his gradual fulfilment of the prophecy's many criteria. This highly mechanistic basis for the development of a supposedly romantic relationship largely deprives it of any possibility of passion (as, perhaps, does the casting of Crosby as the male lead), and their marriage at the end of the film is perfunctory as a plot denouement. Like other Irish film heroines of this era, however, Conn begins the narrative as a housekeeper for her father, and indeed is represented as particularly effective in her nurturing domesticity.[25]

All of these immediately post-war films, then, feature Irish heroines whose principal appeal to their Irish-American suitors is based upon a maternal sexuality and the capacity to provide a secure domestic haven from violence or corruption. Martin McLoone has argued that:

> A paradoxical stereotype of Irish womanhood thus emerged – a strong-willed, independent woman nonetheless committed to conservative social values. This woman had two manifestations – the mother (often a widow) and the feisty but highly moral colleen (the older and the younger self, the mother and the daughter). The radical conservatism implicit in these cinematic representations is crucial for understanding the complexities of Irish-American cultural identity and for assessing the impact of genre stereotypes of the Irish in general.[26]

This figuring of the Irish woman during the late 1940s and early 1950s plays interestingly against the social and economic changes which took place within Irish America and United States' society generally in the aftermath of the Second World War. One of the primary effects of the war for the United States had been the increasing economic and public sphere prominence of women. Through both direct war-work and the indirect replacement of men in vital civilian services, American women had been both forced and encouraged to enter previously male worlds of paid employment.

This had inevitably produced greater social and economic freedom for women than they had previously enjoyed, and one of the most notable features of the immediate post-war years was the active rolling back of these boundaries of female activity and power. Often referred to as the 'back to the home' movement, women's paid employment was directly restricted, and popular culture reflected and projected an image of acceptable femininity as being almost entirely bounded by domestic concerns.[27] Such an agenda betrayed very clear anxieties about the femininity of post-war American women, and the use of 'Irish colleens', positioned as instinctive nurturers and homemakers, as romantic partners appropriate for heroic Irish-American men, suggests an imaginative retreat to Ireland as a source of non-threatening femininity.

Such images of Irish women as unthreateningly feminine were also echoed in tourist promotional material of the post-war years. In *O'Hara's Holiday*, made during the 1950s, the Irish-American policeman, O'Hara, meets Kitty, a Dublin girl, during his visit to Ireland. Despite her Dublin background, O'Hara actually meets Kitty near Kenmare, where she first appears on screen seated against a picturesque rural landscape, and wearing a traditional tweed shawl.[28] This introduction of Kitty, who marries O'Hara at the end of his brief holiday in Ireland, is remarkably similar, visually, to the cover photograph used for the *National Geographic Magazine*'s March 1961 special feature on Ireland. The cover shows an un-named young woman, her head draped in a green shawl, in the grounds of Ashford Castle, and is captioned 'Colleen in green exemplifies two of Ireland's prides, beautiful women and handsome woollens'.[29] *O'Hara's Holiday* goes further, apparently suggesting that both might be considered as souvenirs of a visit to the country.

This gendering of the diaspora relationship to Ireland is further highlighted by the ways in which Irish men are represented as a contrast to the Irish-American romantic lead in popular narratives of the time. If the act of emigration is presented as a masculinising process, meaning that the Irish woman represents a less threatening form of femininity than the Irish-American woman, then the Irish man must represent a less impressive form of masculinity than his Irish-American counterparts. The long-established tradition within colonial discourse of representing Irish men as feminised had of course frequently been evident in Hollywood narratives before. However, in the post-Second World War period it became especially conspicuous, particularly in the contexts in which it was negatively compared to the idealised strength of Irish-American masculinity. Indeed, the peculiarly dark overtones of the Bing Crosby film *Top O' the Morning*, which confounds genre expectations in ways for which the film's resolution never fully accounts, are largely based upon particularly stark condemnations of the feminised Irish man.

When Crosby's insurance investigator arrives in the village from which the Blarney Stone has been stolen, he encounters the local Garda investigation, run by Barry Fitzgerald as Sergeant McNaughton (whose daughter Crosby will eventually marry), and his deputy, Hughie. Sergeant McNaughton is positioned as a rather tragically inadequate policeman, desperate for the community respect he knows he has never earned, and much of the film's action revolves around Crosby's benevolent attempts to allow him to take the credit for solving the mystery of the Stone's disappearance, thus allowing him to retire with dignity. Equally, Hughie is immediately established within the narrative as a comic stage-Irishman – ineffectual, excessively deferential, and highly feminised in his lack of agency. The film's gradual (but startlingly violent) revelation that this recognisably comic character is in fact both a thief and murderer provides for an unexpected reversal of Ireland's predominant Hollywood image as a rural idyll. If, however, this use of the stage-Irishman is read through the desire to highlight the unacceptable and even threatening nature of such feminised masculinity, then its function becomes clearer, despite, or even because of, the havoc it wreaks with the film's narrative structure.

The damaged and untrustworthy nature of Irish male sexuality was also central to a more acclaimed film from the late 1950s, *Shake Hands With the Devil* (1959), starring James Cagney. Set during the fight for Independence, it is the story of an Irish-American medical student who becomes unwillingly involved with a unit of the IRA, led by his surgical professor, Sean Lenihan, played by Cagney. The gender relationships portrayed in the film are notable for a number of interconnected reasons. First, the Irish women characters are presented as not only sexually active, but in the most unacceptable ways possible. In the film's early story in Dublin, members of the unit are betrayed to the British military by a girl clearly intimated to be working as a prostitute serving the local barracks. Later on, in the sequences set in a village on the coast, the unit is aided by Kitty, the local prostitute and barmaid, who appears in a crucial scene on a beach at dawn with Cagney's Lenihan. In this scene, the second aspect of the film's examination of Irish sexuality is explored, as Kitty accuses Lenihan of using his publicly puritan disapproval of her sexual availability as a smokescreen for his desire for her. When she further denounces him as, in effect, a violent misogynist due to sexual inadequacy, Lenihan physically attacks her and leaves her lying on the ground, later killing her on a false charge of informing. As John Hill has commented of Cagney's appearance in *Shake*

Hands With the Devil, 'violence against women had, of course, been a characteristic of the Cagney persona ever since Tom Powers had assaulted his mistress with a grapefruit in *The Public Enemy* in 1931...In casting him as the IRA leader in *Shake Hands With the Devil,* it was inevitable that many of these associations would follow...it is, thus, women, rather than the British, who most unsettle the IRA man's composure and inspire his most vicious outbursts.'[30]

What is notable about the shift of casting and therefore representation between 1931 and 1958, however, is that, where in *The Public Enemy* Cagney had been playing a violent and emasculated Irish-American man, in *Shake Hands With the Devil* this persona had crucially been transposed to an Irish man, while the film's Irish-American hero retains and redeems his masculinity by exercising socially acceptable violence through his final shooting of Lenihan at the end of the film. While *Shake Hands With the Devil*'s representation of Irish women is highly unusual for the time, operating as it does in stark contrast to the more typically maternal Irish 'colleen', in doing so it also highlights the lack of negotiable ground for Irish female sexuality. Where *The Quiet Man* and other films present the Irish woman as an eroticised but socially conformative maternal figure, *Shake Hands With the Devil* foregrounds the catastrophic results of Irish female eroticisation outside the bounds of domesticity, leaving little if any room for manoeuvre between the two positions.

THE ROSE OF TRALEE

It was into this arena of gender representations that there appeared one of the most long-running and high-profile public practices of symbolic gendering across the Irish diaspora. In 1959, the first International Rose of Tralee Festival was organised by local businesses in the town of Tralee, County Kerry. Originally called the Festival of Kerry, it was designed to boost the number of visitors to the town, and to this end was timed to coincide with its traditional August race meeting. The centrepiece of the Festival, then as now, was the Rose of Tralee competition, in which a young woman of Irish heritage is chosen as the year's 'Rose', according to a set of rather vague, but long-standing, criteria.

It is crucial to the Festival's self-promotion and ongoing success that it has always insisted that the Rose competition is not a beauty pageant. Instead, it uses for its judging criteria the words of the eponymous ballad, in particular the repeated lines:

> She was lovely and fair as the rose of the summer,
> Yet 'twas not her beauty alone that won me;
> Oh no, 'twas the truth in her eyes ever dawning,
> that made me love Mary, the *Rose of Tralee*...

The festival has therefore consistently held that its Rose is chosen on the grounds of the 'truth in her eyes ever dawning' – intangible though that quality must be – rather than on the grounds of physical attractiveness. The ballad itself refers to the well-known story of a doomed love affair between William Pembroke Mulchinock, a landowner's son, and Mary O'Connor, a local servant girl, during the 1840s. As the origin of a diaspora pageant, the story contains useful connections to the Irish-American diaspora, albeit less triumphant than most popular narratives of emigration. According to legend, William Mulchinock, returning to Tralee to find his lost love, Mary O'Connor, learns that she has died and, having married another woman, emigrates to the United States to begin a new life. On the failure of his marriage, however, he returns to Ireland, and, having spent his last years in alcoholism, dies and is eventually buried next to Mary O'Connor. This story of frustrated love, unsuccessful marriage and emigration, alcoholism and tragic death might seem an unpromising basis for a celebratory festival of diaspora girlhood, but the Rose of Tralee has nevertheless maintained it as the centrepiece of its competition for more than forty years. Contestants therefore seek to emulate Mary O'Connor's symbolic position as an exemplar of Irish femininity – attractive but also competent and reliable.

The Rose of Tralee's origins in the late 1950s place it within a very significant time in the development of beauty pageants themselves. A profoundly American cultural invention, having their origins in the fairground attractions of Atlantic City, New Jersey, during the 1880s, beauty pageants had long struggled to achieve an image of respectability and chastity against long-standing allegations of immorality and corruption among both the contestants and judges. In the Miss America contest, for example, the transformation of the contest into an activity for respectable young women was marked by the fact that, in 1938, the talent competition was added for the first time, in 1945 a college scholarship fund was added to the prizes, and in 1948 the winner began to be crowned in her evening gown, rather than a swimsuit.[31] In particular, the Second World War, and the utilisation of beauty queens in the drive to sell war bonds, had 'symbolized a shift in contests away from their side-show roots and toward professionalism, careers, scholarships, and a definition of beauty that included deportment and citizenship. With this shift, beauty pageantry became part of middle-class civic boosterism.'[32] Arriving onto the international pageant circuit at this time, which was also one of the formative moments of Irish-American entry into the American middle-classes, the Rose of Tralee competition fulfilled a particular role in the definition and validation of middle-class ethnically Irish womanhood. Given the preference at the time, as discussed above, for idealisations of Irish over Irish-American femininity, this function of gender-validation by the diaspora's ethnic homeland is likely to have played a particularly strong role in its success.[33]

The Rose of Tralee's insistence that it is not a beauty contest rests not only on its emphasising of the 'truth in her eyes ever dawning', but also on the centrality of the competition's 'talent' section and omission of a swimsuit section. The contestants appear in evening wear, are interviewed by the compere, and then perform a song, poem or dance. The judges decide upon the winner, not, supposedly, on her looks, but 'based instead on character, personality and traditional Irish values'.[34]

These criteria for an Irish diaspora beauty pageant, founded during the late 1950s, are therefore grounded in the domestic ideals of Irish femininity of the era. Not only is there an emphasis in the competition's structure upon the Roses' competence rather than decorativeness, there is also a strong emphasis on their family structures and backgrounds. During the contestants' interviews, they are ritually asked to describe their diaspora descent, such as the names and origins of their emigrant ancestors, as well as to identify any known relatives living in Ireland. Combined with the long-established tradition of family members cheering from the auditorium and being shown on camera as their Rose describes the family, this process works to embed young diaspora women within both a strong family background and a network of Irish ethnicity. And while the Rose of Tralee includes competitors from all parts of the Irish diaspora, not only does the United States send more competitors than any country other than Ireland itself, but the contest is also strikingly similar in form to a specifically American type of such contests. In its emphasis upon the contestants' Irish lineage and community involvement, the Rose of Tralee competition fulfils the criteria of a 'community queen pageant', outlined by Robert H. Lavenda as follows: 'at the pageant, as each young woman is introduced, a universal formula is followed: her name is announced, followed by the name of her parents. Candidates in community queen pageants are grounded in their communities, located precisely in the town's social world.'[35] While the pageants Lavenda is describing are small-town events in the mid-western United States, the Rose of Tralee Festival can usefully be considered as a diaspora hybrid of such competitions, designed to place young Irish diaspora women within the validating framework of community approval.

The Festival's role of validation for each new generation of young Irish-American women, positioned as they had always been as the bearers of ethnic identity and pride, began at a time when Irish America was frequently referred to in terms of blood-lines and therefore ethnic distinctiveness. In 1960, during Kennedy's successful presidential campaign, an admiring *Time Magazine* article had commented that the 'Kennedy clan' resembled a 'meadow full of Irish thoroughbreds'.[36] The following year, *Life Magazine* published a two-part special feature on Irish America, entitled 'The Lusty Heritage of The Irish in America', and referring in its sub-headings to the community as 'A Handsome, Hearty Breed'.[37]

The language used in these approving descriptions of Irish America is revealing in its emphasis upon the concept of 'breeding' and 'stock', made particularly explicit in the *Time Magazine* evocation of race-horses. In the light of depictions of Irish America at this time, the Rose of Tralee competition, as a diaspora hybrid of 'community queen' pageants, can be seen as a device by which the entwined concepts of femininity and ethnicity were proudly displayed as endlessly self-renewing within the diaspora, and, crucially, validated by the 'homeland' itself.

THE TROUBLES

Between the end of the Second World War and the mid-1960s, as has been discussed above, representations of the gendered relationship between Ireland and Irish America tended to be focussed upon fictional narratives, principally those produced by Hollywood. One of the other notable features of this period was the almost total absence of news or current affairs coverage from Ireland reaching Irish America.[38] This situation therefore allowed the idealised, fictional images of Irishness, both male and female, to flourish largely unchallenged within the diaspora. As the 1960s progressed, however, political events in Northern Ireland began to produce new images of Irish men and women, neither of whose enacting of gender roles necessarily fitted the established codes of representation to which the diaspora had become accustomed. In particular, the widespread publicity given to the Northern Ireland Civil Rights Association (NICRA) during the late 1960s, followed by the even greater coverage of the Troubles after 1969, produced images of the Irish man and woman which seriously disturbed existing representations. Not only would this negotiation between traditional and developing gender representations of Ireland be played out in sharply influential current affairs accounts of Ireland over the coming decades, it would also come to have a strong influence upon fictional narratives of Irishness produced within the United States in later decades.

The new awareness of contemporary Irishness within the United States diaspora was to begin with a particularly notable departure from the domesticated colleen of previous decades' depictions of Irish women. Bernadette Devlin's role as a leader of the NICRA campaign, and then as an MP in the British parliament, attracted the first significant coverage in the United States of Irish events since well before the Second World War. As a young, fashionable and, perhaps most significant of all, assertive woman, Devlin became the focus of considerable attention within the international news media. Of her emergence into the news spotlight, Fergal Tobin has commented, 'she was elected and made an electrifying maiden speech in the House of Commons on the day she took her seat... Now she was playing a role to which her politics seemed best suited: not a cautious, prevaricating parliamentarian, but *La Passionaria*, the very spirit of a people in revolt.'[39]

Tobin's use of the descriptive term *La Passionaria* is revealing of the way in which Devlin would come to be represented in the mainstream press of both Britain and the United States. *La Passionaria* was the epithet given to Dolores Ibarruri, a celebrated anti-fascist fighter in the Spanish Civil War, and much-invoked figurehead of the Republican movement. As such, the application of this term to Devlin, while appearing to celebrate her political leadership and unorthodox style, in fact re-incorporates her within the role of symbolic figure, automatically removed from real agency or power. This process of relegation to figurehead crucially revolved around very sexualised representations which concentrated upon Devlin's gender.

The *New York Times*, in its coverage of Bloody Sunday, gave great prominence to Devlin's response the following day in the British parliament, when she crossed the floor of the House and slapped Sir Reginald Maudling, the British government spokesman on Northern Ireland. The paper reported her actions in some detail, describing 'her hair whirling' as she attacked Maudling.[40] Such descriptive language is suggestive of a dervish or, more appropriately, a banshee, one of the feared spirit-women of Irish mythology. The *Washington Post* also covered the story the following day. Indeed, they gave more space to Devlin's actions in the House of Commons than to the events on the streets of Derry on Bloody Sunday itself. The *Post*'s story made detailed reference to the disparity in size between Devlin and Maudling, detailing his 6 feet height and 220lb weight by comparison to her 5 feet and 90lb build. Having established their vital statistics, the paper described Devlin during the attack as 'white-faced, in a short blue dress, black hair streaming down to her sides'.[41] The reference to her 'short' dress is not coincidental, and highlights one of the most recurring aspects of Devlin's media representation. Both papers used a widely syndicated *Associated Press* photograph of Devlin leaving Westminster after this event. The photo is taken from a low vantage point as she walks down a short flight of steps, thus emphasising the shortness of her skirt – a clothing style which was, in 1972, entirely typical for young women, but one which in Devlin's case was consistently used to emphasise her eroticised femininity at the expense of her political agency. Writing of J. Bowyer Bell's *The Irish Troubles: A Generation of Violence*, an exhaustive chronological account of this era of Irish history, for example, David Lloyd has commented on its 'stylistic affectations and penchant for metonymic detail (Bernadette Devlin, for example, is virtually inseparable from her mini-skirt at every appearance)'.[42]

By ascribing to Devlin the symbolic qualities of a national figurehead such as Ibarruri, the mythic ones of a banshee, or the metonymic association with an item as trivial as a particular article of clothing, all of these representations of her worked to account for her popularity while reducing her significance as a committed political activist. In doing so, they followed in a long tradition of marginalising the work of female activists, typically in order to maintain the intense masculinisation of nationalist resistance move-ments and project women's roles in events onto their bodies. This manoeuvre therefore attempts to continue their positioning as that of figureheads, specifically designed to channel masculine energies towards protection and defence of the symbolic 'homeland'. Devlin's refusal to occupy this role in the accepted fashion – indicated by her outspoken pursuit of a more active agenda – resulted in a represen-tational dissonance. It is in this dissonant representation that her frequently mentioned mini-skirt became such a powerful 'metonymic detail', standing as it also did in many other contexts during the late 1960s for this excess of symbolic power. Within the context of Irish-American conceptions of Irish femininity, however, this appears to have been particularly problematic, given the contin-ued power of longer-standing conceptions regarding Irish femininity.

It is worth following the ways in which this 'dissonance' regard-ing Irish femininity was negotiated throughout the coming decade of the 1970s and early 1980s. While the majority of gendered repre-sentations of the Troubles have, for obvious reasons, been male (as will be discussed in more detail below), there were other moments, besides Devlin's early appearance, when images of Irish women have been especially dominant. The most noticeable of these was during and immediately after the 1981 hunger strikes.

One of the most conspicuous aspects of the Irish-American press coverage of the hunger strikes and the aftermath of the strikers' deaths is the prominence of their younger, female relatives. This is particularly noticeable in the coverage of hunger strikers' funerals, with considerable space given to photographs of grieving young women with downcast eyes, and dressed in black. Newspapers such as the *Irish People* also tended to publish stories during the months following the funerals, which concentrated on interviews with and prominent photographs of these women, who were usually the sisters or young wives of the men who died. Marcella and Bernadette Sands, sisters of Bobby, as well as the wife and the ten-year-old daughter of Joe McDonnell, were all represented in this way. The *Irish People* carried a long interview with Bernadette Sands about her brother and the effect of his death shortly after his funeral, accompanied by large photographs emphasising her youth, sadness and good looks. Such representations were, of course, recalling those of the nineteenth century, in which Erin was frequently portrayed as a young woman grieving for Ireland – the Irish-American press photographs of young female mourners, such as Bernadette and

Marcella Sands, at the hunger strikers' gravesides are highly reminiscent of nineteenth-century depictions such as those of Erin
mourning for Parnell.[43]

Representations of Irish men during the Troubles were, by
contrast, centred upon the concept of masculine aggression, whether
this was presented positively or negatively. While media outlets such
as the Irish-American press tended to concentrate upon Irish male
heroism, often downplaying aggression in favour of narratives of
self-sacrifice on behalf of their (typically feminised) nation, the
mainstream media and Hollywood began to display increasing
hostility to the concept of Irish masculinity. As has been noted
earlier, the geo-politics of the 1970s and 1980s tended to reinforce
the 'special relationship' between the United States and Britain,
largely centred on a common interest in 'anti-terrorism' policies.[44] As
such, within the context of events in Northern Ireland, Irish men
became closely associated with 'terror' in the mainstream imagination. In just one example, the *Philadelphia Inquirer*, in May 1981,
featured a cartoon of a 'wild mob' of Irishmen, heavily armed with
guns and bombs, bearing Bobby Sands' coffin. The cartoon's caption
features one of the men saying to another: 'I was afraid he'd never
die.'[45] While this manoeuvre maintained the representational gulf
between Irish and Irish-American men which had opened up following the end of the Second World War, it did so in different terms.
Where previously Irish masculinity had been positioned as being in
question and feminised by comparison to Irish-American equivalents, now it was repositioned to the opposite end of the spectrum –
while Irish-American masculinity was presented as comfortingly
domesticated and channelled into 'acceptable' outlets, Irish men
were instead represented as savagely outside of social controls upon
male violence. In effect, this was in many respects a return to the
version of Irish masculinity prevalent in the United States during the
nineteenth century, that of the wild, socially dangerous 'Paddy'.

While this manifestation of Irish male archetypes would begin to
emerge in feature films with increasing frequency during the late
1980s and early 1990s, an early example of American nervousness
about heroic representations of the Irish man has been highlighted
by Diane Negra in her study of television advertising. With particular reference to the Irishman "Sean", a recurring character of the
long-running Irish Spring Soap advertisements, Negra comments
upon the way in which this character's physicality altered throughout the 1970s, pointing out that, 'while in the early ads, Sean is

played by a tall broad-shouldered actor who distinctly resembles John Wayne as he appeared as Sean Thornton in *The Quiet Man*, the casting choices clearly change as the ads progress. Looking at the ads in sequence, "Sean" grows progressively smaller in stature.'[46] Negra comments that this change in representation is hard to account for, except by reference to the changing political climate of the decade, and its effects upon popular conceptions of Irish masculinity: 'by the 1970s, imagery of empowered Irishmen would have acquired inevitable and uncomfortable connotations of terrorist representation, as news accounts of the troubles circulated worldwide ... in the series of ads produced by the Irish Tourist Board, these problems necessitate that young Irish men become virtually invisible in the Ireland those ads depict.'[47]

Equally hard to account for, without similar reference to the events in Northern Ireland, and their frequent domination of the news media, is the decreasing level of Irish themes or even characters from fictional narratives produced in the United States during the 1970s and 1980s. This absence of Irish representation is particularly notable given that these two decades saw a significant rise in interest in its ethnicity by the Irish-American diaspora, along with similar trends in other European ethnic groups in the United States. While, however, there was a steady flow of Italian-American narratives from Hollywood studios following the successes of *The Godfather* and *The Godfather Part II* in 1972 and 1974, no Irish-American equivalents were produced. Following the publishing success of Leon Uris' 1976 novel *Trinity*, for example, a film version might have been expected, but, despite the fact that in October 1976 Uris was reported as being 'in Ireland scouting for locations for the shooting of the movie version of his best-selling novel', the film was never made.[48]

In other areas of representation, Ireland also became noticeable largely by its absence between the outbreak of the Troubles in 1969 and the end of the 1980s. *National Geographic Magazine*, for example, published a cover story about Ireland in September 1969. The story, entitled 'The Friendly Irish', featured a cover picture of a smiling young woman, captioned 'Fair daughter of Erin, Judith Woodworth typifies the youth of the Irish Republic, where an improving economy offers new opportunities'. The long illustrated story within the magazine, presumably written during the summer of 1969, and which does not mention Northern Ireland at all, would have appeared as already anachronistic by the time it was published in September.[49] However, Ireland did not feature again in a major story in the magazine until April 1981, a gap of more than eleven years. This edition discussed the Troubles under the heading 'War and Peace in the North'. The editorial article stated that:

> For 12 years the sectarian conflict in Northern Ireland has been like a black hole, drawing in and devouring every material hope of ending it... Yet there is wide interest in the world for the end of this agony. The Irish emigrants who went out to the United States, Canada, Australia, and other parts of the world have had an impact upon their adopted lands. Their descendants do not want to look back upon Ireland in sorrow and shame.[50]

The cover photograph of this edition, uniquely for Irish stories since the magazine introduced cover pictures, was an aerial photograph of the Inismore landscape, rather than of a woman or children, as had always been the practice before. Both the editorial and the choice of cover photograph of the 1981 magazine suggest ambiguous American attitudes to Irishness during this period, as they, like the Bord Fáilte adverts Negra refers to, avoid images of Irish people in favour of largely empty landscape images. The striking absence of people, male and female, in Irish tourist advertising of the time was highlighted by Robert Ballagh in 1980, when he complained that 'you have Bord Fáilte eulogizing roads where you won't see a car from one end of the day to the other: it's almost as if they're advertising a country nobody lives in'.[51] Barbara O'Connor has also commented upon the extent to which tourist advertising of Ireland during this period presented it as 'empty space'.[52]

This ambiguity is also made clear in one of the few American-produced fictional narratives of this period to engage directly with Irishness, the 1981 ABC/EMI television mini-series *The Manions of America*, starring Pierce Brosnan.[53] This series, over a total of six broadcast hours, followed the emigration from Ireland in 1845 and rise to prosperity in the United States of the Manion family, headed by Brosnan's character, Rory Manion. As an epic diaspora family narrative, in which, in keeping with the Hollywood narrative tradition, individuals stand as representative figures for wider associations, the ethnicity of the central characters is highly gendered. Most strikingly, for an era when representations of Irish masculinity were largely avoided due to their connotations of terrorism, Brosnan's character is an Irish nationalist, whose direct involvement in violent resistance against British rule is the main catalyst for his escape to the United States. Settling in nineteenth-century Boston (which reveals itself in long-shots to be Trinity College, Dublin), Manion is reunited with his Anglo-Irish fiancée, Rachel Clement, and much of the narrative chronicles their rise to property- and business-owning success as their family acquires respectability and influence in the city. Despite this American success story, Manion is presented as an Irishman who never abandons his political commitment to Ireland. As the series draws to a close, Manion, now a middle-aged man, is shown risking his life and all of his family's prosperity to return to Ireland with a shipment of explosives for a nationalist uprising, only just escaping once more to the United States when this mission fails.

The series' presentation of Manion as a passionate Irish nationalist and romantic hero appears therefore to counteract the prevailing tendency to erase such portrayals of Irish masculinity from popular narratives at this time. However, its narrative reveals some significant internal tensions, most of which centre upon the characters' personal and therefore gendered relationships. First, there is the central relationship of the story, that between Rory Manion and Rachel Clement. Rachel is not merely Anglo-Irish, but English-raised, and the story opens as she and her father arrive from England for the first time to take up their inheritance of the 'Big House' of Manion's village. It is made very clear that she has no real understanding of Irish society or politics, and it is this position as an outsider that allows Rachel to (more or less convincingly) bypass the social barriers to her relationship with Manion, her stable-boy. This cross-class romantic alliance of an Irishman with an Anglo-Irish or English woman, an alliance which is at least partly responsible for their decision to emigrate to the United States, is a recurring theme of later-twentieth-century narratives of Irish America. Repeated again in *Far and Away* (1992), this theme and its connotations will be discussed in more detail below.

The continued relationship, after their marriage in Boston, between Rory and Rachel Manion is presented in a number of problematic ways, most of which reflect principally upon Rory's specifically Irish masculinity. Their marriage is depicted as a passionate one, based on an explicit sexual attraction. This depiction of Irish eroticism, however, is swiftly displaced into a tragic maternal narrative, as Rachel not only miscarries but is told that her life will be threatened by further pregnancies, which thus forbids any further sexual relationship between her and Rory. The series then begins to present Rory's 'passionate' nature (in which sexuality and political conviction are intrinsically linked) as excessive. This is depicted first through his developing liaison with a much younger woman, the daughter of a friend and contemporary of his, and second through Rachel's decision to risk her own life by another pregnancy, largely, it is implied, in order to save her marriage. Rory's ill-fated return to Ireland and active nationalist resistance coincides with the culmination of this dangerous pregnancy, and he returns to Boston from the failed attempt at revolution in Ireland just in time to witness Rachel's death while she gives him his long-desired son, the first 'Manion of America'. By linking Rory's sexual and political passions, *The Manions of America* eventually represents them as not only excessive but also destructive, despite his more or less maintained position as the narrative's romantic hero.

IRISH AND IRISH-AMERICAN MASCULINITIES

After the absence of Irish representation in American popular culture during the 1970s and 1980s, the 1990s were characterised by a significant number of films dealing with Irish themes or characters, and often featuring Irish actors.

Produced in 1992, *Far and Away* is, in most respects, a very typical retelling of the establishment of the Irish-American diaspora – it positions the act of emigration as part of a search for liberty and prosperity, following a meritocratic struggle for freedom from a colonial and class-dominated society. Equally typically, the film develops this narrative through a romantic relationship, in which the central characters, played by Cruise and Kidman, stand as a symbolic 'pioneer mother and father' of the later-generation diaspora they will help to establish. What is notable about the film's treatment of this familiar story, however, is that it employs a remarkably similar cross-class romance narrative to that used more than a decade earlier in *The Manions of America*. As in that mini-series, the central couple consists of a Catholic Irish man and a landlord's daughter. In both cases, these narratives posit a desire for escape from the restrictions of social class as much as from colonial experience as a reason for emigration and therefore a foundational motivation for the diaspora itself. While this presentation of the United States as a haven from European class systems is by no means unusual within the context of any immigrant group's story, the consistency with which, in the case of Irish emigrant romances, the female character is either English or Anglo-Irish, points towards a developing theme of scripting and casting. By doing this, productions therefore remove Irish Catholic women (in reality the single largest emigrant group from Ireland to America) from a central role in their narratives. A similar process of ethnically gendered representation would occur in the later, and infinitely more successful film, *Titanic*, in 1997. As Martin McLoone has commented of that film's early scenes of socialising among the steerage passengers, 'under the cultural leadership of the Irish ... The contrast that the film sets up is, therefore, as much about ethnicity as it is about class – the communal and public world of ethnic diversity juxtaposed to the stifling and individualistic world of WASP privilege.'[54]

What McLoone might have added here is that such representations are also as much about gender as they are about class or ethnicity. It is the Irish Catholic (and therefore working-class) man whose energy and cultural exuberance acts as a liberating force for an English or Anglo-Irish (and therefore aristocratic) woman, allowing her to make use of the freedoms offered by the New World. With reference to the discussion above concerning the act of emigration itself functioning as a process of masculinisation for both sexes, it would appear, in these cross-class romance narratives, that the female characters' higher social status also acts to 'protect' them from the loss of femininity which lower-class Irish Catholic women might be seen to experience as a result of emigration.

Also released in 1992, *Patriot Games* was the first of two remarkably similar depictions of pathological Irish masculinity; it would be followed in 1997 by *The Devil's Own*, both films using the classic 'IRA gangster' format to project their Irish representations. Although their plots are superficially different, both *Patriot Games* and *The Devil's Own* centre upon increasingly violent contact between male IRA activists and an idealised Irish-American family, who in both cases are ultimately saved by their father-figures. Not only do the films therefore have in common their use of lone Irish men threatening the safety and stability of an Irish-American family unit, but, significantly, in both cases the heroic Irish-American paterfamilias is played by Harrison Ford.

The connections between Ford's star persona and the concept of heroic patriarchy are highly significant in the ways they are contrasted with Irish masculinity. By the 1990s, Ford was a major Hollywood star, largely as a result of the box-office success of the

Indiana Jones cycle of films, which had nostalgically reintroduced the stoical hero to Hollywood action stories. And in 1988 he had starred in *Frantic*, in which he played a man rescuing his wife from kidnappers, a process which also involved choosing to remain faithful to her despite the availability of a much younger woman. This established him as a 'heroic husband', a persona which was repeated in the 1993 production of *The Fugitive*, where his character, Dr Richard Kimble, proves himself innocent of his wife's murder, bringing the real killer to justice in the process. *Patriot Games* and *The Devil's Own*, then, were released at the height of Ford's signification of an old-fashioned heroic family man. *Patriot Games* in particular is distinguished by its presentation of an idealised – and Irish-American – family. This is reinforced by the casting of Anne Archer as Ford's on-screen wife, who is pregnant throughout the film. In the early 1990s, Archer's star status was largely based upon her role as the idealised and ultimately triumphant wife in the hugely successful *Fatal Attraction* (1987), a film with a long after-life in the popular imagining of contemporary American family values. *Patriot Games*, then, presented a powerful depiction of a model Irish-American family, through both the internal logic of the film and the external logic of the stars' public personae, a depiction matched to an only slightly lesser degree by that of *The Devil's Own* five years later.

10. The Irish-American *pater familias* – Harrison Ford presides over the family dinner table at the beginning of *The Devil's Own* (1997).

In opposition to this representation of Irish-American family values, both films posit a pathological, savage and yet also largely sexless version of Irish masculinity. *Patriot Games* casts Sean Bean as a rebel IRA man who seeks revenge against Ford's Jack Ryan for the death of his brother in a failed assassination attempt on a member of the British royal family. To this end he follows Ryan back to the United States, specifically targeting his family for attack. His murderously expressed affection for his brother is the sole display of emotional attachment made by Bean's character throughout the film, thus depicting him as a brutalised threat to wider American family or social values. Similarly, in *The Devil's Own*, Brad Pitt plays an IRA man placed as a lodger with the unwitting O'Meara family, thus bringing Irish violence into the middle-class Irish-American home in the most literal fashion. The casting of Brad Pitt, an established Hollywood leading man, in the role of the IRA man would suggest an unusually heroic depiction, and indeed McLoone points out that 'he is probably the screen's most attractive IRA man ever and he is certainly the most smoothly efficient in the tradition of the American hero ... The film's strength as a genre piece is that it sets in conflict two equally attractive American heroes.'[55] Despite this generic attractiveness, however, Pitt's character does not have any emotional or sexual relationships which compare to those of the character played by Ford, and, as with Bean's IRA man in *Patriot Games*, is presented as an example of the ways in which Irish masculinity has been damaged by the brutalising effects of the Troubles. In both films, this is played out narratively through the contrasting of the Irish-American family men's roles as public servants against the Irish men's roles as loners whose values and loyalties are tribal rather than civic. As the promotional slogan for *The Devil's Own* expressed this manifestation of competing masculinities, 'one man trapped by Destiny, another bound by Duty'.

Later in the 1990s several independent Irish-American films were released, dealing with the social experience of the new generation of largely illegal Irish immigrants in New York. Of these, *2By4*, made in 1998, portrayed the marginalised and lonely existence of a group of construction workers whose monotonous and exploitative employment is relieved only by extravagantly destructive alcohol and drug-use. *2By4* is a particularly clear departure from traditional narratives of Irish emigration and Irish-American community life in that its story revolves around the after-effects of sexual abuse together with the expression of male homosexuality.[56] Johnnie, the film's central character, is gradually forced to accept his emerging memories of abuse by his uncle (now his employer in New York) as well as his previously repressed sexual orientation.

11. Irish masculinity bringing violence into an Irish-American home – Harrison Ford is attacked as a result of taking in Brad Pitt's on-the-run IRA man in *The Devil's Own* (1997).

One of the film's more significant manoeuvres is the way in which it intertwines ethnic and sexual identities within its narrative. As McLoone has argued, 'there is no sentimental ethnic solidarity... across the different ethnic divides and the Irish workers are shown to be unthinkingly racist in their attitudes to other minorities. The film's final denouement is initiated after a particularly ignorant display of racial abuse by the main protagonist.'[57] As well as the hostility between, for the most part, equally marginalized contemporary minority groups, the film also displays some intriguing hierarchies of ethnic sexuality and desirability. When Trump, Johnnie's abusive uncle and construction boss, uses the mens' wages to pay for violent gay sex, it is with an African-American prostitute whose ethnicity is very clearly marked as being the basis for his appeal. Equally, during Johnnie's excursions into New York's gay bars and brothels, he is usually a rare white face among predominantly African-American and Latino crowds. It is in this context that his whiteness, along with a style of dress which displays his blue-collar, manual-worker status, becomes gendered in a very specific way. In these scenes set in the city's gay community, Johnnie's raw physicality is starkly contrasted with the spectacular and theatrical display of African-American and Latino drag queens, as well as the fey presence of Christian, the very young white Australian he picks up in one of the bars. In the hierarchical relationships between different ethnic minorities which the film presents, then, the Irish male is positioned, in effect, as 'rough trade'. This representation within the context of gay sexual politics is also mirrored in the world of work, where they perform hard manual labour.

Far removed though *2By4* is from the style, content or form of representation in films such as *Patriot Games*, *The Devil's Own* or *Far and Away*, its socio-sexual representation of Irish masculinity is in fact similar to that of these more standard Hollywood narratives, and in all of these films, Irish masculinity is associated with a low social status. This similarity between mainstream Hollywood and relatively avant-garde film portrayals of Irish masculinity is sugges- tive of a deeply embedded archetype working within both forms of representation. Moreover, when it is directly compared to Irish- American masculinity, as in *Patriot Games* or *The Devil's Own*, it is typically found to be inferior or damaged. Equally, in sexual rela- tionships, Irish men are frequently depicted as being the subject of social descending for their partners, whether these are English women or Latino drag queens. As will be discussed below, such a classification of inter-ethnic sexual relationships does not rest on a simplistic denigration of Irishness *per se*. Instead, there appears to be a graduated and highly complex web of comparative hierarchies. For example, while Irish masculinity is frequently compared negatively with Irish-American masculinity, it may appear as a positive feature when it is presented as a marker of generalised ethnicity contrasted with a lack of any ethnic identification at all, as in *Titanic*. There is also, from the 1990s onwards, a clear tendency for both Irish and Irish-American masculinities, even when marking a low socio- economic status, to be presented as positive examples of a predominantly white, working-class, masculine heroism, as in the film *The Matchmaker* and the television series *The Fighting Fitzgeralds*.[58]

DISAPPEARING IRISHWOMEN

Another feature of *2By4* is its presentation of the contemporary Irish-American experience as a resolutely male one – an impression only added to by its unusual focus on Irish homosexuality. This is in fact entirely in keeping with what has been probably the single most dominant trend in American representations of Irishness during the last decade of the twentieth century – the clear absence of Irish (or, for the most part, Irish-American) women from narrative representations of any kind. During the revival in Irish-themed films during the 1990s, representation has been heavily gendered in that Irishness has become almost entirely associated with maleness. None of the 1990s films dealing with Irishness discussed above has any Irish (with the exception of Anglo-Irish) women characters, to the extent that narrative credibility is occasionally strained apparently for the sake of excluding them. The rebel IRA cell in *Patriot Games*, for example, has one female member – yet for reasons which remain completely unexplained within the film, she is actually an Englishwoman who periodically masquerades as Irish during para-military operations (this masquerade of Irish femininity, designed to seduce and then execute a senior IRA commander, consists of little more than the wearing of nothing but a long red wig along with her black underwear, but is nevertheless successful).

This absence of Irish women from American popular culture, maintained for more than a decade even in the face of narrative inco-herence, appears to point towards a consensus rejection of Irish femininity as a suitable object of desire in the late twentieth century. Given the difficulty of proving a negative, it is hard to account for this absence of Irish femininity from popular representation. However, by examining both the function of the Irish male repre-sentations which have flourished during the same period and the predominant models of ethnic femininity from which Irish women have apparently been excluded, it seems possible to suggest at least some plausible reasons for this dominant trend.

The 1990s were marked by frequent representations of Irish masculinity in the United States, in fictional narratives on film and television, in the news media coverage of the developing peace process, as well as in other cultural forms, particularly that of music. This was matched by the rapid Hollywood success of Irish actors such as Liam Neeson, Gabriel Byrne, Stephen Rea, Aidan Quinn and Colm Meaney, as well as their identifiably Irish-American counter-parts Matthew McConaughey, Denis Leary and Edward Burns. All of these actors have, at some point during the decade, worked on Irish-themed films and television, and their Irish ethnicity has also been a very important part of the star personae they have brought to other narratives.

While, as has been discussed above, those fictional narratives which have represented Irish masculinity in connection with Ireland itself have tended to concentrate upon a damaged and 'savage' sexu-ality, other narratives have used the gendered ethnicity of

Irish-American male sexuality as a way of recuperating white work-ing-class masculinity within an American context. Films such as *The Brothers McMullen* (1995) and *She's The One* (1996), as well as television shows such as Denis Leary's New York police sit-com *The Job* (2000) and Edward Burns' family sit-com *The Fighting Fitzgeralds* (2001) have all produced a heroic representation of specifically Irish-American blue-collar codes of behaviour and belief, a strain of popular representation which works against the predom-inant conventions of white middle-class or non-white working-class narratives in contemporary American culture since the 1980s.[59]

By comparison to this valorisation of white working-class masculinity, popular representations of ethnically distinct femininity have come, throughout the course of the 1990s, to focus increasingly upon Southern European or Latina women as idealised objects of desire. The careers of Hollywood actresses such as Penelope Cruz, Marisa Tomei and Jennifer Lopez among others have been based largely upon the representation of their 'Southern' femininity as warm, eroticised and authentically 'unrepressed'.[60] Indeed, the rapidly changing ideals of female physicality that have radiated out to all of the Western world from Hollywood from the late 1980s onwards could also be analysed in tandem with the rising popular-ity of this 'Southern' femininity; in particular, the uniform equation of bronzed skin and voluptuous body shape (naturally or otherwise in both cases) with female sexual attractiveness.

While the shift in idealised femininity should not be misinter-preted as a wholly approving response to Southern European or Latina female sexuality, it is clear from the developing careers of this new generation of actresses during the 1990s that they are increas-ingly associated with a now positively represented physical exuberance, eroticism and emotional openness. Such qualities are, of course, very different from the traditional representations of Irish femininity, which have tended to centre upon functional maternal-ism, stoical dependability and, above all else, chastity. It is this association between Irish female sexuality and traditional ideas of chastity which is perhaps the key to its lack of appeal in contempo-rary representations of ethnic femininity, and also the nexus around which these cultural associations are combined with more literal, physical markers of women as objects of sexual desire. In 2001 an article in the *Dubliner* magazine, entitled 'Whatever Happened to the Irish Actress?', attempted to delineate the reasons for their lack of success equivalent to their male counterparts. Citing the earlier examples of Maureen O'Hara, Greer Garson and Anjelica Huston, the article does concede that, 'while European actresses like Marlene Dietrich and Ingrid Bergman were defining screen seductiveness, Belfast-born Garson was the window-dressing in countless bland matinées. O'Hara epitomised de Valera's vision of the happy maiden (with a strong and fiery nature for good measure)...However, the Milltown lass was more girl-next-door than the subject of wicked fantasies.'[61]

The article goes on to refer to Grace Kelly as an Irish-American 'sex symbol', but in fact even this is revealing of the nature of ethnically Irish female sexual representations. While Kelly undoubtedly presented a more glamorous and sophisticated star persona than O'Hara's 'girl-next-door', it was nevertheless based on an icy unattainability, which, while perhaps not explicitly connected to her Irish ethnicity, may well have been bolstered by it. In more contemporary representation, where 'southern' female sexuality is, in Negra's description of Tomei's persona, presented as that of 'the restorative and primordial feminine',[62] and therefore as authentically 'natural' and unrepressed, Irish women's association with chastity is now positioned as a form of sexual repression, or even sexual pathology, in its subjugation of physical desire to social conventions. Ruth Barton has suggested that 'there is perhaps something just too imperious about the Maureen O'Hara type, too castrating, to cut much ice in a studio environment dedicated to the pursuit of blockbusters aimed at teenage boys'.[63]

This is borne out with great clarity in *Only the Lonely*, one of the very few 1990s Hollywood narratives to represent Irish women at all. Produced in 1991, it was Maureen O'Hara's first feature film in nearly twenty years, and provides a revealing re-reading of the ethnically specific femininity with which she was so long associated. O'Hara plays Rose, the widowed Irish mother of John Candy's lonely middle-aged policeman, Danny. The film's plot centres upon Rose's response when Danny, who lives at home with her, meets and falls in love with a young Polish woman. Rose meets this challenge to her domestic routine with her son, which is presented as a parody of marriage, with cruel disapproval and overtly racist attempts to sabotage the relationship, in a determination to maintain control over her son's life even at the expense of his happiness.

As McLoone has commented of the relationship between this casting of O'Hara and that of her role as Mary Kate in *The Quiet Man*: 'Maureen O'Hara was to play the other side of the duality of Irish stereotypical women when she returned to the screen after a long absence in 1991 to play the widowed mother who still regulates her son's sex life in Chris Columbus' romantic comedy *Only the Lonely*.'⁶⁴ McLoone points here towards the way in which O'Hara's character serves not only as a potential 'sequel' to her role as Mary Kate in *The Quiet Man*, but also to a much bleaker and less affectionate reading of Irish femininity. Rose is shown as not only controlling and destructive of her son's attempts at romantic and sexual happiness, but also as cold and repressed with regards to her own sexuality, demonstrated through her inability to accept affection or companionship from her Greek neighbour, played by Anthony Quinn. This darker interpretation of the Irish woman's traditional representation as a maternal and chaste figure is explicitly tied, within the film, to her racism (O'Hara's character, during the course of the film, racially abuses an almost exhaustive range of America's ethnic minorities), which is in turn, of course, tied to her own whiteness. Although *Only the Lonely* produces a narrative resolution to this conflict between mother and son which, by the end of the film, allows Candy's character to find romantic happiness and retain his mother's affection, this resolution is at best strained, and is still predicated upon the explicit need for Candy, as the Irish-American man, to escape from the Irish woman – an almost exact reversal of the process in earlier films such as *The Quiet Man*, where the Irish-American man is 'rewarded' with an Irish woman.

Given the lack of representation of Irish or Irish-American women within wider popular culture during the 1980s and 1990s, the continuation of Irish America's enthusiastic participation in the still popular Rose of Tralee competition is a notable exception in its celebration of Irish and Irish-American femininity. What is also noticeable about the competition during the late twentieth century is the extent to which it has, rather than attempting to 'modernise' itself, remained fundamentally unchanged from its 1950s origins. The contestants have, in common with the entrants to most beauty pageants, become increasingly more middle-class and academically qualified, and they have also tended to travel to Ireland with their boyfriends as well as their families.⁶⁵ However, they must still be single, under twenty-six, with no children, and be judged according to the same criteria as were outlined above. The continuance of the Festival's highly unusual (within the context of international pageant procedures) provision of 'escorts' for the Roses throughout the duration of the contest only underlines the extent to which it is a celebration of traditional concepts of Irish femininity, given that the Festival very clearly structures the escorts' role as that of chaperones rather than 'dates' (the Festival's determination to maintain this platonic, chaperoning and 'traditional' role for escorts was under-lined in 1994, when two escorts were dismissed for 'inappropriate' behaviour during the competition).[66]

Irish America's continuing enthusiasm for the contest, however dated its concept and ideologies may appear to Irish audiences, may be related to the highly specific culture of beauty pageants in the United States, a culture which is particularly removed from European attitudes to such events. The continuance of the Rose of Tralee competition's celebration of the traditional image of Irish or Irish diaspora femininity as competent, wholesome and evincing a strong family-based identity therefore may well be more closely connected to the continuance of such imagery in American beauty pageants in general than to its specific connections to contemporary Ireland.[67]

CONCLUSION

This chapter has attempted to analyse the shifting conventions of gender and sexual representation of Irish ethnicity in American and Irish-American popular culture during the later twentieth century. Through an examination of the differences in representation not only of male and female but also of Irish and Irish-American arche-types throughout this period, it becomes possible to understand more clearly the importance of gender to the process of ethnic repre-sentation in a diaspora culture such as that of Irish America.

What emerges from this chronological analysis, then, is the extent to which Irishness has been consistently identifiable, in these texts, with heavily gendered archetypes whose power has remained reso-nant within popular cultural forms across many decades. This chapter has not been concerned with the 'truth' of these representa-tions. To concentrate upon this, through the examination of concepts such as 'stereotyping', is to overlook the more valuable understanding of the *functions* of gendered ethnicity in popular representation. Irishness, as expressed through representations of individualised gender and sexual roles, has been central to the production and circulation of cultural ideologies in the Irish-American diaspora as well as in the wider American society. In

particular, the intersections between Irish and Irish-American representations are revealing of the ways in which the diaspora
community has utilised gendered imaginings of Ireland in order to
negotiate their own identities in both national and international
contexts.

The texts examined in this chapter reveal a complex and varying
system of interactions between gendered and sexualised ethnic identities, including Irish and Irish-American as well as male and female,
heterosexual and homosexual. Moreover, it is frequently in the interactions among these identities, rather than with other, non-Irish,
archetypes, that Irish ethnicity has been most frequently and popularly represented. In particular, for much of the late twentieth
century, the encounter between Irish-American masculinity and Irish
femininity has been the predominant trope. The reasons for this are
deeply rooted in the ways in which the two nations themselves were
gendered. Indeed, what emerges most clearly from this examination
of gendered representations within the Irish-American diaspora is
the extent to which the national identities of both Ireland and the
United States are reflected and negotiated within these gendered
narratives. Most of the changes in representation of gendered ethnicities can therefore be mapped onto changes within the relationship
between the two national identities throughout the twentieth
century.

The centrality of gender roles to concepts of national identity, as
well as the particular complexity of diasporic identities within
nationalist frameworks, are therefore clear in the ways in which
Irishness and Irish-Americanness are both gendered and sexually
linked in many popular narratives.

In early twentieth-century narratives, for example, when America
was still pursuing an assimilationist policy, Irish masculinity was
presented as either questionable or threatening – in both cases due
to its perceived closeness to a 'mother' Ireland. Following the end of
the Second World War, however, after Irish-American men were
considered to have 'proved' both their masculinity and patriotism in
military service, their masculinity was frequently figured as being
quintessentially heroic. It is no coincidence, then, that it was during
this period that the Irish-American man was frequently the centre of
narratives in which he married an Irish girl, thus completing an
Oedipal rite of passage to manhood. The beginning of the Troubles
in the late 1960s, however, once more raised the spectre of dangerously 'tribal' Irish masculinity – which was then contrasted with the

civic responsibility of its Irish-American equivalents. Since the late 1980s, however, the developing project of recuperating working-class white masculinity has begun to co-opt Irishness with increasing frequency, as a result of its position as an 'acceptable' form of whiteness. The development of the peace process in Northern Ireland, from the mid-1990s, has obviously aided this project, as it begins to liberate Irish masculinity from tropes of violence.

Depictions of femininity, on the other hand, tended to centre on young Irish-American women during the early twentieth century, with an emphasis upon their supposedly successful assimilation. Those of the 1940s to the 1960s, however, foregrounded Irish women as salvational guardians of traditional femininity, and in particular as appropriately feminine and maternal partners for heroic Irish-American men. In the 1970s and early 1980s, when the predominant images of Irishness were those occurring in the news media, women tended to be presented only occasionally, and then as mourning mothers, wives and daughters, a reversion to an even older trope of representation, originating in the nineteenth century. From the early 1980s, however, female Irishness became an increasingly rare form of representation – not, it would appear, because that particular archetype no longer has any meaning in the popular imagination, but because the meaning it does have no longer serves a useful function in negotiating current anxieties and desires concerning ethnic and national gender roles for the diaspora.

These shifting patterns of representation, then, indicate the extent to which gendered and sexualised archetypes have been central to the negotiation of Irish America's identity during the later twentieth century. Such archetypes, in their particular diasporic forms, have played a crucial role in defining and redefining the Irish-American place within the national and international relationships which have themselves been heavily gendered. The correlation between ethnicity and gender, in a diasporic context, is therefore revealed as a circular and self-perpetuating process in which both sides are positioned and repositioned as functions of identity according to the needs of both the diasporic community and the wider American society.

NOTES

1   John Hill, 'Images of Violence in Irish Cinema', in Kevin Rockett, Luke Gibbons and John Hill (eds), *Cinema and Ireland* (London: Croom Helm, 1987), p. 150.

2   Benedict Anderson, *Imagined Communities: Reflections on the Origin and Spread of Nationalism* (London: Verso, 1991), p. 143.
3   Andrew Parker, 'Introduction', in Andrew Parker et al. (eds), *Nationalisms and Sexualities* (London: Routledge, 1992), p. 6.
4   Ibid.
5   Nira Yuval-Davis, 'Gender and Nation', in Rick Wilford and Robert L. Miller (eds), *Women, Ethnicity and Nationalism: The Politics of Transition* (London: Routledge, 1998), p. 29.
6   Andrew Parker has commented that 'in anti-colonial struggles...feminist programs have been sacrificed to the cause of national liberation and, in the aftermath of independence, women have been consigned to their formerly "domestic" roles', and Sarah Benton has argued that Irish nationalism was influenced by the British and American association of both personal and national self-control with the virtues of 'manliness'. See Andrew Parker, 'Introduction', p. 7, and Sarah Benton, 'Women Disarmed: The Militarisation of Politics in Ireland 1913–23', *Feminist Review*, 50, Summer 1995, p. 148.
7   Anne McClintock, '"No Longer a Future Heaven": Gender, Race and Nationalism', in Anne McClintock, Aamir Mufti and Ella Shohat (eds), *Dangerous Liaisons: Gender, Nation and Postcolonial Perspectives* (Minneapolis: University of Minnesota Press, 1997), p. 92.
8   David Savran, *Taking it Like a Man: White Masculinity, Masochism and Contemporary American Culture* (New Jersey, NJ: Princeton University Press, 1998), p. 269.
9   Cited in Savran, *Taking it Like a Man*, p. 270.
10   Cited in Parker, 'Introduction', p. 5.
11   See Chapter 2, above, for a fuller explanation of the 'melting-pot' thesis and the historical development of its influence on Irish-American ethnicity.
12   Kevin Rockett, 'The Irish Migrant and Film', in Patrick O'Sullivan (ed.), *The Irish World Wide: History, Heritage and Identity, Volume III: The Creative Migrant* (Leicester: Leicester University Press, 1994), p. 175.
13   Diane Negra, *Off-White Hollywood: American Culture and Ethnic Female Stardom* (London: Routledge, 2001), p. 26.
14   Ibid., p. 52.
15   Peter Quinn, 'Looking for Jimmy', *The World of Hibernia*, Vol. 4, No. 4, Spring 1999, pp. 125–30.
16   Bronwen Walter, *Outsiders Inside: Whiteness, Place and Irish Women* (London: Routledge, 2001), p. 64.
17   Peter Quinn, 'Looking for Jimmy', p. 125.
18   Ibid.
19   *The Quiet Man*, dir. John Ford (Republic Studios, 1952).
20   Des McHale, *The Complete Guide to The Quiet Man* (Belfast: Appletree, 1999), p. 52.
21   Luke Gibbons, *The Quiet Man* (Cork: Cork University Press, 2002), p. 59.
22   Ibid., p. 73.
23   Elizabeth Butler-Cullingford, *Ireland's Others: Gender and Ethnicity in Irish Literature and Popular Culture* (Cork: Cork University Press, 2001), p. 169.
24   Luke Gibbons, 'Romanticism, Realism and Irish Cinema', in Kevin Rockett, Luke Gibbons and John Hill (eds), *Cinema and Ireland* (London: Croom Helm, 1987), p. 228.
25   Ruth Barton points out that *Top O' the Morning* prefigures *The Quiet Man* in other, more general ways, arguing that: 'It knowingly plays nostalgia off against comedy, inviting its audience to enjoy and recognise its sentimental vision (and to buy its soundtrack). Just as *The Quiet Man* was to do, it cele-

brates Ireland as it has been constructed by the emigrant imagination, as a country far removed from America by time and space.' Ruth Barton, *Acting Irish in Hollywood: From Fitzgerald to Farrell* (Dublin: Irish Academic Press, 2006), p. 38.

26   Martin McLoone, *Irish Film: The Emergence of a Contemporary Cinema* (London: British Film Institute, 2000), p. 50.

27   American television portrayed this domesticated agenda with particular frequency, in programmes such as the sit-coms *Father Knows Best*, produced by CBS/NBC from 1954 to 1962, and *I Love Lucy*, produced by CBS from 1951 to 1956. The films and star personae of a number of Hollywood actresses during the 1950s were also influential in this regard, most notably the career and public image of Doris Day.

28   *O'Hara's Holiday*, dir. Peter Bryan (Tribune Films Incorporated 1960). In only a slightly different storyline, the travelogue *Honeymoon in Ireland*, dir. unknown (Bord Fáilte, 1963), features Bill, a non-Irish-American man, visiting Ireland on a honeymoon with Irish-born Mary. Again, it is noticeable that an Irish woman is presented as an ideal partner. For further discussion of both tourist films, see Chapter 3 above.

29   *National Geographic Magazine*, March 1961, p. 297.

30   John Hill, 'Images of Violence', in Kevin Rockett et al., *Cinema and Ireland*, p. 166.

31   The effort to imbue beauty pageants with an air of respectability is almost as old as the pageants themselves. P.T. Barnum had first tried to promote such events in 1854, but had been unable to persuade 'decent' young women to compete. As early as the 1880s, pageants were offering bridal trousseaux as prizes in an effort to signal their innocence and suitability for marriageable girls. See Colleen Ballerino Cohen, Richard Wilk, with Beverly Stoeltje, 'Introduction: Beauty Queens on the Global Stage', in Colleen Ballerino Cohen, Richard Wilk and Beverly Stoeltje (eds), *Beauty Queens on the Global Stage: Gender, Contests and Power* (London: Routledge, 1996), p. 4, and Elwood Watson and Daray Martin, 'The Miss America Pageant: Pluralism, Femininity and Cinderella All in One', *Journal of Popular Culture*, 34(1), Summer 2000, pp. 109–10.

32   Colleen Ballerino Cohen et al. (eds), *Beauty Queens on the Global Stage*, pp. 4–5.

33   Of course, the Rose of Tralee competition has always appealed to the world-wide Irish diaspora, and as such has had great popularity far beyond Irish America. Nevertheless, as the history of beauty pageants indicates, even those held outside the United States have been strongly influenced by American values and popular cultural forms, and therefore it seems reasonable to conclude that the Rose of Tralee would have had a particularly well-understood place in Irish-American culture.

34   J. Cyril Gavaghan and Gene O'Donnell, 'The *Rose of Tralee*: 'The Greatest Free Show on Earth'?', in James J. Ward (ed.), *Cases in Marketing Management and Strategy* (Dublin: The Marketing Institute Ireland, 1998), p. 45.

35   Robert H. Lavenda, "It's Not a Beauty Pageant!' Hybrid Ideology in Minnesota Community Queen Pageants', in Colleen Ballerino Cohen et al. (eds), *Beauty Queens on the Global Stage*, p. 35.

36   *Time Magazine*, 11 July 1960, p. 20. See Chapter 1, above, for a full discussion of the uses and importance of John F. Kennedy's ethnicity during his presidential campaign of 1960.

37   *Life Magazine*, 17 March 1961, p. 113.

38   See Chapter 1, above, for a fuller discussion of the lack of news coverage of Ireland in the mainstream American press, prior to the outbreak of the Troubles.

39   Fergal Tobin, *The Best of Decades: Ireland in the 1960s* (Dublin: Gill and Macmillan, 1996), p. 230.

40   *New York Times*, 1 February 1972, p. 2.

41   *Washington Post*, 1 February 1972, pp. 1–2.

42   David Lloyd, *Ireland After History* (Cork: Cork University Press, 1999) p. 59.

43   See *Irish People*, 23 May 1981, p. 3, and 'Glasnevin', *Weekly Freeman*, 11 October 1891, in L. Perry Curtis Jr., *Images of Erin In the Age of Parnell* (Dublin: National Library of Ireland, 2000), p. 22.

44   See Chapter 1, above, for a full discussion on the importance for Ireland of the 'special relationship' between the United States and Great Britain.

45   *Philadelphia Inquirer*, 6 May 1981, p. 21.

46   Diane Negra, 'Consuming Ireland: Lucky Charms Cereal, Irish Spring Soap and 1–800–Shamrock', in *Cultural Studies*, Vol. 15, No. 1, January 2001, p. 85.

47   Ibid., p. 88.

48   *Irish Echo*, 9 October 1976, p. 13.

49   *National Geographic*, September 1969, p. 1.

50   *National Geographic*, April 1981, p. 2.

51   Robert Ballagh, 'Getting Away From Outworn Shibboleths of Irishness', *Sunday Independent*, 9 November 1980, p. 12.

52   Barbara O'Connor, 'Myths and Mirrors: Tourist Images and National Identity', in Barbara O'Connor and Michael Cronin (eds), *Tourism in Ireland: A Critical Analysis* (Cork: Cork University Press, 1997), p. 74.

53   *The Manions of America* (ABC/EMI, 1981).

54   Martin McLoone, *Irish Film*, p. 45.

55   Ibid., p. 66.

56   The film's agenda to represent Irish homosexuality is somewhat undermined by its use of childhood sexual abuse as an apparently causal explanation for the central character's adult sexuality, as well as by its consistent linking of male homosexuality to sado-masochism. It is, nevertheless, a groundbreaking attempt to represent Irish sexuality as being more diverse than is usually allowed, even within the independent film industry.

57   Martin McLoone, *Irish Film*, p. 196.

58   *The Fighting Fitzgeralds* (NBC, 2001) and *The Matchmaker*, dir. Mark Joffe (Polygram/Working Title, 1997). For more discussion of *The Matchmaker*, see Chapter 2, above.

59   For a discussion of this mobilisation of an 'innocent' Irish-American masculinity, see Diane Negra, 'Irishness, Innocence, and American Identity Politics before and after September 11', in Diane Negra (ed.), *The Irish In Us: Irishness, Performativity, and Popular Culture* (Durham: Duke University Press, 2006), pp. 354–71.

60   An especially striking example of this representation of 'Southern' femininity as emotionally open and healing is that of *Spanglish*, dir. James L. Brooks (Columbia Pictures Corporation, 2004). The film centres upon the relationship between a white upper-middle-class family and their Mexican maid. The maid, played by Spanish actress Paz Vega, is presented throughout as emotionally intuitive and a restorative force for family values within the household. Her 'warm' femininity is contrasted throughout in an extremely positive way to that of Téa Leoni's wife and mother, while Leoni is presented in the film as exceptionally 'white', both physically and culturally.

61 'Whatever Happened to the Irish Actress?', *Dubliner*, November 2001, Issue 9, p. 17.
62 Negra, *Off-White Hollywood*, p. 150.
63 Barton, *Acting Irish in Hollywood*, p. 224.
64 Martin McLoone, *Irish Film*, p. 50.
65 As Gavaghan and O'Donnell note, 'In 1992, with the exception of one who was still studying, all entrants had primary degrees in subjects as diverse as fine arts and political science and several were studying for post-graduate degrees'. See J. Cyril Gavaghan and Gene O'Donnell, 'The *Rose of Tralee*', p. 48.
66 *Irish Times*, August 1994, p. 5.
67 The Rose of Tralee's continuing appeal to Irish America is in some contrast to its reception in other quarters. The local organising committees of the United Kingdom broke away from the official Tralee Festival and established their own Irish Rose competition in 2000, after a disagreement about funding allocations – a decision which also suggested a willingness by the Irish-British diaspora to perform their own validations of ethnic ideals. In Ireland itself, the Festival's on-stage competition is televised live over two nights, and achieves very high audience figures, usually ranking only slightly below the Eurovision Song Contest in RTE's list of most-watched programmes. This comparison is significant for more than mere viewing figures, however, as the Rose of Tralee audience in Ireland is divided between a traditional constituency who enjoy it at face value and a mainly younger audience who tend to watch it ironically, as they would any other beauty pageant or, indeed, the Eurovision Song Contest. See the *Guardian*, 21 August 2000, for a discussion of the conflict between the Festival and its British organising committees, and J. Cyril Gavaghan and Gene O'Donnell, 'The *Rose of Tralee*', for detailed viewing figures for the Festival on RTE during the 1990s.

5

Mapping the Diaspora: Theorising Irish-American Identity

DIASPORA STUDIES

WITHIN RECENT cultural and postcolonial studies, much work has been produced on both the concept of diasporas, and their position within the (typically) metropolitan centres in which they are concentrated.[1] There have, since the 1990s, been an increasing number of attempts to define and characterise the nature and form of diasporas across the world. One of the most innovative and influential exponents of this work has been James Clifford, whose radical redevelopment of his own field of anthropology has had a lasting impact upon the ways in which diasporas are considered. Insisting upon the need to focus on a wider conception of 'native' identities, Clifford argues that

> diasporic conjunctures invite a reconception – both theoretical and political – of familiar notions of ethnicity and identity... Unresolved historical dialogues between continuity and disruption, essence and positionality, homogeneity and differences (cross-cutting 'us' and 'them') characterize diasporic articulations. Such cultures of displacement and transplantation are inseparable from specific, often violent, histories of economic, political, and cultural interaction, histories that generate what might be called *discrepant cosmopolitanisms*.[2] [original emphasis]

Within his own discipline, Clifford has produced a radical change in the way that populations which have developed significant diasporas have been assessed and studied – most significantly, perhaps, by challenging the concept of the 'native'. As Appadurai has commented, in traditional discourse, 'natives are not only persons who are from certain places, and belong to those places, but they are also those who are somehow incarcerated, or confined, in those places'.[3]

Clifford's reconceptualising of what he terms 'dwelling-in-travel' has done much to shift this perception of 'native' cultures, seeing the development of diasporic perspectives as offering a challenge to the essentialising nature of ethnicity, bound as he sees it to place and concepts of 'home'.[4] As an alternative to that form of ethnicity, Clifford instead celebrates the hybridity he sees as existing in the 'discrepant cosmopolitanisms' of diasporas, arguing that they 'mediate, in a lived tension, the experiences of separation and entanglement, of living here and remembering/desiring another place'.[5] As Floya Anthius has pointed out, Clifford sees the hybridity of diaspora cultures acting as a challenge to ethnic identities founded on essentialism and concepts of purity, preferring instead to concentrate upon 'routes' rather than 'roots'.[6]

Largely because of his focus upon hybridity, Clifford rarely attempts to define categories and schemas into which different diasporas may be put, arguing instead that 'we should be wary of constructing our working definition of a term like *diaspora* by recourse to an "ideal type", with the consequence that groups become identified as more or less diasporic, having only two, or three, or four of the basic six features'.[7] This rejection of schematic definitions is in sharp contrast to other theorists, whose attempts to develop categories of diasporic experience have marked one of the other major tendencies of the last decade of diaspora studies. Robin Cohen, for example, has proposed a 'diasporic rope' consisting of seven identifying 'strands'. These are:

> 1) a collective memory and myth about the homeland; 2) an idealization of the supposed ancestral home; 3) a return movement [actual or in support for homeland activities ie. revolution, business, etc]; 4) a strong ethnic group consciousness sustained over a long time; 5) a troubled relationship with the host society; 6) a sense of solidarity with co-ethnic members in other countries; 7) the possibility of a distinctive, creative, enriching life in tolerant host countries.[8]

This 'diasporic rope' echoes a similar schema of 'shared characteristics' of diasporas suggested by William Safran in 1994.[9] Such approaches are inclined to lead to the development of hierarchical structures of diasporas, with some being categorised as being more authentically diasporic than others. While comparative studies of the differences between individual diasporas obviously have their uses, such a process of measurement leads, as Clifford points out, to a practice of exclusion or, at the very, of least hierarchical ranking. Instead, Clifford suggests, 'a polythetic field would seem most conducive to tracking (rather than policing) the contemporary range of diasporic forms'.[10]

Despite these theoretical differences among Clifford and other critics such as Cohen and Safran, there are also significant similarities between their approaches which have important implications for the study of the Irish-American diaspora. The most important of these is a widespread assumption that the diasporic condition is one experienced almost exclusively by non-white populations, and also that these diasporas are formed through the process of moving from the developing world into the West. This can be seen, for example, in the lists included in Cohen's table of horticultural 'types' of diasporas. One of the very few diaspora theorists to mention the Irish experience even in passing, Cohen nevertheless does not discuss it in any detail at all. Many other theorists, such as Clifford, Hall or Appadurai, do not give the Irish (or any other white diasporas) any consideration at all. Instead, diaspora theory has tended to develop around considerations of population movements from areas such as India, Africa, South-East Asia and the Caribbean, towards areas such as Britain, the United States and other Western nations. While the reasons for such studies are both obvious and valid, the lack of attention paid to certain other groups, of whom the Irish would be just one, suggests a number of underlying assumptions regarding the nature and acceptable form of diasporas.

A highly notable feature of diaspora studies over the last decade is that, due perhaps to its origins in both anthropology and post-colonial studies, little if any attention has been paid to the movement of white populations, whether from the absolutely privileged West of nations such as Britain, Canada or the United States, or the relatively privileged West such as Ireland or Southern Europe. Indeed, it is worth noting that to speak of a 'United States diaspora', for example, appears oxymoronic within the context of diasporic theory, despite the fact that there are indeed American communities in almost every major city around the world. This suggests that there is a strong assumption within such theory that diasporas are not only racially defined by non-whiteness (under which there lies another assumption that Americans are exclusively white), but also presumed to be indefinitely excluded and non-privileged within their host societies. This therefore excludes absolutely privileged emigrant groups such as Americans from being considered as diasporic, as their movement, even in its first generation, is enacted within a rhetoric of agency and advantage. Commenting upon this within a discussion of the recurring botanical metaphors of diaspora, Malkki has argued that this situation is mirrored by the differences between a transplantation and an uprooting, suggesting that 'the notion of transplantation...generally evokes live, viable roots. It strongly suggests, for example, the colonial and postcolonial, usually privileged, category of "expatriates" who pick up their roots in an orderly manner...in uprooting, the orderliness of transplantation disappears. Instead, broken and dangling roots predominate – roots that threaten to wither.'[11]

However, this approach also has important implications for a relatively privileged population such as the Irish-American diaspora. As such, it is in many ways in keeping with certain schools of thought within the Irish-American historical academy. The Irish-American achievement of a notable degree of relative privilege, from approximately Kennedy's 1960 election onwards, was almost immediately followed by pronouncements that their new-found social mobility had resulted in a 'withering' of the diasporic roots.[12] Thus the identities of diasporic groups such as Irish America, with histories of parlous first-generation emigration, followed by long struggles to achieve stability, are frequently pathologised not only in their first-generation form, for being 'uprooted' from their original homeland, but also in their later generations, for becoming fully 'embedded' in their new location.

The gendered nature of many discussions of diaspora and ethnicity has only recently begun to be analysed from a theoretical perspective which seeks to deconstruct the masculinisation of the topic. Within a specifically Irish context, the work of Hasia Diner and Ide O'Carroll from the 1980s onwards sought to reinscribe the female experience of emigration from Ireland to the United States into discussions of the history of the Irish diaspora.[13] Focusing particularly upon the nineteenth- and early twentieth-century histories of Irish America, their work was an invaluable retrieval of what was, in fact, a major feature of emigration from Ireland and settlement in the United States. The specifics of the individual and group experience of Irish women migrants to America, having been largely overlooked prior to this period, have since become increasingly well-archived and analysed.

However, there still remains a considerable amount of work to be done on the gendered nature of theoretical and historical frameworks of thought regarding the processes of migration, settlement and diaspora-formation. Given the extent to which the concepts of nations and nationality themselves have historically been gendered, along with the equal extent to which travel, and therefore migration, have also been considered in terms of underlying assumptions about the travelling subject's gender, the entire process of diaspora-formation needs to be reconsidered in ways which delineate and problematise such assumptions.[14] It is precisely the gendering of both the nation and its citizens/subjects that in turn has led to influential genderings of diasporas, albeit through complex processes of association. If the nation, as it is conceived of as a home, has, in virtually all patriarchal societies, been gendered as female, while 'her' citizens/subjects have been gendered as male, this has clear implications for the process of leaving home, and also of course for the later process of establishing a new home elsewhere.

As Bronwen Walter has argued, for example, with regard to Brah and Clifford's theories of diaspora as 'dwelling-in-displacement': 'The place which is present in notions of both placement and displacement is "home".'[15] And the concept of 'home' of course is always already gendered as female, whether in the literal form of a home, established and maintained by a woman as 'home-maker', or in the symbolic form of a national home, characterised as a nurturing female body – in the Irish case, that of 'Mother Ireland'. In both cases, this 'home' is associated, as are its female occupants, with tradition, cultural preservation and, above all else, stability. As Doreen Massey has argued: 'The most common formulations of the concept of geographical place in current debate associates [sic] it with stasis and nostalgia, and with an enclosed security.'[16] To return to Walter's argument, however, the connections made between 'home' and gendered national or diasporic identities become particularly clear when the subject of migration and resettlement is raised. As Walter notes: 'The phrase "a woman's place is in the home" denotes simultaneously a social position and a geographic location, and implies the binary opposite for men.'[17] The implications of this long-standing set of associations for women with stability, home and tradition and those for men with movement, travel and modernity have obvious connections to the ways in which specific diasporas such as Irish America have been conceptualised and represented. In particular, they highlight the roots of a subtle but long-standing connection made between leaving the feminised national home in Ireland and a process of 'masculinisation through migration' to diaspora nations such as the United States. The implications of this process for both Irish men *and* women are obviously very important not only for the ways in which the Irish-American diaspora would be represented within the United States, but also for the ways in which its continued connections to Ireland would be viewed.[18]

The practice of identifying continued Irish-American interaction with Ireland, especially that centred around a 'return' to the homeland, with sentiment, irrationality and even un-Americanness, can therefore be traced in part to the underlying gendered associations of both Irish and American identities, as well as those of the diaspora themselves. Diaspora studies therefore need not only to interrogate the specifically different experiences of individual diasporic women and their identity-formation, but also to extend this interrogation into the gendered nature of many of the theories underpinning the ways in which diasporic identity is formed.

The political associations between a diaspora such as Irish America and its Irish homeland can also be seen to occupy a theoretical terrain riven with many of the central questions raised by diaspora theory, as well as those of ethnic identity and history within the United States. In the 1960s, Thomas N. Brown argued that earlier, nineteenth-century Irish-American political interventions in Ireland had been predicated upon a belief that the diaspora's citizen status within the United States would remain open to question until the Irish in Ireland were also citizens of an independent nation; he suggested that 'Irish nationalism was its unifying cement and the establishment of Irish freedom an important purpose. But in fact Irish-American nationalism was directed chiefly toward American, not Irish, ends. A free Ireland would reflect glory on the Fenians, but of more immediate and practical value was the use of the Brotherhood as an American pressure group.'[19]

This argument raises interesting questions about the complexity of diasporic ethnic and civic identities, and again highlights the extent to which such identities have been poised within the 'diasporic space' of their hyphenated ethnicities. In the post-Independence era of this study, it is noticeable that Irish-American political involvement with Ireland has continued to focus around the remaining aspect of British colonialism in the Irish State, in the form of the ongoing disputes in Northern Ireland. Following Brown's argument, it is interesting to consider that one motivating factor for this ongoing political intervention by later-generation Irish Americans is a residual feeling of unease about Irish-American status within the United States, while this aspect of colonial history in their ethnic homeland remains unresolved. Such a motivation would be underpinned by understandings of the concepts of nation, state and citizenship which are shared by both Ireland and the United States, concepts which rest upon ideas of agency, self-determination and independence. Such concepts are underpinned by, among other things, a highly gendered understanding of citizen status.

Yuval-Davis cites Rebecca Grant as arguing that national-citizen identities have predominantly been conceptualised as masculine, due to the early theories of nation–states propounded by Hobbes and Rousseau. Where Hobbes saw the nation-state's embodiment of the movement from nature to culture as being based on aggression, Rousseau characterised it as being based in reason. Both such characteristics, she points out, were considered 'male' attributes.[20] As such, therefore, Irish America's ascent to full citizen status within the United States, begun through the masculinising process of emigration, requires that the ethnic homeland also completes its masculinising journey to the status of independent nation–state. The irony of this process, of course, is that, in order for later-generation Irish Americans to exert diasporic influence in this regard, they must display a sense of loyalty to and identification with the 'mother' land, thus risking a questioning of the very masculinity which they seek to bolster. Such questioning does occur in, for example, Benedict Anderson's assessment of diasporic interventions in homeland conflicts. He writes dismissively of the diasporic subject's involvement in the conflicts of an 'imagined Heimat', where 'he does not intend to live, where he pays no taxes, where he cannot be arrested, where he will not be brought before the courts, and where he does not vote: in effect, a politics without responsibility or accountability'.[21] The similarity of this final assessment to the phrase 'power without responsibility', along with the negatively feminised associations of that phrase, are clear. While diasporic involvements in the politics of their ethnic homeland do raise a number of important questions regarding their place within the circuit of knowledge and experience of those debates or conflicts, condemnations such as Anderson's do not deal sufficiently with the changed circumstances of late twentieth-century mechanisms of information exchange, or indeed with the complex processes of diasporic national identifications. As Jolle Demmers has argued in her assessment of diasporic interventions in homeland conflicts, an important shortcoming of most theories of nationalism is that they 'all stressed the centrality of territory and boundaries: ethnic or national boundaries should not cut across political ones'.[22]

Another recurring debate surrounding diasporic cultures is that of terminology, and the perceived ideology underlying the different terms available. A wide array of terms is potentially applicable to the many different diasporas in different historical and geographical situations. As well as 'diaspora' itself, there are also immigrants; exiles; refugees; asylum-seekers; expatriates; nomads; guest-workers and cosmopolitans; as well as a host of finely delineated hyphenated terms such as, to cite just one, Black-British, which is used specifically to denote a British-born citizen of African or Caribbean descent. Clearly, not all of these terms could ever be used as synonyms for each other – there is a clear difference of both agency and intention between a cosmopolitan and an asylum-seeker. Indeed, the principal differentiation which can be applied to these terms is one of privilege (in absolute or relative terms). While refugees, asylum-seekers and guest-workers all clearly suggest a lack of privilege and influence, expatriates and cosmopolitans indicate a high status within their host society as well as their country of origin. The remaining terms, such as immigrants, exiles, nomads and diaspora itself, however, are ambiguous in this aspect of their meaning, and the extent to which they indicate a group's social, cultural or economic advantages or disadvantages becomes strongly dependent upon the context within which they are used.

While most 'immigrants' and 'exiles' tend, particularly in the first generation, to be at least relatively unprivileged, this is not necessarily a universal feature of these terms, and, crucially, this may change dramatically over succeeding generations. And, while 'nomad' is superficially suggestive of non-Westernised, economically disadvantaged groups, the adoption of the term by theorists such as Deleuze and Guattari as being descriptive of a profoundly Westernised 'nomadology', created within postmodern and globalised cultures and economies, has created a new double meaning for the term.[23] The term 'diaspora' has also been criticised by a number of theorists, and rejected by some societies, for its perceived depoliticisation of the processes of emigration and of the disadvantage that created it. From the perspective of the nation of origin, Floya Anthius has argued that 'some nations are reluctant to use the term diaspora to describe their *émigrés*, for it takes on a subversive meaning in the context of the nation-building project or contestation'.[24] Citing the example of Cyprus, Anthius describes the official designation of second- and third-generation Cypriots abroad as 'migrants' in order to 'retain the group' as part of a national project. In the case of Irish America (and Irish populations in the rest of the world), David Lloyd has expressed deep concerns regarding the adoption of the term 'diaspora' as a group descriptive. Highlighting the extent to which emigration from Ireland has become naturalised and therefore depoliticised, Lloyd cites the adoption of the term 'diaspora' for Irish America as one of the ways in which this is achieved. Arguing instead for the continued use of the term 'emigration', he suggests that:

> The term itself bears for us the reminder of the political and economic legacies of colonialism and, particularly where Irish emigrants meet those from other nations, the shock of recognition of our alignment with the postcolonial world that so many would have us forget... Where the invocation of 'diaspora' tends to emphasize, and even to celebrate, the mostly *cultural* by-products of nearly two centuries of Irish migrations, that of emigration keeps in mind both the economic and political reasons for our leaving and helps to affirm the vital relation between our historical experience and that of other decolonising societies.[25]

It is clear that the need for alignment with the rest of the postcolonial world (including that within the United States) is vitally important for Irish America, as will be outlined below. Equally, the uneasy tension which has often been noted between Ireland and its diaspora is partly explained by successive Irish governments' apparent eagerness to naturalise and then ignore the scale of emigration from the state. However, Lloyd's insistence on the need for the term 'emigrants' as a descriptor which will help to achieve the goals of solidarity with other diasporas and recognition from the Irish state is problematic for later-generation communities. 'Emigrants' is necessarily suggestive of the first generation: those who were born in Ireland and moved to the United States. As such, their experience, both as individuals and as a group, is identifiably different from that of their descendants in later generations. While, as this book has described throughout its chapters, those later generations' cultural identity is significantly formed by the first generation's experiences of displacement, exile and trauma, this occurs through a process of *inheritance* and transmission, followed by specific types of cultural performativity, rather than through first-hand experience.

As such, this later-generation identity is formed precisely through the 'cultural by-products' that Lloyd describes, and the term 'diaspora' as a descriptor of this group preserves the vital distinction between first and later generations. Rather than creating the naturalisation of the original causes of emigration, which Lloyd rightly desires to avoid, this distinction allows for precisely those causes to be acknowledged in the experiences of first-generation emigrants, while also allowing for an examination of the different processes of cultural inheritance experienced by later generations. The over-celebratory nature of some assessments of the Irish-American 'diaspora' – often those which invoke the concept of 'hybridity' – certainly needs to be addressed, but it seems essential to do so within the conceptual framework of the term 'diaspora' itself, rather than allow the term to be captured by those with an agenda based upon such over-celebration. The reclaiming of 'diaspora' as a concept which can be utilised within a critical and nuanced examination of later-generation Irish-American cultural transmission and interaction with Irish culture also provides a vital opportunity to reconnect the project to wider theoretical considerations of postcolonial diasporas in precisely the way advocated by Lloyd, and which will be discussed in more detail below.

CENTRES AND PERIPHERIES

Most of the assessments described above, analysing diasporic community formations, tend to emphasise the cultural processes and tensions created by those processes of the contact and negotiation between the subaltern/diasporic peripheries and the imperial/metropolitan centres in which such contact takes place. Very little attention appears to have been paid, however, to the reverse relationship between the diaspora and its original 'homeland'.[26] Within this theoretical lacuna there appear to be a number of revealing and often contradictory assumptions about that relationship.

The first assumption which appears to be evident in the lack of attention paid to the relationship between diasporas and their cultural/national origins is one of a relatively straightforward dualism inherent to – and embodied in – the 'hyphenated' identities of diasporic communities. So, to return to the specific concerns of Irish-Americans, the community is viewed as comprising of two distinct and always differentiated cultural influences. The hyphen therefore serves more than a linguistic purpose in suggesting the continuing cultural separation between the two influences at work in such a community. This apparently inherent division between America and Ireland was, of course, partly a result of Irish America's participation in the American nation-building project, in which ethnicity and tradition were to be rejected in favour of the perceived dynamism of modernity. Indeed, the retention of ethnic affiliations which pre-dated those of American identity was explicitly regarded as a threat to the coherence of the American state by the early twentieth century, as witnessed by Woodrow Wilson's statement during the First World War that 'hyphenated' Americans were undesirable. The power attributed to the 'hyphen' in ethnic identity was seen as a challenge to the 'melting-pot' process upon which the American project was founded, and it is significant within this context to remember that Wilson's warning against multiple loyalties was specifically aimed at the Irish-American population, whose continuing connections to Ireland were perceived as a threat to the American war alliance with Britain. So, in this example, we can see a clear illustration of the positioning of a diaspora's attachments to their homeland as being unacceptable and not only a potential obstacle to full participation in the American project, but even perhaps a cause of outright disloyalty to it.

However, from the Irish perspective, the need for a clear and hier-archical division between Ireland and its diaspora was also created by the centrality of ideas of cultural essentialism and 'purity' within the cultural nationalist project in Ireland from the end of the nine-teenth century onwards. This insistence on the distinctive and 'uncontaminated' nature of Irishness placed Irish-Americans, even those of the first generation, in a difficult relationship to post-Independence Ireland. While their support for an independent Ireland was both expected and accepted by their home country (led, of course, by de Valera, an Irish-American himself), their literal and symbolic distance from cultural nationalism's narrow definitions of Irishness ensured that their diasporic culture – particularly in its links to popular cultural forms such as Hollywood cinema – was regarded with suspicion as a foreign and 'contaminating' influence within Ireland. A clear example of this approach by the state was the priority given to establishing film censorship by the new Free State

Parliament.[27] Of course, a similar movement towards draconian censorship was soon underway in the United States too, spearheaded, as in Ireland, by the Catholic Church. However, the censorship of film in Ireland also defined its moral guardianship according to concepts of national origins explicitly based upon notions of cultural purity. As Louisa Burns-Bisogno comments of James Montgomery, the first Irish Film Censor, 'in many instances Montgomery banned films with little or no explanation. However, comments in his notes reflect his perception of American cinema as immoral and destructive to marriage and the family, a very real danger to Catholic Ireland.'[28] Irish-Americans, then, were placed in a difficult position in terms of identity formation. While, within America, their Irishness was perceived as both too strong an influence and in itself an inherent threat to their Americanness, within Ireland their exposure to American culture was seen as having contaminated their Irishness, and that American culture was itself seen as inherently threatening to Irish values and therefore, by extension, to the state itself. It appeared that not only were 'hyphenated Americans' unwanted, but so too were 'hyphenated Irish'.

This chapter argues, however, that the diasporic cultural space is located precisely within the space of that hyphen, and that it is only through this recognition that the diasporic relationship to the originating culture can be assessed. And it is at the moment of 'return', particularly in the case of the second generation onwards, that the tensions in this relationship became apparent. The return to 'home' requires a negotiation not only of the elisions of both time and space which are inherently a part of a diaspora's experience, but also of these hierarchies of cultural power constructed around the relationships to both the metropolitan centre and the originating periphery.

The second assumption which appears to be revealed by cultural theory's lack of attention to diasporic relationships to 'home' is intimately connected to the concept of postcolonial hybridity, and provides a revealing critique of its positioning within postcolonial theorising. When the theoretical analysis of diaspora identities is conducted only within the context of the diaspora's positioning in relation to its contact with and power relations to its metropolitan/ imperial 'host' culture, this places the originating culture of the diaspora in a revealing double bind. First, within this theoretical structure, the colonial or postcolonial 'homeland' is implied as a fixed cultural entity in its historical influence upon its diaspora. That relationship is therefore not seen as sufficiently dynamic to inform the process of that diaspora's developing hybridity – indeed, it would even appear to be seen as a hindrance to such a development. Second, and following on from this positioning of the 'homeland', there is the development of a hierarchy of postcolonial culture and influence in which the diaspora appears to be placed ahead of its originating culture, apparently due largely to its contact and connections to the metropolitan centre. It is at this point that the lack of theoretical attention paid to the diaspora's relationship to its 'home' begins to reveal a latent acceptance of colonial/metropolitan hierarchies of difference and power.

Within this context, the influence and continuing meaning (particularly for later generations) of the originating culture for postcolonial diasporas is constructed as one based on sentiment and nostalgia, the ultimate expression of which, perhaps, is the desire or intent of executing a 'return' to that originating location. And, given the ideological positioning of themes such as nostalgia by many cultural critics, once any ongoing relationship between the diaspora and its homeland is constructed in this manner, it becomes excluded from the perceived cultural dynamism of postcolonial hybridity.[29]

These critical tensions between postcolonial diasporas and their 'home' cultures are mirrored in the approaches taken to the historical development of diasporic movement itself. There are two distinct approaches which have been predominant in the critical assessment of diasporas, both of which not only have strong implications for the Irish-American diasporic relationship, but also point towards the tensions which appear to be inherent between Ireland and its diaspora.

The first of these noticeable critical approaches to the development of colonial and later postcolonial diasporas has been what might be termed a hierarchy of exile, in which both entire diasporic communities and their individual members have been made subject to a kind of grading schema according to the perceived levels of colonial/dictatorial persecution inherent to their act of emigration. Within this schema, the greater the degree of forced, politically motivated emigration for the first generation, the greater the degree to which the diaspora can claim a moral authority in its contemporary form. Equally, the degree of mobility between the diasporic space and the original 'homeland', for the diaspora as a whole or for its individual members, is often conceived of in moral terms. In one of the most striking examples of this hierarchical system, Aijaz Ahmad, describing the notion of exile, explains:

And I do not mean people who live in the metropolitan countries for professional reasons but use words like 'exile' or 'diaspora' – words which have centuries of pain and dispossession inscribed into them – to designate what is, after all, only personal convenience. I mean, rather, people who are prevented, against their own commitment and desire, from living in the country of their birth by the authority of the state – *any* state – or by fear of personal annihilation.[30]

This 'true' form of exile is therefore favourably contrasted with the 'opportunistic' movement of those who choose to leave their home without this impetus of terror. While Ahmad does not explicitly discuss the position of diasporic individuals of later generations who may choose to 'return' to their ethnic homeland under less perilous conditions than their ancestors left it, there is a strong implication that they too would be acting according only to 'personal convenience', and therefore excluded from any 'moral' hierarchy of diasporic conditions.

This hierarchical system has increasingly been challenged in recent years, but, as with other assessments of diasporic culture discussed above, only within the context of the insights it provides into the relationship between diasporic communities and their metropolitan 'hosts'. The structures of power and tension between those diasporas and their originating cultures, which have been produced by the still widespread acceptance of this 'hierarchy of exile', have yet to be sufficiently examined.[31]

In the analyses described above, then, diaspora cultures are critiqued according to degrees of oppression, and characterised by 'morally' motivated attacks upon the movements of those diasporic individuals who are seen to be operating from an 'elitist' position of cultural and economic power. What this manoeuvre reveals is not only, in quite explicit terms, a condemnation of individuals who have failed to (sufficiently) experience the colonial validation of persecution, but also an explicit condemnation of those individuals' likely continuation of mobility – including their possible decision to return home. This refusal to admit the validity of experience for diasporic individuals whose movements have been largely motivated by choice contains, therefore, a continuation of the belief described above that the 'return journey' is culturally and ideologically unsound on the grounds of its presumed connections to nostalgia and an essentialised culture.

Discussions of 'rootedness' on the one hand, and 'cosmopolitanism' on the other, when examining diasporic cultural formations rather than specific individuals, also tend to outline moral impera- tives; imperatives which are frequently contradictory. Rootedness, as has been discussed above, is often critiqued as being essentialised and even racialised. Floya Anthius has insisted that

> there does not exist any account of the ways in which diaspora may indeed have a tendency to reinforce absolutist notions of 'origin' and 'true belonging'...For a discourse of antiracism and social mobilisa- tion of a transethnic (as opposed to transnational) character cannot be easily accommodated within the discourse of the diaspora, where it retains its dependence on 'homeland' and 'origin', however reconfig- ured...It fails to provide a radical critique of ethnic rootedness and belonging, as exclusionary mechanism, in social relations.[32]

In this analysis, therefore, an ongoing attachment to a particular ethnic or national homeland, as a basis for a shared cultural perspec- tive, becomes suspect due to its apparently conservative and exclusionary nature. Irish America, for example, is often accused of maintaining an exclusionary white ethnicity, and of demonstrating a conservative nostalgia in its ongoing connections with the Irish 'homeland'.

In other accounts of diasporic formations, however, it is precisely the *lack* of such attachments which provokes suspicion and oppro- brium. The perceived cosmopolitanism of diasporic individuals and groups is frequently ascribed to a privileged and even exploitative position outside of firm national and ethnic affiliation. As was discussed above, critics such as Ahmad have characterised 'cosmopolitan' movement, typically between a homeland and a metropolitan centre, in just these terms. There is a direct connection between this accusative use of the term 'cosmopolitan' and the perceived nature of later-generation, white diasporas such as Irish America. Their relatively privileged role within their host society (in contemporary terms, if not historically), along with their European origin, gives them the opportunity to identify with their ethnic origins selectively and from a secure position, as has been described by a number of critics.[33] As such, their decisions to do so – whether in the form of material, cultural or tourist consumption – risk cate- gorisation as being self-interested and insincere exploitations of their heritage.

Accusations of both exclusionary rootedness and exploitative rootlessness are not only inappropriately moralistic in most cases, but also raise the fundamental question of what position in relation to their cultural heritage diasporas such as Irish America could take which would be deemed 'morally' acceptable.

DIASPORIC SPACE

A product first of colonialism and then later of other forms of political oppression as well as global capitalism, there are many examples of diasporas around the world operating in widely differing ways according to their cultural structures. However, all diasporas have certain experiences in common. The most crucial is that they have their origins in an experience of spatial displacement which also created a temporal rupture in their development of cultural identity; and this act of dislocation, and its reverberations through subsequent generations, is of crucial importance to the development of diasporic identity, whether the original act of departure was voluntary or not. Describing the Caribbean diaspora, Stuart Hall argues: 'We might think of black Caribbean identities as "framed" by two axes or vectors, simultaneously operative: the vector of similarity and continuity: and the vector of difference and rupture.'[34]

So, for example, as Irish citizens emigrated or were exiled to the 'New World' over several centuries, they were broken from their temporally and spatially rooted history, only to establish another in America or Australia, and then yet another in Britain and the rest of the European Union. At the beginning of the postcolonial era, during cultural nationalism, they attempted to rediscover and suture their history across space and time by reassociating their present cultures with those of their past, as shown by the 'Irish spiritual empire, as well as the still thriving interest in Gaelic culture across the world'.[35] In later years, they and other diasporic cultures have also, with the development of a 'compressed' global space, redefined their culture across scattered geographical locations, producing Irish cultural and – significantly – economic diasporas which do not operate within traditional national borders. So there are connections of Irish cultural identity among parts of America, Ireland and Europe, just as there are Asian cultural networks linking Kashmir, Paris and Mauritius.

A feature of diasporic cultural identity which arises from its temporal and spatial shifts and flexibility is therefore a form of hybridity, in that a workable and meaningful whole is created – and continues to be created within changing circumstances – from parts originating from a variety of influences, through time and across space. This hybridity and eclecticism of cultures is not the same as an 'homogenisation', in that not only are different aspects of a culture appropriated by different diasporas, but, more significantly, they are assigned different meanings within their given contexts. And, as Stuart Hall points out when speaking of the Caribbean, 'sameness' and 'difference' change their meanings according to where the observer is positioned – a realisation which, in itself, is a product of changing concepts of time and space, in which there is no longer a fixed centre from which to observe:

> Visiting the French Caribbean for the first time, I also saw at once how different Martinique is from, say, Jamaica: and this is no mere difference of topography or climate. It is a profound difference of culture and history. And the difference *matters*. It positions Martiniquains and Jamaicans as *both* the same *and* different. Moreover, the boundaries of difference are continually repositioned in relation to different points of reference. Vis-à-vis the developed West we are very much 'the same'... And yet, vis-à-vis one another, Jamaican, Haitian, Cuban, Guadeloupean, Barbadian, etc... [36]

This formulation of cultural identities which are very specific to the postcolonial and postmodern era is based upon the breakdown of spatial barriers which defined spaces as inevitably separated from each other if they were to have meaning, as well as on the breakdown of concepts of time as linear and necessarily unbroken. Diasporic cultural identities have been forged precisely at the moments of historical rupture and geographic displacement. This is then combined with the effects of transnational capital to create dynamic and evolving communities who, as it were, 'feed' cultural expressions back and forth across time and space, creating meaning out of the very instability which this process recognises and works from.

This concept of 'sameness' and 'difference', which Hall describes in terms of interconnected diasporas' relationships to each other, also has a profound role to play in the relationships between those diasporas and their originating cultures. Again, the boundaries of that 'sameness' and 'difference' are continuously repositioned according to the point of reference. So, returning to the relationship between Irish America and Ireland, the 'sameness' which Irish-Americans are seen to have in relation to Ireland is a product of their positioning within wider American society, as a form of continuity with and inheritance from their common Irish cultural background. So this 'sameness' is a relative perception, made against the Irish-American diaspora's 'difference' from other ethnic and diasporic communities within the United States.

Yet seen against the reference point of contemporary Ireland, this same diasporic group is often seen in terms of its 'difference' from Irish culture, by virtue of both the cultural influence of those very American ethnic groups who identify the Irish-Americans as 'the same' as the Irish, and by the temporal and spatial ruptures inherent to their diasporic status, which have, as it were, created new trajectories of Irishness according to the historical and geographical breaks and splits which formed them.

This approach to the relationship between Irish America and Ireland opens up new possibilities for assessing the relationship and influences between the two communities, while avoiding the creation of hierarchies of exile and essentialism which are evident in the approaches described above. If, instead of positioning Irishness and Irish-Americanness against each other in a rigidly dualistic comparison of cultural templates, we rather, as Stuart Hall argues with regard to Martiniquains and Jamaicans, accept the two cultures as being '*both* the same *and* different', then we not only overcome the hierarchical and essentialist frameworks of reference within which diasporic cultures tend to be perceived, but also open up new ways of examining both cultures.

This approach has particularly profound implications for the examination of points of contact between Ireland and Irish America, particularly those created by acts of 'return' to Ireland by members of the Irish diaspora. In particular, it allows for a re-examination of the concepts of 'sentiment' and 'nostalgia', an attitude to Ireland which Irish-Americans in particular are perceived to hold, and of which the 'return' visit is regarded as the most extreme expression. These accusations – for accusations they certainly are – of sentimentality and nostalgia originate from the hierarchical perceptions of Irishness which were discussed earlier.[37] Irish-American cultural meaning is, within this schema, not only perceived to be one originating from invention and a highly selective collective memory, but also one which refuses, when confronted with the 'truth' of either historical or contemporary Ireland, to accept or even recognise this 'reality'.

This intertwining of 'sameness' and 'difference' is taken up in a revealing way in the work of Avtar Brah. Theorising, in effect, the hyphenated space of diasporic identity, she suggests that this specifically diasporic space is one which 'includes the entanglement, the intertwining of the genealogies of dispersion with those of "staying put". The diaspora space is the site where the native is as much a diasporan as the diasporan is the native.'[38] In this discussion, those whom Brah describes as 'natives' who have 'stayed put' are in fact those born to the region of settlement by diasporic groups – in the case of her specific analysis, white British people living among immigrant communities within Britain. In this respect, her analysis contains similarities to those other approaches, described above, which examine diaspora relationships to the metropolitan centre to the exclusion of their relationships to former homelands. However, in the case of Irish-Americans, it also seems useful to apply this schema in reverse, and consider the entanglement of such a diaspora with those who 'stayed put' in their native space of Ireland. This would then extend the 'diasporic space' Brah outlines to include that between and among Ireland and Irish America; a space which is also rich with the diasporic processes she describes as placing 'the discourse of 'home' and 'dispersion' in creative tension, *inscribing a homing desire while simultaneously critiquing discourses of fixed origins*' [original emphasis].[39] Particularly when read through Stuart Hall's imagining of a simultaneity of cultural performance under diasporic conditions, this approach raises significant new opportunities to consider the specific performances of later-generation Irish-American diasporic identity.

HISTORIES OF THE IRISH DIASPORA

When examining the relationship between Ireland and its diaspora, it is worth considering the nature and development of that diasporic culture. The magnitude of the Irish diaspora's importance to the development and re-development of Irish identity in the twentieth century may be seen initially in an examination of the numbers alone. At the beginning of the twenty-first century, the population of Ireland was, using rounded figures, either almost four million or five-and-a-half million, depending upon how Ireland itself is defined, and whether the population of Northern Ireland is included in the count.[40] The number of the world's population who consider themselves to be ethnically Irish is generally accepted as being around seventy million, of whom approximately forty million are Irish-American.[41] The difficulties of definition inherent in this apparently simple demographic statistic in themselves point to both the power and the tensions inherent in the relationship between Ireland and its extended population.

If there are serious difficulties still involved in the 'mere' statistical definition of the population of Ireland itself, with questions of identity centred around the recognition of borders, religion and ethnicity, then how much greater do these issues become when considering the identity of the 'hyphenated' Irish around the world? And beyond this point of questioning that diaspora's claims on the term 'Irish', there remain the difficulties inherent for a small nation, preoccupied for much of this century with self-definition and determination, in accommodating the demands made upon it by an extended diaspora that is now at least twelve times the size of the home population.

Since the 1990s, there has been a renewed consideration of this issue, principally embodied in President Mary Robinson's 1995 speech to the Houses of the Oireachtas, in which she explicitly positioned herself as the president of a nation not defined by borders alone, by making reference to the Irish diaspora, and stating not only that her presidency would 'cherish' them, but also that:

> The men and women of our diaspora represent not simply a series of departures or losses. They remain, even while absent, a precious reflection of our own growth and change, a precious reminder of the many strands of identity which compose our story... They know the names of our townlands and villages. They remember our landscape or they have heard of it.[42]

This statement, by the Irish head of state, appears to indicate a resolution of many of the historic difficulties connected to definitions of Irishness. It is suggestive of a new era in which there now exists an all-inclusive recognition of the rights of the diaspora – in all of its forms – to a sense of belonging in the 'homeland'. It is interesting to note, for example, that in the same speech, when discussing specific projects which were aiming to provide linkages to the diaspora, Robinson mentioned the Irish Genealogical Project, saying that 'one of the most understandable and poignant concerns of any diaspora is to break the silence: to find out the names and places of origin. If we are to cherish them, we have to assist in the utterly understandable human longing.'[43]

This reference to the 'understandable human longing' to trace diasporic ancestral history does appear to indicate a new-found sensitivity to the specific experiences and processes of identity formation of the diaspora.[44] The remaining practical restrictions on such claims, however, indicate continued tensions in the relationship. Ireland remains one of the few Western nations, for example, which does not grant its citizens abroad the right to participate in the democratic process at home; Irish citizens who are out of the country at the time of an election may not vote, no matter how temporary their absence. By contrast, British subjects may continue to vote at home for fifteen years after their departure.

One of the central bases for this cultural tension has been the issue of first-generation emigrants' decision to leave Ireland, and the motivations which prompted this decision. This has been a persistent area of dispute among scholars attempting the difficult task of tracking first-generation emigrants' journeys from Ireland to the United States and the rest of the world. The assignment of motivation to emigrants is a highly controversial subject, as it is inevitably seen to reflect upon both the Irish population who stayed in Ireland and upon the contemporary diaspora.

In its most extreme, but not infrequent, form, this debate is one which might be termed the 'Darwinist' critique of the diasporas' relationships with their homelands – the argument that, of colonised populations such as the Irish, it was either the 'brightest and the best' or those who were 'surplus to requirements' who left. This establishes yet another layer of hierarchy within diaspora theorising, in which the diaspora populations are dualistically positioned as either superior or inferior to those who chose or were forced to stay behind. As usual with any such hierarchical arrangement, its inversion or reversion by opposing groups always fails to challenge the use of a hierarchy of difference as the framework for such a relationship. Examining Irish emigration, for example, Donald Akenson explains:

> There have been various attempts at developing models of migration in order to explain why some sorts of people migrate and others do not. The most venerable goes back to the 1880s when E. G. Ravenstein worked out a set of 'laws' of migration. In folk culture, explanations abound. Probably, most members of the Irish diasporate would probably agree that the able and the ambitious were the ones who emigrated, while those who were left behind believe it was the restless and undisciplined who left.[45]

This description of the varying interpretations placed upon the act of emigration is revealing of the tensions which have long been assumed to remain between the Irish and their diaspora.

This tension was considerably exacerbated by Kerby Miller's ground-breaking study of the Irish diaspora in the United States, *Emigrants and Exiles: Ireland and the Irish Exodus to North America*. An exhaustive archival study, *Emigrants and Exiles* nevertheless theorised the creation of Irish America through the lens of American assimilationist history. The key conclusion, signalled in its title, was that the immigrant generation and their immediate descendants were more or less 'coerced' into regarding the act of emigration as one of forced exile, largely in order to provide a psychological justification for what would otherwise have been seen as a betrayal of their identity and nationality. The basis for Miller's argument that Irish emigrants to the United States were ambitious individualists who felt the need to disguise this aspect of their decision to leave Ireland is his highly controversial reading of the psychological and cultural effects of Irish Catholicism. The Ireland they left, he argues, was one with a culture which was 'conservative and collective', largely as a result of religious influences on society.[46] This continued to reverberate in the United States for both the emigrant generation and beyond, he suggests, claiming, 'in short, emigration still posed severe social, cultural, and even psychological problems for many Catholics caught between individual necessity or ambition on the one hand and communal customs and obligations on the other'.[47]

As a result, Miller suggests that emigrants were subject to enormous guilt at their choice of 'freedom' in the United States, a guilt which was exploited by nationalists across several generations. He describes this process as having begun in the ritual of pre-emigration 'American wakes', and argues that:

> Finally, the same guilt, refracted through the stark memories of the American wakes, provided fertile ground for the appeals of Irish-American nationalists that emigrants 'do something' for Mother Ireland. Images of their mother's tears, their father's graves, their parents' hypothetical sufferings from poverty, English oppression, or their children's alleged 'ingratitude': all these were the nationalists' stock-in-trade, just as they had been the prevalent themes of the songs sung at the moment when the emigrants had been most vulnerable.[48]

The psychological manoeuvre which Irish-Americans used to reconcile this tension, Miller then argues, is to recast their choice of
emigration as a 'forced exile' from Ireland, as this then allowed them
to assuage their guilt at this decision.

In his slightly later study of the Irish diaspora, Donald Harman
Akenson, while praising Miller's archival scholarship, criticises his
assessments of Irish America's 'disadvantages' in their new lives as
being the result of their Catholicism.[49] With a clear reference to
Miller's approach, Akenson declared himself opposed to 'trying to
guess the psychological, emotional, and intellectual processes that
preceded all of the millions of individual decisions to leave'.[50]
Nevertheless, Akenson does follow a similar line of argument to that
of Miller in his own evaluation of the diaspora's position as 'exiles'.
He disputes this term's accuracy, and insists that those who
propound it are not allowing the migrant generation 'their dignity as
intelligent, self-aware responsible persons, each of whom made a
conscious decision to leave Ireland'.[51] Obviously, this assessment of
emigration as a deliberate and willing act has implications for the
development of later generations' identity. This is a topic Akenson
does not engage with directly, although his assertion that, like other
groups, the Irish diaspora has members who 'strongly wish to
believe certain romantic or inaccurate generalizations about their
own past ... that they were exiled from Ireland rather than that they
left by choice',[52] as well as his posed but unanswered question, 'for
how long does a sense of ethnicity last?' are strongly suggestive of
his position on the subject.[53]

Despite the differences between their assessments of Catholicism's
influence, however, Miller and Akenson share a number of key ideological assumptions about Irish America. The first of these is a
privileging of a 'theological' explanation for the diaspora. While
Miller sees Irish America's Catholicism as being central to its sense
of 'exile' from Ireland, Akenson famously highlights the fact that the
majority of ethnically Irish-Americans are of Protestant descent.[54]
While both of these assertions, within the terms made by their
authors, have great significance for later-generation Irish-Americans,
neither Akenson nor Miller extend their conclusions to discuss the
specific issues of cultural identity formation for emigrants' descen-
dents which their work implies must exist.

The second, and most far-reaching, assumption of both Miller and
Akenson's work is that, if the diaspora was created by men and
women who made some degree of active choice regarding their deci-

sion to leave Ireland, then the term 'exile', with its accompanying sensations of loss, pain and nostalgia across that and subsequent generations, is inappropriate or even malevolent. What both Miller and Akenson are describing, is, essentially, economic emigration from Ireland. The tone and method of analysis both use to describe this, however, effectively naturalises the economic hardship which caused emigration; neither scholar provides any explanation of the causes of this poverty, implying instead that this state of affairs was in some way integral to Ireland, rather than the result of the very particular set of political and economic circumstances of colonial administration. Under such an analysis, continuing interest or attachment to Ireland after emigration is presented as 'romantic' or even pathological, rather than an eminently understandable response to displacement forced by social and economic circumstances beyond the emigrants' control.

This implication of Irish-American cultural pathology in continuing to look towards their 'homeland' as a source of identity is, as was suggested above, partly grounded in the disciplinary limitations of work such as Miller's and Akenson's. Both scholars are positioned within a canon of American historical and sociological thought which has its original basis in the assimilationist ideology of the nineteenth and early twentieth century. This necessarily structures the maintenance of ethnic identities within later generations as being at best based on inaccurate facts, or at worst a pathological response which, it is implied, is 'un-American'. Other contributors to the field have been more explicit in their condemnation of such ethnic attachments. Arthur M. Schlesinger, in *The Disuniting of America*, has argued that not only is the development of a 'historical identity' by ethnic groups with the United States a predominantly elitist movement, but also that it constitutes a 'counter-revolution against the original theory of America'.[55] Referring specifically to what he refers to as 'ethnic cheerleading' among the Irish, Schlesinger argues that non-Anglo-Saxon white groups such as the Irish, Italians and Jews in America have no need to retain such ethnic identities, on the grounds that 'Europe has reigned long enough; it is the source of most of the evil in the world anyway'.[56]

ETHNICITY STUDIES IN THE UNITED STATES

Schlesinger's anti-European sentiments reveal his ideological connections to a strain of American historiography which has been fundamental to the construction of diaspora groups such as the Irish in the United States. Originating with Frederick Jackson Turner's 'frontier thesis' in 1893, the settlement of the United States by European immigrant groups was defined as a conclusive break with their past and history; this in turn led to the assimilationist policies of the early twentieth century, in which ethnic identities were to be abandoned through a process of Americanisation, a process generally referred to as the 'melting-pot'. It was at this point that the concept of a generational progression through the process of Americanisation become so central to historical thinking within the academy. While first-generation immigrants were accepted as having a large degree of irremovable ethnic identity, this was popularly believed to be 'educated out' during the second generation, and extinct by the third. Werner Sollors has commented of the centrality of this generational theorising within American historiography that, 'in America, more than Europe, generational imagery – in both its positivist and its romantic-historical versions – has provided a mental map for newcomers and their descendants'.[57]

In a not dissimilar fashion to that of the metaphor of rootedness within diaspora theorising, the 'mental map' of generations has, within American ethnic history, created a system of thought concerning ethnic identity which has tended to obscure as much as illuminate the processes of similarity and difference within diaspora groups. Indeed, the lengthy and ongoing struggle between adherents and opponents of the 'melting-pot' thesis has perhaps been one of the major factors in creating and maintaining a theoretical divide between American ethnic history and diaspora studies; two disciplines which might otherwise have been expected to have close and fruitful intellectual ties.[58]

The issue of white ethnicity within the United States is a complex and highly contested area. In order to examine what relevant connections might exist between these two subjects, therefore, it is necessary to explore some of the central debates in the discussion of ethnic identification during the period of this study. The essential contestation contained within discussions about ethnicity in the United States is its apparent contradiction of the 'melting-pot' theories so central to the country's late nineteenth- and early twentieth-century nation-building project. Recent research suggests that neither term is a direct opposite of the other, but the assumption that they are oppositional has been the basis of much of the discussions of ethnicity for the last century. One of the first challenges to the belief in the 'melting-pot's' dominance came from the social scientist Marcus Hansen, who as early as the 1930s propounded the idea of a 'third-generation return' to ethnic culture. Written during a period of strong attachment to the idea of the 'melting-pot', however, Hansen's ideas were largely ignored until their rediscovery and reprinting by Daniel Moynihan in the late 1950s, when the persistence of ethnicity was beginning to attract renewed attention within academic research, if not among more general audiences.

Hansen's theory, put briefly, was that, while first-generation immigrants retained strong attachment to their original cultures, the second generation were characterised by what he termed 'fleeing sons', who completely rejected their ethnicity in favour of self-conscious Americanisation, as they 'wanted to lose as many of the evidences of foreign origin as they could shuffle off'.[59] By contrast to this, the third-generation 'returning grandsons' displayed considerable attachment to their ethnic origins, thus completing a three-generation cycle of ethnic identification patterns while seeking to 'satisfy some human longings that corn bread and apple pie can never appease'.[60] Hansen's work, though referred to as a foundational text of contemporary American ethnicity studies, has been consistently attacked by other theorists on a number of grounds. Aside from understandable, if anachronistic, criticisms of the anecdotal nature of his research, the ideological context of this area of social studies is evident in many of the dismissals of his theories. In particular, much of the debate surrounding the degree and nature of ethnicity retention among 'old-stock' European-immigrants such as the Irish – as well as Poles, Italians, Germans and Scots – has revealed a continuing difficulty in defining what ethnicity actually means for later generations, and whether different kinds of identification are all to be considered as equal. This has led, in some of the more extreme cases, as mentioned above, to the development of a kind of hierarchy of ethnic identification, based largely upon concepts of ghettoisation contrasted with social mobility. The attainment of middle-class socio-economic status by significant numbers of a diasporic group is often considered antithetical to strong ethnic affiliations. In the case of Irish-Americans, this argument has been repeatedly rehearsed regarding the development of so-called 'lace curtain Irish', who moved out of the old neighbourhood communities into non-ethnically-specific suburbs. This in itself is revealingly reflective of the fact that frameworks of thought associated with the 'melting-pot' theory are still deeply embedded in many approaches to this issue. In other words, ethnic affiliation and cultural performance are seen as profoundly first-generation and working-class activities, which will disappear once future generations gain the social mobility assumed to be the result of an American upbringing.

Another early exploration of the persistence of ethnicity among later-generation immigrants in the United States was Oscar Handlin's study *The Uprooted*, first published in 1951. Turning from an examination of immigrant impact on the United States to an examination of migration's impact on the immigrants themselves, Handlin described the experience of displacement and alienation. Using the familiar imagery of rootedness, he argued that: 'The immigrants lived in crisis because they were uprooted. In transplantation, while the old roots were sundered, before the new were established, the immigrants existed in an extreme situation. The shock, and the effects of the shock, persisted for many years; and their influence reached down to generations which themselves never paid the cost of crossing.'[61]

Handlin discussed in detail the generational progression of this experience of displacement, directly contesting the melting-pot assumptions of a decreasing feeling of ethnicity, as well as addressing the continued ties to 'old countries', through letters, chain immigration and remittances.[62] Showing considerably more sympathy towards these ongoing feelings of connection with ethnic homelands than scholars such as Miller would nearly forty years later, Handlin acknowledged the inherited nature of such alienation for later generations, arguing, 'to the son now looking back it seems the movement comes untimely to a close. The ideals of the nest, remembered even at the height of flight, have triumphed. Men weary of a century and more of struggle, impatient of the constant newness, more eagerly than ever hunger for the security of belonging.'[63] In the main, however, the melting-pot thesis remained dominant in the immediate aftermath of the Second World War, as it was assumed that old-stock European immigrant groups in the United States no longer needed to consider themselves part of a diasporic culture.

President Kennedy's election in 1960 was widely seen at the time as marking the socio-economic breakthrough of white ethnicities, and Irish-Americans in particular, into the upper echelons of American power. The importance of the attainment of political power at a national level by an Irish-American Catholic was rapidly reflected in commentaries on the new position of the diaspora in the popular American imagination. In the mid-1970s, Lawrence McCaffrey declared that 'the Irish are even numbered among the so-called beautiful people – part of the Kennedy heritage. On television handsome men, women and children wearing Irish knit sweaters and with Irish names like Kevin, Brian, Sean, Sheila and Maureen sell cars, soap and toothpaste.'[64] McCaffrey's association between the apparently new marketability of Irishness and Kennedy's election was no coincidence. At the same time, again connected to commentary on the 1960 presidential election, there was a resurgence of scholarly interest in white ethnicities, marked most notably by *Beyond the Melting Pot: The Negroes, Puerto Ricans, Jews, Italians and Irish of New York City*, published in 1963 by Nathan Glazer and Daniel Patrick Moynihan. Glazer and Moynihan's work heralded a resurgence of interest in the subject. As it had also been Moynihan who 'rediscovered' Hansen's earlier work, the concept of the 'third-generation return' also began to receive critical attention at this time. As was mentioned above, much of this attention was critical of Hansen's conclusions; and much of that criticism centred (as it still does) around the issue of ethnicity's complex relationship to both culture and social structure. In effect, most social scientists who conducted studies in this area made more or less explicit distinctions between social structures and cultural practices and identifications, almost always privileging social structures above culture in terms of significance and value. This meant, in effect, that white ethnic groups were seen as jettisoning their cultural ethnicity with increasing speed the further they became socially and economically assimilated into American society.[65]

Given the emphasis on generational impacts in ethnic identification within Hansen's work, it is interesting to note the similar emphasis shown in a number of the criticisms of his theories. Vladimir C. Nahirny and Joshua A. Fishman, for example, in 1965, critique Hansen's concepts of 'fleeing sons' and 'returning grandsons' by arguing that the second-generation 'fleeing sons'' apparent determination to escape their ethnicity is an indication of its continuing power over them, inherited from their first-generation immigrant fathers. By contrast, they see the 'returning grandsons' of the third generation as being free to feel 'interest' in their heritage precisely because it has no real significance within their lives. They assert that 'they need not emphasise their Americanism by dissociating from ethnicity because their Americanism is unstrained and their ethnicity is attenuated'.[66] Furthermore, Nahirny and Fishman argue that cross-generational levels of ethnic identification cannot be assumed to be merely a question of degree, but must also be examined in terms of the nature of that identification; in other words, that the forms and practices of ethnicity also change across generations.

The enormous social changes within American immigrant groups throughout the twentieth century – particularly those relating to social mobility, geographical dispersion and the impact of the civil rights movement on many aspects of social organisation – are of obvious relevance to this issue of varying styles of ethnic identification across generations. The concept of attenuated ethnicity acquired through a process of social mobility across generations, and leading to the development of a new form of ethnic identification, was also reflected in the work of Herbert Gans, whose theories of 'symbolic ethnicity' were built upon the recurring belief among social scientists throughout the 1970s and early 1980s that social structures were of greater significance than cultural identifications. As Mary Waters comments, he 'views this symbolic identification as more or less a leisure-time activity. Individuals identify as Irish, for example, on occasions such as Saint Patrick's Day, on family holidays, or for vacations... Gans also wonders how such symbolic ethnicity can continue when the actual ethnic collectivity that the individual claims to belong to continues to recede.'[67]

The rise of multiculturalism, following the battles of the civil rights movement, and the renewed and sustained interest in ethnicity shown by Americans from all backgrounds, provoked further academic research into the nature and meaning of this contemporary expression of individual and collective identity. As was mentioned above, however, the process of these investigations, as well as the conclusions drawn from them, have often been as revealing of the ideological assumptions of those conducting the study as they have been of the subject itself.

A number of detailed sociological studies investigating connections between ethnic background and individual identity have been conducted over the last twenty years within both specific ethnic groups, including Irish-Americans, and a wider population sample in the United States. These have included the work of Richard Alba, Mary Waters, Rosenweig and Thelan, George Lipsitz and Reginald Byron.[68] It is worth noting that, despite these scholars' differing ideological positions and conclusions on the subject of white ethnicities in contemporary American society, they all share a disciplinary approach to their research which is grounded primarily in sociology.

Indeed, sociological research, both quantitative and qualitative, has been the most common form of American scholarship to engage with white diasporas within the United States over the last twenty years. Without contesting the value or importance of this work, it has tended to view the groups it studies as more or less assimilated ethnic minorities *within* the clearly demarcated borders of both American society and sociological systems of thought. As a result, it has tended to have little engagement with international diaspora theory, or indeed theories such as postcolonialism or cultural studies. Instead, these studies function more as examinations of immigration into American society – therefore perpetuating more or less precisely the disciplinary lacuna which Handlin was aiming to address up to fifty years earlier.

The extent to which these disciplinary limitations are largely specific to studies of diaspora groups within America is evident in the differences between examinations of Irish America and the Irish in Britain. While contemporary studies of the Irish population living in Britain also have a strong leaning towards sociology, many also engage with cultural theory. Bronwen Walter, for example, in a study which largely concentrates on the Irish, and Irish women in particular, in Britain, has argued of the term 'diaspora' that it is 'a spatial concept in a multitude of ways. In descriptive terms, it refers to the long-term settlement which follows people's scattering or dispersal from their "original" homeland. But contemporary cultural understandings parallel this "closed" definition with a more "open" symbolic spatiality, which combines the separate locations of origin, travel and settlement into a "third space".'[69] Walter also develops and applies Avtar Brah's theories of 'diaspora space', and Lavie and Swedenborg's concept of diasporic culture as a 'third space'.[70] By reading her own sociological research through the theoretical concepts proposed by those engaged in systems of thought influenced by the study of postcolonialism and cultural representation, Walter attempts to recentre the Irish diaspora in Britain within a wider disciplinary perspective, an approach rarely taken by scholars examining the Irish-American diaspora.

CONCLUSION

First-generation emigrants' arrival from Ireland into host countries such as the United States, whether in the nineteenth or twentieth centuries, occurred under conditions of exclusion and deprivation at least partly equivalent to those of other, non-white, contemporary diasporas. However, the majority of contemporary Irish-Americans are now later-generation middle-class and at the very least relatively privileged within American society. They, along with groups of similar history and European ethnic background, are therefore excluded from most discussions of diaspora experience. Rather than suggesting that Irish America is not a valid diasporic group, this seems to suggest instead a limitation of diaspora theory itself, possibly due to its strong disciplinary link to anthropology. Despite the groundbreaking work of James Clifford and other 'radical' anthropologists, there appear to remain disciplinary predispositions towards the study of the 'Other' to the exclusion of groups apparently part of the Western 'Self'. By contrast, the study of diasporas such as contemporary Irish America within the postcolonial framework of diaspora theory, far from marking a conservative 'turn', is in fact an essentially radical project.[71] By examining the relationships and connections (as well as differences) between white European diasporas such as Irish America and those of non-white and non-European diasporas, it may be possible to interrogate the race and class-based ideologies which have traditionally structured the critiques of diasporic cultures. The study of Irish America within the terms of diasporic theory also provides a useful framework of analysis for examining a diaspora which has developed well beyond the first and second generations, therefore offering opportunities to examine contrasts and similarities for the more recently developed diasporas, which are the more popular subjects of study within this discipline.

From the disciplinary perspective of Irish studies, the benefits of examining Irish America through the critical framework of diaspora theory are also significant and potentially radical. Since the mid-1980s, a number of critics within the discipline have developed what has become known as the 'postcolonial turn' in Irish studies, seeking as they do so to examine Irish history and culture within the comparative framework offered by other ethnic and national groups which also experienced colonialism and anti-colonial nationalism. Theorists such as Luke Gibbons, Seamus Deane and David Lloyd, among many others, have engaged with postcolonial theories such as those of Franz Fanon, as well as the Subaltern studies group of Indian cultural theorists, the 'Black Atlantic' analysis of black British critics such as Paul Gilroy and Stuart Hall, and poststructuralist theorists such as Michel Foucault and Jacques Derrida.[72] This project has been wide-ranging and dramatic in its impact upon the study of Irish history, society and culture. In particular, it has enabled a valuable new approach to Ireland's experience of global forces such as colonialism and, later, globalisation. The particularities of Irish history, as an ostensibly white, Christian, European nation, which was nevertheless subject to the forces of European colonialism, have provided a useful and dynamic contrast and comparison to the experiences of other postcolonial societies, and enabled the entire process of colonialism and postcolonial resistance to be interrogated from a fresh and revealing perspective. In particular, they have allowed the dynamics of race and ethnicity within colonial experience to be examined with a clarity which has been beneficial to both postcolonial theory and Irish studies.

While the large-scale emigration from Ireland which created the first generation of Irish-Americans, and their experience upon arrival, has been given some consideration through a similar theoretical lens, however, the continuing development of later-generation Irish America during the latter half of the twentieth century has received very little critical analysis using the theoretical tools of postcolonialism or cultural theory.[73] There has been a particular sensitivity, it appears, among those critics who might have engaged with this project, towards the dangers of claiming a continuing level of marginalisation or 'victimhood' for the now largely prosperous and privileged later-generation Irish-Americans comparable to that of later-arriving, largely non-white immigrant groups. The conservatively inspired recuperation of whiteness in some quarters of United States culture over the last decade of the twentieth century has undoubtedly influenced this sensitivity, unsurprisingly, given the extremist nature of some of its proponents.[74] The development of this backlash against multiculturalism, affirmative action policies, and other belated recognitions of the extent of the racially determined nature of American society nevertheless makes the project of reconnecting the experiences of and remaining influences on European diasporas such as Irish America all the more vital. Such backlashes and revisions of American ethnic history need to be countered by the establishment of more radical solidarities between earlier immigrant groups such as Irish America and more recent arrivals. The most fruitful way to achieve this would seem to be an analysis of both historical and contemporary Irish America through the perspectives offered by postcolonial and cultural theory. As David Lloyd has argued of this development's relevance to Irish

America, 'the recent intensification of racialized politics in the United States, by which recent Irish immigrants, whether documented or undocumented, are directly and acutely addressed, demands our response. This is a moment in which Irish migrants must either choose solidarity with people of colour or once more hide under the veil of our whiteness.'[75] And, reconnecting this issue with Irish identities and Irish studies' intellectual practice, Luke Gibbons has insisted that 'the capacity of a society to retrieve the memory of its own unacknowledged others – those who paid the price in different ways for its own rise to prosperity – is a measure of its ability to establish global solidarities with 'the other' without, both at home and abroad'.[76]

It is also the argument of this chapter, then, that the analysis of later-generation Irish America, specifically in respect of its relationship to Ireland, through the perspective of postcolonial diaspora theory, has important implications not only for the development of ethnic history in the United States, but also for the continued development of Irish studies as a discipline which recognises and engages with global forces and events. The exclusion of the diaspora (within the United States and beyond) from considerations of Irish identity and culture has been challenged in recent years. However, much of this challenge has, ironically, come from the revisionist 'camp' of Irish studies, those who seek to downplay the impact or even existence of colonial and neo-colonial forces on Irish history and culture. This co-opts the diaspora, especially Irish America, as a dynamically hybrid force acting upon what is portrayed as an insular and self-pitying traditional nationalist Irishness in the name of liberating globalisation.[77] The integration of Irish-American experience into a postcolonial analysis of Irishness would act as a direct challenge to this project, recovering diasporic Irishness for a more radical imagining of Irish studies by continuing its extending of connections between the specifics of the discipline and their implications for a more internationalist analysis. As Gibbons has argued:

> Globalisation without this radical memory is indeed a one-way street, cutting off one of the most vital and deeply rooted sources of solidarity with the plight of developing nations and the casualties of the world-system. Rather than reverting to the inward gaze of an old-fashioned nationalism (itself a caricature of the past), the postcolonial turn in Irish criticism ... represents an attempt to extend the horizons of the local to distant and often very different cultures, beyond the comforting cosmopolitanism of the West.[78]

NOTES

1   See Homi Bhaba, *Nation and Narration* (London: Routledge, 1990), as well as Nikos Papastergiadis, *Dialogues in the Diasporas* (London: Rivers Oram Press, 1998).

2   James Clifford, 'Travelling Cultures', in Lawrence Grossberg, Cary Nelson and Paula A. Treichler (eds), *Cultural Studies* (London: Routledge, 1992), p. 108.

3   Arjun Appadurai, 'Putting Hierarchy in its Place', *Cultural Anthropology*, Vol. 3, No. 1, 1988, p. 37.

4   James Clifford, 'Travelling Cultures', p. 103.

5   James Clifford, 'Diasporas', *Cultural Anthropology*, Vol. 9, No. 3, 1994, pp. 310–11.

6   Floya Anthius, 'Evaluating 'Diaspora': Beyond Ethnicity?', *Sociology*, Vol. 32, No. 3, August 1998, p. 568. Also see Clifford's own detailed exposition of this concept, in James Clifford, *Routes: Travel and Translation in the Late Twentieth Century* (Cambridge, MA: Harvard University Press, 1997).

7   James Clifford, 'Diasporas', p. 306.

8   Robin Cohen, *Global Diasporas: An Introduction* (London: UCL Press, 1997), pp. 184–7.

9   William Safran, 'Diasporas in Modern Societies: Myths of Homeland and Return', in *Diaspora: A Journal of Transnational Studies*, Vol. 1, No. 1, 1994, pp. 83–4.

10 James Clifford, 'Diasporas', pp. 306–7.

11 Lisa Malkki, 'National Geographic: The Rooting of Peoples and the Territorialization of National Identity Among Scholars and Refugees', *Cultural Anthropology*, Vol. 7, No. 1, 1992, pp. 31–2.

12 Lawrence McCaffrey, *The Irish Diaspora in America* (Bloomington: Indiana University Press, 1976), p. 178.

13 Hasia Diner, *Erin's Daughters in America: Irish Immigrant Women in the Nineteenth Century* (Baltimore, MD: Johns Hopkins University Press, 1983), and Ide O'Carroll, *Models for Movers: Irish Women's Emigration to America* (Dublin: Attic Press, 1990).

14 For a fuller discussion of the gendering of nations and national identities, as well as that of diasporas, see Chapter 4.

15 Bronwen Walter, *Outsiders Inside: Whiteness, Place and Irish Women* (London: Routledge, 2001), pp. 194–5.

16 Doreen Massey, *Space, Place and Gender* (Cambridge: Polity Press, 1994), p. 167.

17 Walter, *Outsiders Inside*, p. 196.

18 For a full discussion of the ways in which the Irish-American diaspora has been represented in terms of gendered ethnic identities, see Chapter 4.

19 Thomas N. Brown, *Irish-American Nationalism 1870–1890* (Philadelphia: JB Lippincott Company, 1966), p. 41.

20 Nira Yuval-Davis, 'Gender and Nation', in Rick Wilford and Robert L. Miller (eds), *Women, Ethnicity and Nationalism: The Politics of Transition* (London: Routledge, 1998), p. 24.

21 Benedict Anderson, 'Long-Distance Nationalism: World Capitalism and the Rise of Identity Politics', *The Wertheim Lecture*, Amsterdam (Amsterdam: Centre for Asian Studies, 1992), p. 11.

22 Jolle Demmers, 'Diaspora and Conflict: Locality, Long-Distance Nationalism, and Delocalisation of Conflict Dynamics', in *Javnost – the Public: Journal of The European Institute for Communication and Culture*, 1 Diasporic Communication, Vol. IX (2002), p. 93. For a detailed discussion of the

processes of Irish-American interventions in Irish politics, see Chapter 1.

23   Gilles Deleuze and Félix Guattari, *A Thousand Plateaus: Capitalism and Schizophrenia*, trans. Brian Massumi (London: Athlone Press, 1996), pp. 381–4.

24   Floya Anthius, 'Evaluating "Diaspora"', p. 569.

25   David Lloyd, *Ireland After History* (Cork: Cork University Press, 1999), pp. 103–4.

26   A notable exception to this is the work of Hamid Naficy, such as 'Framing Exile: From Homeland to Homepage', in Hamid Naficy (ed.), *Home, Exile, Homeland: Film, Media, and the Politics of Place* (London: Routledge, 1999).

27   Kevin Rockett, 'History, Politics and Irish Cinema', in Kevin Rockett, Luke Gibbons and John Hill (eds), *Cinema and Ireland* (London: Croom Helm 1987), p. 40.

28   Louisa Burns-Bisogno, *Censoring Irish Nationalism: The British, Irish and American Suppression of Republican Images in Film and Television, 1909–1995* (London: McFarland & Company, 1997), p. 43.

29   See Robert Hewison, *The Heritage Industry* (London: Methuen, 1987), David Lowenthal, *The Heritage Crusade and the Spoils of History* (Cambridge: Cambridge University Press, 1998), Alan O'Day, 'Revising the Diaspora', in D. George Boyce and Alan O'Day (eds), *Modern Irish History: Revisionism and the Revisionist Controversy* (London: Routledge, 1997), and Roy Foster, *The Irish Story: Telling Tales and Making It Up in Ireland* (London: Allen Lane, 2001).

30   Aijaz Ahmad, *In Theory: Classes, Nations, Literatures* (London: Verso, 1992), p. 85.

31   See Caren Kaplan, *Questions of Travel: Postmodern Discourses of Displacement* (Durham, NC: Duke University Press, 1998), pp. 105–12.

32   Floya Anthius, 'Evaluating "Diaspora"', p. 577.

33   See Mary Waters, *Ethnic Options: Choosing Identities in America* (Berkeley: University of California Press, 1990), and Reginald Byron, *Irish America* (Oxford: Oxford University Press, 1999), as well as the more detailed discussion of 'symbolic ethnicities' below.

34   Stuart Hall, 'Cultural Identity and Diaspora', in Patrick Williams and Laura Chrisman (eds), *Colonial Discourse and Postcolonial Theory* (London: Harvester Wheatsheaf, 1993), p. 395.

35   Terence Brown, *Ireland: A Social and Cultural History 1922–1985* (London: Fontana Press, 1985), p. 35.

36   Brown, *Ireland: A Social and Cultural History*, p. 35 and Hall, 'Cultural Identity and Diaspora', p. 396.

37   For further discussion on such hierarchical perceptions of Irishness, see Michel Peillon, 'Tourism – the Quest for Otherness?', *The Crane Bag Book of Irish Studies*, Vol. 8, No. 2 (Dublin: Blackwater Press, 1984), pp. 165–8.

38   Avtar Brah, *Cartographies of Diaspora: Contesting Identities* (London: Routledge, 1996), p. 209.

39   Ibid., p. 192.

40   See <http://www.nicensus2001.gov.uk/nica/common/home.jsp> for details of the 2001 census figures for Northern Ireland. Also see <http://www.cso.ie/census/Census2002Results.htm> for details of the 2002 census figures for the Republic of Ireland. Both accessed July 2006.

41   Donald Harman Akenson, *The Irish Diaspora: A Primer* (Belfast: Institute of Irish Studies, 1996), p. 15, and Byron, *Irish America*, p. 275.

42   Mary Robinson, 'Cherishing the Irish Diaspora': An Address to the Houses of the Oireachtas, February 1995, <http://www.rootsweb.com/~irlker/diaspora.html>. Accessed July 2006.

43   Ibid.

44   For a detailed discussion of this trend in Irish-American identity formation, see Chapter 2.
45   Akenson, *The Irish Diaspora*, p. 36.
46   Kerby A. Miller, *Emigrants and Exiles: Ireland and the Irish Exodus to North America* (Oxford: Oxford University Press, 1985), p. 121.
47   Ibid., p. 240.
48   Ibid., p. 568.
49   Akenson, *The Irish Diaspora*, pp. 237–40.
50   Ibid., p. 38.
51   Ibid., p. 37.
52   Ibid., p. 274.
53   Ibid., p. 218.
54   Ibid., pp. 219–24.
55   Arthur M Schlesinger, *The Disuniting of America* (New York: Norton 1992), p. 43.
56   Ibid., p. 64.
57   Werner Sollors, *Beyond Ethnicity: Consent and Descent in American Culture* (Oxford: Oxford University Press, 1986), p. 211.
58   See Alan O'Day, 'Revising the Diaspora', pp. 197–210, for a thorough historical overview of the literature and discussions in this field.
59   Marcus Hansen, 'The Problem of the Third Generation Immigrant', in *Augustana Historical Society Publications* (Rock Island, IL: Augustana Historical Society, 1938), p. 7.
60   Ibid., pp. 8–9.
61   Oscar Handlin, *The Uprooted: The Epic Story of the Great Migrations that Made the American People* (New York: Grosset and Dunlap, 1971), p. 6.
62   Handlin noted that: 'By 1860, the Irish alone were sending back four or five million dollars a year... Such contributions recognized the continued connectedness with the old place. In time, that was further strengthened by involvement in nationalistic movements which established a political interest in the affairs of the Old Country, an interest the peasants had not had while they were there.' Ibid., p. 260. This last statement is, in the Irish case, debatable, but it does highlight Handlin's sensitivity to the complexities of the diaspora's specific and ongoing relationship to their homeland.
63   Ibid., p. 306.
64   Lawrence J McCaffrey, *The Irish Diaspora in America*, p. 172. For a more detailed discussion of the implications of Kennedy's election for Irish America, see Chapter 1, as well as Chapter 3 for an examination of the commodification of Irishness within the United States.
65   See John Ibson, 'Virgin Land or Virgin Mary? Studying the Ethnicity of White Americans', *American Quarterly*, Vol. 33, Issue 3 (1981), pp. 284–308 for a detailed discussion of the research into white ethnicity up to the date of publication. Ibson pays particularly close attention to the assumptions made within many studies about social mobility and the effect of these assumptions on the conclusions drawn, pointing out that, 'as Americans are prone to forget, the existence of social mobility and its cultural meaning are different matters', p. 303.
66   Vladimir C. Nahirny and Joshua A. Fishman, 'American Immigrant Groups: Ethnic Identification and the Problem of Generations', *The Sociological Review*, 13 (1965), p. 312.
67   Cited in Mary Waters, *Ethnic Options*, p. 7.
68   See Richard Alba, *The Transformation of White America* (New Haven, CT: Yale University Press, 1990), Mary Waters, *Ethnic Options*, Roy Rosenzweig and David Thelen, *The Presence of the Past: Popular Uses of History in American*

Life (New York: Columbia University Press, 1998), George Lipsitz, *The Possessive Investment in Whiteness: How White People Profit from Identity Politics* (Philadelphia: Temple University Press, 1998), and Reginald Byron, *Irish America*. For a fuller discussion of these works, with particular reference to their implications for Irish-American cultural identities, see Chapter 2.

69 Bronwen Walter, *Outsiders Inside*, p. 8.

70 Smadar Lavie and Ted Swedenburg, 'Introduction: Displacement, Diaspora, and Geographies of Identity', in Smadar Lavie and Ted Swedenburg (eds), *Displacement, Diaspora, and Geographies of Identity* (Durham, NC: Duke University Press, 1996), pp. 13–18.

71 The introduction of the models of cultural theory and, most particularly, post-colonial theory, into Irish studies has been highly controversial. It is outside the scope of this book to examine the full implications of these controversies. However, the published exchanges on Irish postcolonialism between Luke Gibbons and Francis Mulhern are indicative of the strength of the debate. Francis Mulhern, 'A Nation, Yet Again: The Field Day Anthology', in Francis Mulhern, *The Present Lasts a Long Time: Essays About Cultural Politics* (Cork: Cork University Press, 1998), Luke Gibbons, 'Dialogue Without the Other? A Reply to Francis Mulhern', *Radical Philosophy*, 67, Summer 1994, pp. 28–31, and Francis Mulhern, 'Postcolonial Melancholy', in Francis Mulhern, *The Present Lasts a Long Time: Essays About Cultural Politics* (Cork: Cork University Press, 1998). Also see D. George Boyce and Alan O'Day (eds), *The Making of Modern Irish History*, for a wider-ranging discussion of some of the key areas of contestation.

72 The development of Irish 'cultural' studies has been lengthy and wide-ranging. Briefly, however, the first publications of the Derry-based Field Day group in the 1980s were instrumental in its establishment. Other publications of particular significance would include Terry Eagleton, *Heathcliff and the Great Hunger* (London: Verso, 1995), Luke Gibbons, *Transformations in Irish Culture* (Cork: Cork University Press, 1996) and David Lloyd, *Ireland After History*. For a short but effective discussion of the history of this disciplinary turn in Irish studies, see Spurgeon Thompson, 'Introduction: Towards an Irish Cultural Studies', *Cultural Studies*, Vol. 15, No. 1, 2000, pp. 1–11.

73 See Hasia Diner, *Erin's Daughters in America*, and Noel Ignatiev, *How the Irish Became White* (London: Routledge, 1995).

74 One of the more extremist of these recuperations of whiteness is enacted by the League of the South. This far-right organisation, based in the Southern United States, claims that those states of the old Confederacy had a distinctively 'Celtic' ethnicity, encompassing Scottish, Irish, Welsh and Cornish settlement. For a fuller discussion of the ways in which this organisation mobilises a highly specific version of whiteness to buttress its racially defined 'neo-Confederacy', see Euan Hague, 'The Scottish Diaspora: Tartan Day and the Appropriation of Scottish Identities in the United States', in David C. Harvey, Rhys Jones, Neil McInroy and Christine Milligan (eds), *Celtic Geographies: Old Culture, New Times* (London: Routledge, 2002), pp. 149–53.

75 David Lloyd, *Ireland After History*, p. 106.

76 Luke Gibbons, 'The Global Cure? History, Therapy and the Celtic Tiger', in Peadar Kirby, Luke Gibbons and Michael Cronin (eds), *Reinventing Ireland: Culture, Society and the Global Economy* (London: Pluto Press, 2002), p. 100.

77 Fintan O'Toole, 'No Place Like Home', in Fintan O'Toole, *The Ex-Isle of Erin* (Dublin: New Island Books, 1997), and Richard Kearney, *Postnationalist Ireland: Politics, Culture, Philosophy* (London: Routledge, 1997).

78 Luke Gibbons, 'The Global Cure?', p. 104.

Conclusion

IRISH AMERICA IN THE TWENTY-FIRST CENTURY

AT THE TIME of writing, it is of course still too early in the twenty-first century to make clear predictions about the next set of geo-political or socio-economic developments that will have an important impact upon the ongoing cultural relationship between Ireland and Irish America. Nevertheless, the year 2000, as the end of this book's period of study, may also prove to have been the end of an era in at least some areas of interaction between Ireland and the United States. The presidential election victory of George W. Bush in November 2000 was widely predicted to presage a change of direction in United States foreign policy, with particularly noticeable effects for the Northern Ireland peace process, a development in turn likely to affect Irish-American responses to direct political or philanthropic causes in Ireland. The 11 September 2001 attacks on New York and Washington overtook such debates, and, aside from the immediate issue of the United States' specific official reaction to those attacks, raised fresh questions concerning popular American responses to foreign affairs. Those popular responses, centring as they have in many cases around issues of ethnicity as well as definitions of 'terrorism', may well have long-term implications for the interaction between Irish America and Ireland. The Irish-American experience of the 11 September attacks on New York in particular has rapidly been narrativised as one of a specific brand of idealistically American sacrifice and heroism, largely due to the central role and high death toll in the attacks of the (still markedly Irish-American) emergency services. The long-term effects of this upon Irish-American conceptions of geo-politics are not yet determinable, but there are already some indications that it may have a considerable effect upon the Irish-Americans' construction of ethnic identity. The positioning of

Irish America as an idealised – and white ethnic – American identity in the face of foreign – and non-white ethnic – attacks upon the American nation–state has already been noted in some of the immediate responses to 11 September. Diane Negra has commented upon the example of 'The Ballad of Mike Moran', about the New York fire-fighter who shouted out 'Osama, kiss my royal Irish ass!' on stage at a large-scale memorial concert for those who died in the World Trade Center.

> I am Irish and was proud to serve with other firemen,
> Who gave their lives for us that day, each one of them a friend,
> In remembrance of my brothers, who from earthly bonds did pass,
> Osama, step right up and kiss my royal Irish ass![1]

Moreover, Moran was frequently quoted as actually having shouted 'kiss my *white* Irish ass!' at the concert. This small but telling change in vocabulary was also reflected in an episode of Denis Leary's sitcom *The Job*, when Leary's character repeats the phrase during his refusal to participate in what he sees as 'effeminate' anger management group therapy.[2]

On 16 July 2002, the governor and the mayor of New York, along with the Irish president, officially dedicated New York State's Irish Hunger Memorial in Battery Park, itself in the immediate vicinity of the World Trade Centre site. The Memorial is a traditional Famine-era Irish cottage, reconstructed stone by stone. During the ceremony, several references were made by speakers to historical and cultural connections they saw between the two sites. During her tour of the site, President Mary McAleese commented that 'The fire-fighters of Irish extraction who lost their lives [on 11 September] were there only because of the cottage', while Rudolph Giuliani remarked that 'So many times last Fall it was predominantly Irish-Americans who guided us ... We have to learn how to make positive and good things out of bad. I can't think of any group that does this more than the Irish.'[3] The complexities of such comparisons were highlighted, however, by the other comparisons made by the official speakers at the dedication ceremony, who expressed the hope that the Irish Hunger Memorial would serve to remind visitors and governments alike that there are comparative famines in the contemporary world, to which the West has a duty to respond. President McAleese's address to an official dinner the evening before argued that:

There can be no better next-door neighbour for the new memorial, for this is now an area where a bustling noisy city, silently but powerfully holds its most sacred memories. Against that backdrop both physical and psychological, the Irish Famine Memorial evokes memories of a dreadful time in nineteenth-century Ireland that is tragically repeated today in so many parts of our twenty-first century global homeland. The monument is an outward call to conscience and to responsibility, daring us, challenging us to care about the stranger in far off lands who is dying right now of hunger, who is wondering does anyone care and who despairs for his or her children and their future.[4]

At least initially, then, this development within Irish-American identity construction has not appeared incompatible with a continuing identification with Ireland itself. Ireland has largely been seen, in this context, as a loyal ally of Irish America and, indeed, the United States as a whole in its responses to 11 September. One of the only countries in the world to declare a national 'Day of Mourning' only days after the attacks themselves, Ireland was also a non-permanent member of the United Nations Security Council at the time, and in this context was seen by both the American government and people as being sympathetic to its own response to the attacks.

However, as the political situation – and its cultural effect – develops, there are other signs that the interaction between Irish America and Ireland may be complicated by the competing loyalties and representations of Irish-American and Irish identities. For example, the arrest and subsequent trial of three Irishmen accused of being IRA agents working with Marxist FARC guerrillas in Colombia brought into sharp relief the complications of defining 'terrorism', especially from an Irish-American perspective.

Equally, although as yet too early to determine, the development of an increasing hostility between the United States and what Secretary of Defense Donald Rumsfeld has described as 'old Europe' over political and military intervention in the Middle East will have important implications for Irish-American identification with Ireland.[5] If and when Ireland is forced definitively to align itself with one or other of these power blocs, that choice will have ramifications for its relationship with Irish America for years and possibly decades. As yet Ireland, like the United Kingdom, does not seem to have been classified as being part of the 'old Europe', which is rapidly coming to symbolise the antithesis of American ideals. This could rapidly change, however, given the fluidity of the political situation at the time of writing, and the complexities of cultural identification involved for both the Irish and the Irish-American populations. For example, in February 2003, more than 100,000 people took part in a protest march against the pending war in Iraq – one of the largest public protests in Irish history.[6] Despite this, however, the Irish government has, since war began, allowed the US military to use Shannon Airport as a stop-over point for troops travelling to and from Iraq. This is a political–economic relationship which is in transition, and the nature of that transition over the coming years will determine much of Irish America's view of Ireland.

On a cultural level, the dramatic changes to Irish culture and society heralded by the 'Celtic Tiger' economy of the 1990s may also result, in the longer term, in some changes of relationship between Ireland and Irish America. If the growing wealth of Ireland in the early twenty-first century is maintained, Irish-American expectations and experiences of contact with Irish culture may also be changed. The notion of an Irish cultural 'homeland' which is to some degree 'out of time' and a consoling escape from modern American life has always been a complex issue for the Irish-American diaspora, as this book has discussed. However, it may well become a practical impossibility in any form in an Ireland of sustained economic growth, where ordinary suburban homes in the capital routinely cost more than a million euro, and with levels of luxury consumer spending dramatic by even American standards. If, in other words, Ireland becomes a nation where even comfortably middle-class American visitors feel impoverished, then the long-held notion of the country as a link to Irish America's own less prosperous past will be challenged. Equally, if Irish-American identity is a complex construction of white identity within America, the changing demographics of Irish society will also raise questions about this process. The 2006 census revealed that the immigrant population of Ireland is now 10 per cent, with most of these residents originating in China, Nigeria, the Baltic and Eastern European countries such as Poland.[7] Dublin, for example, now contains Chinese, Lithuanian and Russian supermarkets, a Polish-language newspaper and frequent billboard advertisements in several languages, including Polish and Chinese. How many of these residents will settle permanently, thus bringing up their children in Ireland, remains to be seen. However, a proportion of them are already doing so, and Irish schools are currently educating the first generation of Chinese-Irish, Nigerian-Irish and Polish-Irish citizens. This is a change to Irish society which is only just beginning to be negotiated. However, as Irish identity in Ireland becomes less definitively white, Irish-American identity formation will also have to negotiate the changing intersections between ethnicity and Irishness.

The relationship among Ireland, Irish America and the United States as a whole is therefore still in a phase of change, the outcome of which is uncertain. What is undoubtedly clear, however, is that twenty-first century processes of Irish-American identity construction will continue to be as engaged with and influenced by broader social, cultural and political events as they were throughout the twentieth century.

IRISH STUDIES AND POPULAR CULTURE

Some of the historical and ideological reasons for the tensions between Irish and Irish-American cultural identities have, I hope, been explored in this book. I would suggest, however, that the structure and nature of the Irish studies academy are also partly responsible for these tensions, which are reflected within that academy at least as much as they are in the wider culture.

The historical development of Irish studies on both sides of the Atlantic as a recognised (and, crucially, funded) discipline has been such that it continues to be dominated by highly canonical literary criticism and historical enquiry. This is not to suggest that a variety of scholars in both Ireland and the United States have not been engaged in non-canonical work relating to Irish and Irish-American culture, history and politics, much of it innovative and valuable research. It is, however, notably the case that the established networks of scholarly exchange within the discipline, such as university departments, disciplinary associations and conferences, journals and research funding, are overwhelmingly concerned only with the canon of Irish literary and historical study. Serious engagement with contemporary Irish and Irish-American culture, and non-canonical texts from all eras has, largely speaking, been left to individual scholars working in the fields of film, media studies, cultural studies and sociology. And because the established networks of professional exchange and employment within Irish studies often excludes or marginalises both the primary texts and the interdisciplinary approach of this work, it is often being conducted in relative isolation, without the vital support of either funding or peer feedback necessary to useful research. Examples of this would include the recent staging of a major Irish studies conference in the United States which, among more than sixty separate panels, did not contain even one which concentrated on popular culture. Equally, university jobs in Ireland which draw upon expertise in Irish studies are overwhelmingly in English and history departments which have not significantly incorporated interdisciplinary or non-traditional texts or methodologies into their syllabi, thus excluding scholars whose principal work is in these fields.

Irish studies, on both sides of the Atlantic, urgently needs to address these issues. Without suggesting that the study of canonical literary texts or traditional history doesn't remain vitally important, it must also make greater strides to include interdisciplinary methodologies and non-canonical texts. An Irish studies academy which does not, in the early twenty-first century, make a serious study of immigrant identities, consumer culture, popular culture and the practices of everyday life (both contemporary and historical) is rapidly going to appear dangerously divorced from actual Irish culture not only within Ireland itself, but also within the diaspora. An academy which did include these areas of study, moreover, must do so across international borders. Popular culture and the cultural practices of everyday life have never best been studied within frameworks of national identity, given the ways in which their primary texts have tended, almost by definition, to have multiple sources of origin and cultural inheritance, as well as being subject to the flows of international capital. This book has, it is hoped, shown some of the ways in which this has been crucial to the ways in which Irish-American contact with Ireland has been structured during the late twentieth century. It is essential, however, that Irish studies on both sides of the Atlantic recognises how central popular culture and cultural practices are to *all* aspects of Irish culture as it is lived.

NOTES

1 Lyrics available on <http://www.soundclick.com>. Accessed July 2006.
2 Diane Negra, 'Irishness, Innocence, and American Identity before and after September 11', in Diane Negra (ed.), *The Irish In Us: Irishness, Performativity, and Popular Culture* (Durham, NC: Duke University Press, 2006), pp. 362–3. Also see *The Job* (ABC Television, 2001–2002).
3 *The Irish-American Post*, July/Aug 2002/ Vol. 3, Issue 2, see <http://www.irishamericanpost.com>. Accessed July 2006.
4 'Remarks by the President of Ireland, Mary McAleese, at the Irish Famine

Memorial Dinner, Battery Park City', New York, Monday, 15 July 2002. For the full text of this speech, see <http://www.ballinagree.freeservers.com/macaleese.html>. Accessed July 2006.

5   See <http://news.bbc.co.uk/2/hi/europe/2687403.stm>. Accessed July 2006.
6   See <http://www.rte.ie/news/2003/0215/Iraq.html>. Accessed July 2006.
7   *Irish Times*, 20 July 2006, p. 6.

Bibliography

PRIMARY SOURCES

Novels, Poetry and Memoirs

Carey, Alice, *I'll Know It When I See It* (New York: Clarkson Potter, 2002).

Flanagan, Thomas, *The Tenants of Time* (London: Bantam, 1988).

Haley, Alex, *Roots: The Saga of An American Family* (New York: Doubleday, 1976).

Heaney, Seamus, *A Northern Hoard I. Roots, Wintering Out* (London: Faber, 1972).

McCourt, Frank, *Angela's Ashes* (New York: Scribner, 1996).

McCourt, Frank, *'Tis* (New York: Scribner, 1999).

McCourt, Malachy, *A Monk Swimming* (New York: HarperCollins, 1998).

McCourt, Malachy, *Singing Him My Song* (New York: HarperCollins, 2000).

Matieu, Joan, *Zulu: An Irish-American's Quest to Discover her Roots* (Edinburgh: Mainstream, 1998).

Severin, Tim, *The Brendan Voyage* (London: Hutchinson, 1978).

Uris, Leon, *Trinity* (London: André Deutsch, 1976).

Uris, Jill and Leon Uris, *Ireland: A Terrible Beauty: The Story of Ireland Today* (London: Corgi, 1977).

Waters, Maureen, *Crossing Highbridge: A Memoir of Irish America* (Syracuse, NY: Syracuse University Press, 2001).

White, Richard, *Remembering Ahanagran: Storytelling in a Family's Past* (Cork: Cork University Press, 1999).

Archive Files

Congressional Record, Vol. 97, Part 9, 27 September 1951.

The European Recovery Programme: Basic Documents and

Background Information, P. No. 8792 (Dublin 1949).
Pre-Presidential Files, Speech Files, Box 895, Kennedy Library.
T.J. Kiernan Oral History Transcript, Kennedy Library.

Pamphlets and Statements

Byrne, John, 'Artist's Statement' (Dublin: Temple Bar Gallery 2001).
Waterford Crystal Visitor Centre brochure, 2000.
Waterford Wedgwood Company Accounts, 2005, published on <http://www.waterfordwedgwood.com>.

American Newspapers and Magazines

Chicago Irish-American News, Chicago.
Christian Science Monitor, Boston.
Life Magazine, Chicago.
National Geographic Magazine, Washington, DC.
Newsweek, New York.
Boston Globe, Boston.
Chicago Tribune, Chicago.
Irish American Post, Milwaukee, WI.
Irish Echo, New York.
Irish Edition, Philadelphia.
Irish People, New York.
Irish World and American Industrial Liberator and Gaelic American, New York.
New Yorker, New York.
New York Times, New York.
Philadelphia Inquirer, Philadelphia.
Washington Post, Washington, DC.
Time Magazine, Chicago.
TV Guide, Radnor, PA.

British Newspapers and Magazines

Guardian, London.
Observer, London.

Irish Newspapers and Magazines

An Phoblacht, Dublin.
Irish Press, Dublin.
Magill, Dublin.

Dubliner, Dublin.
Irish Independent, Dublin.
Irish Times, Dublin.
Sunday Independent, Dublin.
World of Hibernia, Dublin.
Weekly Freeman, Dublin.

Internet Sites

<http://news.bbc.co.uk/2/hi/europe/2687403.stm>.
<http://www.ballinagree.freeservers.com/macaleese.html> .
<http://www.carrollsirishgifts.com>.
<http://www.celticdragonpubco.com>.
<http://www.cso.ie/census/Census2002Results.htm>.
<http://www.internationalfundforireland.com>.
<http://www.irishamericanpartners.org>.
<http://www.irishnationalcaucus.org>.
<http://www.irishpubcompany.com>.
<http://www.irishshop.com>.
<http://www.irlfunds.org/ww_usa.html>.
<http://www.irlfunds.org>.
<http://www.nicensus2001.gov.uk/nica/common/home.jsp>.
<http://www.philanthropyroundtable.org>.
<http://www.riverdance.com>.
<http://www.rootsweb.com/~irlker/diaspora.html>.
<http://www.rte.ie/news/2003/0215/Iraq.html>.
<http://www.soundclick.com>.
<http://www.tourismireland.com/corporate>.
<http://www.waterford.com>.

Feature Films

Abie's Irish Rose, dir. Victor Fleming (Paramount Famous Lasky
    Corp., 1929), United States.
Birth of a Nation, dir. D. W. Griffith (David W. Griffith Corp.,
    1915), United States.
Brothers McMullen, The, dir. Edward Burns (20th Century Fox,
    1995), United States.
Cohens and the Kellys, The, dir. Harry A. Pollard (Universal
    Pictures, 1926), United States.
Colleen Bawn, The, dir. Sidney Olcott (Kalem Company, 1911),
    United States.

Devil's Own, The, dir. Alan J. Pakula (Colombia Pictures, 1997), United States.

Far and Away, dir. Ron Howard (Universal Pictures, 1992), United States.

Fatal Attraction, dir. Adrian Lyne (Paramount Pictures, 1987), United States.

Fighting Kentuckian, The, dir. George Waggner (Republic Pictures, 1949), United States.

Fighting Sullivans, The, dir. Lloyd Bacon (20th Century Fox, 1944*),* United States.

Frantic, dir. Roman Polanski (Warner Brothers, 1988), United States.

Fugitive, The, dir. Andrew Davis (Warner Brothers, 1993), United States.

Godfather Part II, The, dir. Francis Ford Coppola (Paramount Pictures, 1974), United States.

Godfather, The, dir. Francis Ford Coppola (Paramount Pictures, 1972), United States.

Hiroshima Mon Amour, dir. Alan Resnais (Argos Films, 1959), France/Japan.

His Family Tree, dir. Charles Vidor (RKO Radio Pictures, 1935), United States.

Irene, dir. Alfred E. Green (First National Pictures, 1926), United States.

Lad From Old Ireland, The, dir. Sidney Olcott (The Kalem Company, 1910), United States.

Luck of the Irish, The, dir. Henry Koster (20th Century Fox, 1948), United States.

Matchmaker, The, dir. Mark Joffe (Polygram/Working Title, 1997), United States.

McLintock!, dir. Andrew V. McLaglen (Batjac Productions, 1963), United States.

Nephew, The, dir. Eugene Brady (Irish DreamTime/World, 2000 Entertainment 1998), Ireland.

Only the Lonely, dir. Chris Columbus (20th Century Fox, 1991), United States.

Patriot Games, dir. Phillip Noyce (Paramount Pictures, 1992), United States.

Public Enemy, The, dir. William A. Wellman (Warner Brothers, 1931), United States.

Quiet Man, The, dir. John Ford (Republic Studios, 1952), United States.

Raiders of the Lost Ark, dir. Steven Spielberg (Paramount Pictures, 1981), United States.

Sands of Iwo Jima, The, dir. Allan Dwan (Republic Pictures 1949), United States.

Shake Hands With the Devil, dir. Michael Anderson (United Artists, 1959), United States/Ireland.

She's The One, dir. Edward Burns (20th Century Fox, 1996), United States.

They Were Expendable, dir. John Ford (Metro-Goldwyn-Mayer, 1945), United States.

This Is My Father, dir. Paul Quinn (Filmline International/Hummingbird Communications, 1998), Canada/Ireland.

Titanic, dir. James Cameron (20th Century Fox, 1997), United States.

Top O' the Morning, dir. David Miller (Paramount Pictures, 1949), United States.

2By4, dir. Jimmy Smallhorne (Red Horse Films, 1998), United States.

Television Films and Series

Father Knows Best (CBS/NBC, 1954–62), United States.
Fighting Fitzgeralds, The (NBC, 2001), United States.
Job, The (ABC, 2001), United States.
I Love Lucy (CBS, 1951–56), United States.
Manions of America, The (ABC/EMI, 1981), United States.
Roots (ABC/Warner Bros. Television, 1977), United States.

Short Films

Autumn in Dublin, dir. Terry Wogan (1962), Ireland.
Crystal Clear, dir. Brendan J. Stafford (Eamonn Andrews Studios, 1959), Ireland.
Glimpses of Erin, dir. James A Fitzpatrick (Fitzpatrick Travel Talk, 1934), United States.
Green For Ireland, dir. Arthur Wooster (Arthur Wooster, 1968), United Kingdom/Ireland.
Honeymoon in Ireland, dir. unknown (Bord Fáilte, 1963), Ireland.
Ireland in Spring, dir. Colm O'Laoghaire (Colm O'Laoghaire Productions, 1956), Ireland.
Ireland Invites You, dir. Colm O'Laoghaire (Colm O'Laoghaire

Productions, 1966), Ireland.

Irish In Me, The, dir. Herman Boxer (Universal International Colour/Dudley Pictures Corporation, 1959), United States/Ireland.

No More Yesterdays, dir. Martin Rolfe (Associated British Pathé, 1967), United Kingdom/Ireland.

O'Hara's Holiday, dir. Peter Bryan (Tribune Films Incorporated, 1960), Ireland.

See You At the Pillar, dir. Peter Bayliss (Associated British Pathé, 1967), United Kingdom/Ireland.

Spell of Ireland, The, dir. Danny Devlin (Celtic Films, 1950s), United States.

SECONDARY SOURCES

Books and Journal Articles

Ahmad, Aijaz, *In Theory: Classes, Nations, Literatures* (London: Verso, 1992).

Akenson, Donald Harman, *The Irish Diaspora: A Primer* (Belfast: Institute of Irish Studies, 1996).

Akenson, Donald Harman, *If The Irish Ran the World: Montserrat, 1630–1730* (Liverpool: Liverpool University Press, 1997).

Alba, Richard, *Ethnic Identity: The Transformation of White America* (New Haven, CT: Yale University Press, 1990).

Anderson, Benedict, *Imagined Communities: Reflections on the Origin and Spread of Nationalism* (London: Verso, 1991).

Anderson, Benedict, 'Long-Distance Nationalism: World Capitalism and the Rise of Identity Politics', *The Wertheim Lecture*, Amsterdam (Amsterdam: Centre for Asian Studies, 1992).

Anthius, Floya, 'Evaluating "Diaspora": Beyond Ethnicity?', *Sociology*, Vol. 32, No. 3, August 1998.

Appadurai, Arjun, 'Putting Hierarchy in its Place', *Cultural Anthropology*, Vol. 3, No. 1, 1988.

Arthur, Paul, 'Diasporan Intervention in International Affairs: Irish America as a Case Study', *Diaspora: A Journal of Transnational Studies*, Vol. 1, No. 2, 1991.

Ballagh, Robert, 'Getting Away From Outworn Shibboleths of Irishness', *Sunday Independent*, 9 November 1980.

Ballerino Cohen, Colleen, Richard Wilk, with Beverly Stoeltje,

'Introduction: Beauty Queens on the Global Stage', in Colleen Ballerino Cohen, Richard Wilk and Beverly Stoeltje (eds), *Beauty Queens on the Global Stage: Gender, Contests and Power* (London: Routledge, 1996).

Barry, John G., *The Study of Family History in Ireland* (Cork: Cork University Press, 1967).

Bartlett, Thomas, Chris Curtin, Riana O'Dwyer and Gearód Ó Tuathaigh (eds), *Irish Studies: A General Introduction* (Dublin: Gill and Macmillan, 1988).

Barton, Ruth, *Acting Irish in Hollywood: From Fitzgerald to Farrell* (Dublin: Irish Academic Press, 2006).

Benton, Sarah, 'Women Disarmed: The Militarisation of Politics in Ireland 1913–23', *Feminist Review*, 50, Summer 1995.

Bhaba, Homi, *Nation and Narration* (London: Routledge, 1990).

Bielenberg, Andy (ed.), *The Irish Diaspora* (London: Longman, 2000).

Brah, Avtar, *Cartographies of Diaspora: Contesting Identities* (London: Routledge, 1996).

Brennan, Tim, 'Cosmopolitans and Celebrities', *Race and Class: A Journal for Black and Third World Liberation*, Vol. 31, No. 1, July–September 1989.

Brett, David, *The Construction of Heritage* (Cork: Cork University Press, 1996).

Brown, Terence, *Ireland: A Social and Cultural History 1922–1985* (London: Fontana Press, 1985).

Brown, Thomas N., *Irish-American Nationalism 1870–1890* (Philadelphia: J.B. Lippincott Company, 1966).

Burns-Bisogno, Louisa, *Censoring Irish Nationalism: The British, Irish and American Suppression of Republican Images in Film and Television, 1909–1995* (London: McFarland & Company, 1997).

Butler-Cullingford, Elizabeth, *Ireland's Others: Gender and Ethnicity in Irish Literature and Popular Culture* (Cork: Cork University Press, 2001).

Byron, Reginald, *Irish America* (Oxford: Oxford University Press, 1999).

Cahalan, James M., *Great Hatred, Little Room: The Irish Historical Novel* (Dublin: Gill and Macmillan, 1983).

Callinicos, Alex, *Theories and Narratives: Reflections on the Philosophy of History* (Cambridge: Polity Press, 1995).

Casey, Marian, 'Ireland, New York and the Irish Image in American Popular Culture, 1890–1960', D.Phil. thesis (New York: New York University, 1998).

Chakrabarty, Dipesh, 'Subaltern Studies and Postcolonial Histories', paper delivered to *Explaining Change in Cultural History: 25th Irish Conference of Historians*, NUI Galway, 18–20 May 2001.

Chioni Moore, David, 'Routes: Alex Haley's Roots and the Rhetoric of Genealogy', *Transition*, Issue 64, 1994.

Clifford, James, 'Travelling Cultures', in Lawrence Grossberg, Cary Nelson and Paula A. Treichler (eds), *Cultural Studies* (London: Routledge, 1992).

Clifford, James, 'Diasporas', *Cultural Anthropology*, Vol. 9, No. 3, 1994.

Clifford, James, *Routes: Travel and Translation in the Late Twentieth Century* (New Haven, CT: Harvard University Press, 1997).

Cohen, Robin, *Global Diasporas: An Introduction* (London: UCL Press, 1997).

Connerton, Paul, *How Societies Remember* (Cambridge: Cambridge University Press, 1989).

Coogan, Tim Pat, *The Disillusioned Decades: Ireland 1966–87* (Dublin: Gill and Macmillan, 1987).

Coogan, Tim Pat, *Wherever Green Is Worn: The Story of the Irish Diaspora* (New York: Palgrave Press, 2000).

Corcoran, Farrel, 'The Political Instrumentality of Cultural Memory: A Case Study', *Javnost – the Public: Journal of The European Institute for Communication and Culture*, Vol. 9, No. 3, 2002.

Cronin, Mike and Daryl Adair, *The Wearing of the Green: A History of St Patrick's Day* (London: Routledge, 2002).

Cronin, Sean, *Washington's Irish Policy 1916–1986: Independence, Partition, Neutrality* (Dublin: Anvil Books, 1987).

Curtis Jr., L. Perry, *Images of Erin in the Age of Parnell* (Dublin: National Library of Ireland, 2000).

Curtis, Barry and Claire Pajaczkowska, 'Getting There: Travel, Time and Narrative', in George Robertson et al. (eds), *Travellers' Tales: Narratives of Home and Displacement* (London: Routledge, 1994).

de Certeau, Michel, *The Practice of Everyday Life* (Berkeley: University of California Press, 1984).

Deleuze, Gilles and Félix Guattari, *A Thousand Plateaus: Capitalism and Schizophrenia*, trans. Brian Massumi (London: Athlone Press, 1996).

Demmers, Jolle, 'Diaspora and Conflict: Locality, Long-Distance

Nationalism, and Delocalisation of Conflict Dynamics', *Javnost – the Public: Journal of The European Institute for Communication and Culture*, 1: *Diasporic Communication*, Vol. 9, 2002.

Devlin McAliskey, Bernadette, 'Where Are We Now in the Peace Process?', *Irish Reporter*, 21, February 1996.

Dickson Falley, Margaret, *Irish and Scotch-Irish Ancestral Research: A Guide to the Genealogical Records, Methods and Sources in Ireland, Volume I: Repositories and Records* (Dublin: Genealogical Publishing Co., 1962).

Diner, Hasia, *Erin's Daughters in America: Irish Immigrant Women in the Nineteenth Century* (Baltimore, MD: Johns Hopkins University Press, 1983).

Dodd, Luke, 'Sleeping With The Past: Collecting and Ireland', *Circa* (September/October 1991).

Dooley, Brian, *Black and Green: The Fight for Civil Rights in Northern Ireland and Black America* (London: Pluto Press, 1998).

Eagleton, Terry, *Heathcliff and the Great Hunger* (London: Verso, 1995).

Erie, Steven P., *Rainbow's End: Irish-Americans and the Dilemmas of Urban Machine Politics, 1840–1985* (Berkeley: University of California Press, 1988).

Fanning, Charles (ed.), *New Perspectives on the Irish Diaspora* (Carbondale: Southern Illinois University Press, 2000).

Fitzpatrick, David, *Irish Emigration 1801–1921* (Dublin: Economic and Social History Society of Ireland, 1984).

Foster, R.F., *Modern Ireland 1600–1972* (London: Penguin, 1988).

Foster, R.F., *The Irish Story: Telling Tales and Making It Up in Ireland* (London: Allen Lane, 2001).

Foucault, Michel, *Discipline and Punish* (London: Penguin, 1977).

Foucault, Michel, 'The Order of Discourse', in M. Shapiro (ed), *Language and Politics* (Oxford: Blackwell Press, 1984).

Freud, Sigmund, 'Family Romances', in J. Strachey (ed.), *The Standard Edition of the Complete Works of Sigmund Freud (IX)* (London: Hogarth Press, 1953).

Frow, John, *Time and Commodity Culture: Essays in Cultural Theory and Postmodernity* (Oxford: Clarendon Press, 1997).

Gans, Herbert, 'Symbolic Ethnicity: The Future of Ethnic Groups and Cultures in America', *Ethnic and Racial Studies*, 2, 1979.

Gavaghan, J. Cyril and Gene O'Donnell, 'The Rose of Tralee: "The Greatest Free Show on Earth"?', in James J. Ward (ed.), *Cases in Marketing Management and Strategy* (Dublin: The Marketing

Institute Ireland, 1998).

Gibbons, Luke, 'Romanticism, Realism and Irish Cinema', in Kevin Rockett, Luke Gibbons and John Hill (eds), *Cinema and Ireland* (London: Croom Helm, 1987).

Gibbons, Luke, 'Dialogue Without the Other? A Reply to Francis Mulhern', *Radical Philosophy*, 67, Summer 1994.

Gibbons, Luke, *Transformations in Irish Culture* (Cork: Cork University Press, 1996).

Gibbons, Luke, 'The Global Cure? History, Therapy and the Celtic Tiger', in Peadar Kirby, Luke Gibbons and Michael Cronin (eds), *Reinventing Ireland: Culture, Society and the Global Economy* (London: Pluto Press, 2002).

Gibbons, Luke, *The Quiet Man* (Cork: Cork University Press, 2002).

Graham, Colin and Richard Kirkland (eds), *Ireland and Cultural Theory: The Mechanics of Authenticity* (Dublin: Macmillan, 1999).

Gribben, Arthur (ed.), *The Great Famine and the Irish Diaspora in America* (Amherst: University of Massachusetts Press, 1998).

Gronow, Jukka, *The Sociology of Taste* (London: Routledge, 1997).

Guelke, Adrian, *Northern Ireland: The International Perspective* (Dublin: Gill and Macmillan, 1988).

Hague, Euan, 'The Scottish Diaspora: Tartan Day and the Appropriation of Scottish Identities in the United States', in David C. Harvey, Rhys Jones, Neil McInroy and Christine Milligan (eds), *Celtic Geographies: Old Culture, New Times* (London: Routledge, 2002).

Halbwachs, Maurice, *On Collective Memory* (Chicago: University of Chicago Press, 1992).

Hall, Stuart, 'Cultural Identity and Diaspora', in Patrick Williams and Laura Chrisman (eds), *Colonial Discourse and Postcolonial Theory* (London: Harvester Wheatsheaf, 1993).

Hall, Stuart, 'Notes on Deconstructing the Popular', in John Storey (ed.), *Cultural Theory and Popular Culture: A Reader* (London: Harvester Wheatsheaf, 1998).

Handlin, Oscar, *The Uprooted: The Epic Story of the Great Migrations that Made the American People* (New York: Grosset and Dunlap, 1971).

Hansen, Marcus, 'The Problem of the Third Generation Immigrant', in *Augustana Historical Society Publications* (Rock Island, IL: Augustana Historical Society, 1938).

Healy, James B., *Northern Ireland Dilemma: An American Irish Imperative* (London: Peter Lang, 1989).

Hewison, Robert, *The Heritage Industry* (London: Methuen, 1987).

Hey, David, *Family History and Local History in England* (London: Longman, 1987).

Hill, John, 'Images of Violence in Irish Cinema', in Kevin Rockett, Luke Gibbons and John Hill (eds), *Cinema and Ireland* (London: Croom Helm, 1987).

Hobsbawm, Eric, *On History* (London: Weidenfeld and Nicholson, 1997).

Holland, Jack, 'Noraid's Untold Millions', *Magill*, April 1987.

Holland, Jack, *The American Connection: US Guns, Money and Influence in Northern Ireland* (Boulder, CO: Roberts Rinehart Publishers, 1999).

Ibson, John, 'Virgin Land or Virgin Mary? Studying the Ethnicity of White Americans', *American Quarterly*, Vol. 33, Issue 3, 1981.

Ignatiev, Noel, *How the Irish Became White* (London: Routledge, 1995).

Joyce, William Leonard, *Editors and Ethnicity: A History of the Irish-American Press, 1848–1883* (New York: Arno Press, 1976).

Kaplan, Caren, *Questions of Travel: Postmodern Discourses of Displacement* (Durham, NC: Duke University Press, 1998).

Kearney, Richard, *Postnationalist Ireland: Politics, Culture, Philosophy* (London: Routledge, 1997).

Kenny, Kevin, *Making Sense of the Molly Maguires* (Oxford: Oxford University Press, 1998).

Kenny, Kevin, *The American Irish: A History* (London: Longman, 2000).

Killick, John, *The United States and European Reconstruction 1945–1960* (Keele: Keele University Press, 1997).

Lavenda, Robert H., ' "It's Not a Beauty Pageant!" Hybrid Ideology in Minnesota Community Queen Pageants', in Colleen Ballerino Cohen, Richard Wilk and Beverly Stoeltje (eds), *Beauty Queens on the Global Stage: Gender, Contests and Power* (London: Routledge, 1996).

Lavie, Smadar and Ted Swedenburg (eds), *Displacement, Diaspora, and Geographies of Identity* (Durham, NC: Duke University Press, 1996).

Lavin, Marilyn, 'Consumer Goods: Reinforcers of Irish and Irish-American Identities in the United States', paper delivered at *The Scattering, Ireland and the Irish Diaspora: A Comparative*

Perspective, Irish Centre for Migration Studies, University College Cork, Cork, 24–27 September 1997.

Lee, J.J., *Ireland 1912–1985: Politics and Society* (Cambridge: Cambridge University Press, 1989).

Leslie, Esther, 'Souvenirs and Forgetting: Walter Benjamin's Memory-Work', in Marcus Kwint, Christopher Breward and Jeremy Aynsley (eds), *Material Memories* (New York: Berg Press, 1999).

Linebaugh, Peter and Marcus Rediker, *The Many-Headed Hydra: The Hidden History of the Revolutionary Atlantic* (London: Verso, 2000).

Lipsitz, George, *The Possessive Investment in Whiteness: How White People Profit from Identity Politics* (Philadelphia: Temple University Press, 1998).

Lloyd, David, *Ireland After History* (Cork: Cork University Press, 1999).

Lockwood, Chris, 'Who Are the Customers – What Do They Want?', in *Come Back For Erin?* (Dublin: The National Tourism Council of Ireland, 1977).

Lourdeaux, Lee, *Italian and Irish Filmmakers in America: Ford, Capra, Coppola, and Scorsese* (Philadelphia: Temple University Press, 1990).

Lowenthal, David, *The Past Is A Foreign Country* (Cambridge: Cambridge University Press, 1985).

Lowenthal, David, *Possessed by the Past: The Heritage Crusade and the Spoils of History* (New York: The Free Press, 1996).

Lury, Celia, 'The Objects of Travel', in Chris Rojek and John Urry (eds), *Touring Cultures: Transformations of Travel and Theory* (London: Routledge, 1997).

McCaffrey, Lawrence J., *The Irish Diaspora in America* (Bloomington: Indiana University Press, 1976).

McCaffrey, Lawrence J., *Textures of Irish America* (Syracuse, NY: Syracuse University Press, 1992).

McCaffrey, Lawrence J., *The Irish Catholic Diaspora in America* (Washington, DC: Catholic University of America Press, 1997).

MacCannell, Dean, *The Tourist: A New Theory of the Leisure Class* (New York: Schocken Books, 1989).

McCarthy, John F., 'Ireland's Turnaround: Whitaker and the 1958 Plan for Economic Development', in John F. McCarthy (ed.), *Planning Ireland's Future: The Legacy of T.K. Whitaker* (Dublin: Glendale Press, 1990).

McClintock, Anne, '"No Longer a Future Heaven": Gender, Race and Nationalism', in Anne McClintock, Aamir Mufti and Ella Shohat (eds), *Dangerous Liaisons: Gender, Nation and Postcolonial Perspectives* (Minneapolis: University of Minnesota Press, 1997).

McHale, Des, *The Complete Guide to The Quiet Man* (Belfast: Appletree, 1999).

McLoone, Martin, *Irish Film: The Emergence of a Contemporary Cinema* (London: British Film Institute, 2000).

Malkki, Lisa, 'National Geographic: The Rooting of Peoples and the Territorialization of National Identity Among Scholars and Refugees', *Cultural Anthropology*, Vol. 7, No. 1, 1992.

Massey, Doreen, *Space, Place and Gender* (Cambridge: Polity Press, 1994).

Meagher, Timothy J., *Inventing Irish America: Generation, Class and Ethnic Identity in a New England City, 1880–1928* (Notre Dame: University of Notre Dame Press, 2001).

Metress, Seamus, 'The Irish-Americans: From the Frontier to the White House', in Larry L. Taylor (ed.), *Cultural Diversity in the United States* (Westport, CT: Bergin and Garvey, 1997).

Miller, Kerby A., *Emigrants and Exiles: Ireland and the Irish Exodus to North America* (Oxford: Oxford University Press, 1985).

Mitchell, Arthur, *JFK and his Irish Heritage* (Dublin: Moytura Press, 1993).

Mulhern, Francis, *The Present Lasts a Long Time: Essays About Cultural Politics* (Cork: Cork University Press, 1998).

Mukerji, Chandra and Michael Schudson, 'Introduction: Rethinking Popular Culture', in Chandra Mukerji and Michael Schudson (eds), *Rethinking Popular Culture: Contemporary Perspectives in Cultural Studies* (Berkeley: University of California Press, 1991).

Naficy, Hamid, 'Framing Exile: From Homeland to Homepage', in Hamid Naficy (ed.), *Home, Exile, Homeland: Film, Media, and the Politics of Place* (London: Routledge, 1999).

Nahirny, Vladimir C. and Joshua A. Fishman, 'American Immigrant Groups: Ethnic Identification and the Problem of Generations', *Sociological Review*, 13, 1965.

Nash, Catherine, 'Genealogical Identities', in *Environment and Planning D: Society and Space*, 20, 2002.

Negra, Diane, 'Consuming Ireland: Lucky Charms Cereal, Irish Spring Soap and 1-800-Shamrock', *Cultural Studies*, Vol. 15, No. 1, January 2001.

Negra, Diane, *Off-White Hollywood: American Culture and Ethnic Female Stardom* (London: Routledge, 2001).

Negra, Diane (ed.), *The Irish in Us: Irishness, Performativity, and Popular Culture* (Durham, NC: Duke University Press, 2006).

O'Brien, George, 'The Last Word: Reflections on *Angela's Ashes*', in Charles Fanning (ed.), *New Perspectives on the Irish Diaspora* (Carbondale: Southern Illinois University Press, 2000).

O'Carroll, Ide, *Models for Movers: Irish Women's Emigration to America* (Dublin: Attic Press, 1990).

Ó Ciosáin, Niall, 'Hungry Grass', *Circa*, Summer 1994.

O'Clery, Conor, *Daring Diplomacy: Clinton's Secret Search for Peace in Ireland* (Boulder, CO: Roberts Rinehart, 1997).

O'Connor, Barbara, 'Myths and Mirrors: Tourist Images and National Identity', in Barbara O'Connor and Michael Cronin (eds), *Tourism in Ireland: A Critical Analysis* (Cork: Cork University Press, 1997).

O'Connor, Barbara, '*Riverdance*', in Michel Peillon and Eamonn Slater (eds), *Encounters with Modern Ireland: A Sociological Chronicle 1995–1996* (Dublin: Institute of Public Administration, 1998).

O'Day, Alan, 'Revising the Diaspora', in D. George Boyce and Alan O'Day (eds), *Modern Irish History: Revisionism and the Revisionist Controversy* (London: Routledge, 1997).

O'Hanlon, Ray, *The New Irish Americans* (Boulder, CO: Roberts Rinehart, 1998).

O'Hanlon, Ray, 'The MacBride Principles: Vital Force or Spent Force?', *Irish Echo*, 3–9 November 1999.

O'Hart, John, *Irish Pedigrees; or, The Origin and Stem of the Irish Nation* (Dublin: Gill and Son, 1881).

O'Toole, Fintan, 'No Place Like Home', in Fintan O'Toole, *The Ex-Isle of Erin* (Dublin: New Island Books, 1997).

Papastergiadis, Nikos, *Dialogues in the Diasporas* (London: Rivers Oram Press, 1998).

Parker, Andrew, 'Introduction', in Andrew Parker et al. (eds), *Nationalisms and Sexualities* (London: Routledge, 1992).

Peillon, Michel, 'Tourism – the Quest for Otherness?', *The Crane Bag Book of Irish Studies*, Vol. 8, No. 2 (Dublin: Blackwater Press, 1984).

Pettitt, Lance, *Screening Ireland: Film and Television Representation* (Manchester: Manchester University Press, 2000).

Quinn, Peter, 'Looking for Jimmy', *The World of Hibernia*, Vol. 4,

No. 4, Spring 1999.

Reedy, George E., *From the Ward to the White House: The Irish in American Politics* (New York: Scribner's Sons, 1991).

Rockett, Kevin, 'History, Politics and Irish Cinema', in Kevin Rockett, Luke Gibbons and John Hill (eds), *Cinema and Ireland* (London: Croom Helm, 1987).

Rockett, Kevin, 'The Irish Migrant and Film', in Patrick O'Sullivan (ed.), *The Irish World Wide: History, Heritage and Identity, Volume 3: The Creative Migrant* (Leicester: Leicester University Press, 1994).

Rockett, Kevin, *Still Irish: A Century of the Irish in Film* (Dublin: Red Mountain Press, 1995).

Rockett, Kevin, *The Irish Filmography: Fiction Films 1896–1996* (Dublin: Red Mountain Press, 1996).

Roediger, David R., *The Wages of Whiteness: Race and the Making of the American Working Class* (London: Verso, 1999).

Rosenzweig, Roy and David Thelen, *The Presence of the Past: Popular Uses of History in American Life* (New York: Columbia University Press, 1998).

Safran, David, *Taking it Like a Man: White Masculinity, Masochism and Contemporary American Culture* (Princeton, NJ: Princeton University Press, 1998).

Safran, William, 'Diasporas in Modern Societies: Myths of Homeland and Return', *Diaspora: A Journal of Transnational Studies*, Vol. 1, No. 1, 1994.

Samuel, Raphael, *Theatres of Memory, Volume I: Past and Present in Contemporary Culture* (London: Verso, 1994).

Schlesinger, Arthur M., *The Disuniting of America* (New York: Norton, 1992).

Shannon, William V., 'Northern Ireland and America's Responsibility', *The Recorder* (The American Irish Historical Society), Vol. 36, 1975.

Slater, Eamonn, 'When the Local Goes Global', in Eamonn Slater and Michel Peillon (eds), *Memories of the Present: A Sociological Chronicle of Ireland 1997–1998* (Dublin: Institute of Public Administration, 2000).

Slide, Anthony, *The Cinema and Ireland* (London: McFarland & Company, 1988).

Sollors, Werner, *Beyond Ethnicity: Consent and Descent in American Culture* (Oxford: Oxford University Press, 1986).

Storey, John, *Cultural Studies and the Study of Popular Culture:*

Theories and Methods (Edinburgh: Edinburgh University Press, 1996).

Thompson, Spurgeon, 'Introduction: Towards an Irish Cultural Studies', *Cultural Studies*, Vol. 15, No. 1, 2000.

Tobin, Fergal, *The Best of Decades: Ireland in the 1960s* (Dublin: Gill and Macmillan, 1984).

Turner, Graeme, *Film as Social Practice* (London: Routledge, 1988).

Urry, John, *The Tourist Gaze* (London: Sage, 1990).

Veblen, Thorstein, *The Theory of the Leisure Class* (London: Dover Publications, 1994).

Walter, Bronwen, *Outsiders Inside: Whiteness, Place and Irish Women* (London: Routledge, 2001).

Waters, Mary, *Ethnic Options: Choosing Identities in America* (Berkeley: University of California Press, 1990).

Watson, Elwood and Daray Martin, 'The Miss America Pageant: Pluralism, Femininity and Cinderella All in One', *Journal of Popular Culture*, Vol. 34, No. 1, Summer 2000.

Whelan, Kevin in David Hey (ed.), *The Oxford Companion to Local and Family History* (Oxford: Oxford University Press, 1996).

Williams, Raymond, *Culture and Society 1780–1950* (London: Penguin, 1966).

Wilson, Andrew J., *Irish America and the Ulster Conflict 1968–1995* (Belfast: Blackstaff Press 1995).

Woodham Smith, Cecil, *The Great Hunger, Ireland 1845–9* (London: New English Library, 1984).

Yuval-Davis, Nira, 'Gender and Nation', in Rick Wilford and Robert L. Miller (eds), *Women, Ethnicity and Nationalism: The Politics of Transition* (London: Routledge, 1998).

Index